THE RISE OF THE
BLOGOSPHERE

THE RISE OF THE
BLOGOSPHERE

Aaron Barlow

Westport, Connecticut
London

Library of Congress Cataloging-in-Publication Data

Barlow, Aaron, 1951-
   The rise of the blogosphere / Aaron Barlow.
      p. cm.
   Includes bibliographical references and index.
   ISBN 978-0-275-98996-5 (alk. paper)
  1. Online journalism. 2. Blogs. 3. Cyberspace. 4. Journalism--United States.
I. Title.
   PN478.4.O62B37 2007
   070.4—dc22   2007000052

British Library Cataloguing in Publication Data is available.

Library of Congress Catalog Card Number: 2007000052
ISBN-10: 0–275–98996–8
ISBN-13: 978–0–275–98996–5

First published in 2007

Praeger Publishers, 88 Post Road West, Westport, CT 06881
An imprint of Greenwood Publishing Group, Inc.
www.praeger.com

Printed in the United States of America

The paper used in this book complies with the
Permanent Paper Standard issued by the National
Information Standards Organization (Z39.48–1984).

10 9 8 7 6 5 4 3 2 1

For Jan

A torrent of angry and malignant passions will be let loose. To judge from the conduct of the opposite parties, we shall be led to conclude, that they will mutually hope to evince the justness of their opinions, and to increase the number of their converts by the loudness of their declamations, and by the bitterness of their invectives.

—Alexander Hamilton, *The Federalist Papers*, #1

CONTENTS

PREFACE

In *Consilience: The Unity of Knowledge*, biologist Edward O. Wilson writes that a "balanced perspective cannot be acquired by studying disciplines in pieces but through pursuit of the consilience among them. Such unification will come hard. But I think it is inevitable. Intellectually it rings true, and it gratifies impulses that rise from the admirable side of human nature. To the extent that the gaps between the great branches of learning can be narrowed, diversity and depth of knowledge will increase. They will do so because of, not despite, the underlying cohesion achieved. The enterprise is important for yet another reason: It gives ultimate purpose to intellect. It promises that order, not chaos, lies beyond the horizon. I think it inevitable that we will accept the adventure, go there, and find out."[1] Amen to that!

My own scholarly interests have never been confined to my areas of training, but constantly leach into other fields, extending my curiosity to topics as surprising to me as tomorrow's news. Yet, each time I look back, I discover there is still a consilience, a unity, to my explorations. I may never quite know where I am going, but when I get there I see connections, and the destination seems as if it should have been visible all the time, so obvious is it now.

The destination represented by this book lies well beyond even my scholarly curiosity. Though I did not know it at the time, it was determined by the fact that I am one of those fortunate people with feet on both sides of the contemporary technological divide. From my early years, I was involved in printing, setting type by hand, running presses, melting lead for linotype pigs and pouring stereotype slabs for the local newspaper. Later, I ran automatic-feed letterpresses and offset presses. At that same time, I was beginning to get my first, small experiences with journalism by writing, editing, and mimeographing my own high-school "underground" newspaper. The worlds of job printing and small publications were my own.

Years later, after a short period as a reporter for a small daily newspaper and time editing a tabloid monthly dedicated to environmental causes, I fell in love with the personal computers just starting to have currency. This took me to the other side of that technological divide. Few people have had the luck I have had, to learn both "hot" type printing before it became a novelty hobby and to have been a user of the constantly evolving computers and Internet possibilities of the 1980s and 1990s *and* (going beyond simply that divide) even to have been a long-time student of American writing.

The idea that I would write a book that includes all three of these—printing, computers, and writing—certainly should never have seemed an unlikely task for me to take on.

But it has been. I last held a composing stick in 1980 and had stopped dabbling in journalism by 1985. I even left academia, for what I thought was forever, in 1994.

When I did come back to teaching and to writing, my focus had changed. Popular culture was my new passion, especially as it related to film. My first book was on home viewing of movies, and I felt I would continue to write with an emphasis on the intersection of image and word in American culture.

Our basic natures can't stay hidden for long, however. Over the years, I found myself spending more and more time on the Web—but not reading about movies or discussing them, as one might have thought. I was surfing the blogs, and that started to draw my interest back to the journalism profession that I, like so many Americans (I soon discovered), had been successfully ignoring. Startled by what I found, and concerned, I began to read about its history, trying to figure out what had gone so horribly wrong, making the press a favorite whipping boy where once it had been a respected profession. At the same time I wanted to understand just what, on the blogs, seemed to be going so right.

The result? This book.

ACKNOWLEDGMENTS

This book was inspired by my involvement with the "citizen journalist" group ePluribus Media as it grew from an idea among a number of bloggers to an established online presence with its own blog and Internet journal. Though it would be impossible to list all who have contributed to the group—and to my knowledge of what is really happening in the blogosphere—the following people (some listed by only their blog names) deserve special thanks: Cho, Andrew Brenner, KFred, Susie Dow, D.E. Ford, Todd Johnston, Luaptifer, Tanya, Roxy, Stoy, Rba, Avahome, Lefty Limblog, Kay Shepherd, Timothy D. Smith, BarbinMD, JeninRI, Vivian, Amy Warren, BeverlyinNH, XicanoPwr, Jeff Huber, Intranets, TxSharon, Barbara, Biblio, Welshman, Silence, renarf, Greyhawk, Ilona, and Newton Snookers. There are others, of course—an organization as diffuse and "netroots" as ePMedia sees people come and go, and return. To any I haven't mentioned: you, too, influenced this book. Your omission from this list is my fault only and has nothing to do with the value of your contributions to ePuribus Media or to my learning curve.

In addition, I would like to thank two former colleagues at Kutztown University of Pennsylvania, Marie Squerciati and Matthew Nesvisky, both of whom pointed me in fruitful directions I might otherwise have missed.

INTRODUCTION

When looking at cultural change in America, it is easy to fall into the error of "technodeterminism," the idea that, according to Michael Warner, "technology has an ontological status prior to culture."[1] Warner, a specialist in eighteenth-century media culture, goes on to say that the "assumption that technology is prior to culture results in a kind of retrodeterminism whereby the political history of a technology is converted into the unfolding nature of that technology."[2] Just so. We should never make the mistake of thinking that the blogs that exploded onto the scene over the last five years are nothing more than a function of technology. They are much more than that. In fact, the political blogs have a pedigree as old as that of the United States—older. As I attempt to show in this book, they spring from cultural developments going back to the early eighteenth century.

Certainly, in looking over the backgrounds of political blogs, one quickly finds that blogs are simply *allowed* by technology, not that they are *caused* by technology. The cultural forces that led individuals to adopt the blogs so readily as a means of political expression arose long before the technology appeared. In fact, those forces first arose along with the momentum toward revolution in the middle years of the eighteenth century, only to be suppressed as the growing commercial and professional news media squeezed the public sphere almost to nonexistence.

One critical point to keep in mind while examining the backgrounds of the blogs is that the press, in colonial times and the early years of the republic (up through the presidency of Andrew Jackson), had no distinct role as an entity separate from its utilization. That is, it was simply a part of the democratic process that evolved through the Revolution and beyond. For the five decades following, it became a necessary part of the new democracy, but not a thing in itself. No one at that time could have asked the question journalism scholar Jay Rosen asked at the end of the twentieth century: "What does it take to make democracy work and what should be asked of the press?"[3] "The press" was simply a means or method, not yet a distinct player in American culture. Nothing could be asked of it.

It was not a distinct player in part because of its diffused nature. There was no concentration of media power at all before the 1830s, when Francis Preston Blair became the first to begin real, centralized influence over newspapers even far removed from the Washington, D.C. of his *Globe* and it wasn't until after the Civil War, with the rise of the powerful newspaper chains, that individual media entities could begin to wield real power by themselves. In discussing why he felt the diffuse nature of American journalism was a positive element of the American public sphere, Alexis de Tocqueville wrote that the power of the press was checked by its very ubiquity, that a finite power, scattered so about the nation, could never match what a centralized press could have wielded: "I cannot fancy that a truth so evident still has not become common among us. That those who want to make revolutions with the aid of the press seek to supply it with only a few powerful organs I understand without difficulty; but that the official partisans of the established order and the natural supporters of the existing laws believe that they attenuate the action of the press in concentrating it—that I absolutely cannot conceive."[4] In de Tocqueville's eyes, the grassroots aspect of 1830s journalism was an end in itself, as well as a means for the expression of popular sentiment. He understood quite well that a vibrant, local press serves as a cornerstone of democracy, and that its loss was a loss for the people. After his time, that local aspect of the press was lost in the move toward commercial control of the press and professionalism of its members. Only today, with the ascendancy of the blogs, is there any real reversal, any real move back to the type of journalism de Tocqueville observed.

Actually, there was hardly any such thing as "journalism" in those early days (the word was first used in the 1830s), and "journalist" described a person involved in an activity, not a profession. The "freedom of the press" of the First Amendment to the Constitution referred to no independent societal institution but to a necessary tool of unfettered political debate. Newspapers, instruments of politics, focused on political debate to an extent not seen (on paper) since.

Not seen since. Society changes, and so do its media, especially in terms of what they cover, and they certainly did in the nineteenth century. Unfortunately for many Americans who desired a continued connection with the press and with politics, the changes were such that many felt increasingly alienated from both. But change was inevitable. As Gerald Baldasty, a chronicler of nineteenth-century American newspapers, writes, "The changes in newspaper content across the nineteenth century underscore the extent to which news is a social construct, varying from era to era according to the social forces at work at the time. News is a malleable compound, a synthesis of interests. It is defined through the relationship of the press and society, through the economic forces that shape newspapers as businesses, and through the structure and day-to-day operation of the press itself."[5]

By the Civil War, practitioners of the press had begun to expand the content of their papers and even to see themselves in a new role, with responsibilities to society distinct from those of other businesses and, increasingly, with rights derived from those responsibilities. Professionally, they were beginning to consider themselves not "of " society, but "about" it. Writing some sixty years after the Civil War, Walter Lippmann described the press of his time (pretty much as it had been half a century earlier):

> There is nothing else quite like it, and it is, therefore, hard to compare the press with any other business or institution. It is not a business pure and simple, partly because the product is regularly sold below cost, but chiefly because the community applies one ethical measure to the press and another to trade or manufacture. Ethically a newspaper is judged as if it were a church or a school. But if you try to compare it with these you fail; the taxpayer pays for the public school, the private school is endowed or supported by tuition fees, there are subsidies and collections for the church. You cannot compare journalism with law, medicine or engineering, for in every one of these professions the consumer pays for the service. A free press, if you judge by the attitude of the readers, means newspapers that are virtually given away.
>
> Yet the critics of the press are merely voicing the moral standards of the community, when they expect such an institution to live on the same plane as that on which the school, the church, and the disinterested professions are supposed to live.[6]

On the same plane as community institutions, but also with business parallels (of a special nature), the press existed, in Lippmann's view, in a unique position vis-à-vis society. This view holds today, especially within the journalism community. In fact, the exceptionalism of the media has even been expanded. Leonard Downie, Jr., executive editor of *The Washington Post* (writing with Robert Kaiser, also of the *Post*), goes beyond Lippmann, defining his profession in terms of the positive roles it plays in society: "Good journalism holds communities together in times of crisis, providing the information and the images that constitute shared experience. When disaster strikes, the news media give readers and viewers something to hold on to—facts, but also explanation and discussion that can help people deal with the unexpected."[7]

A separation between the media and the community is unstated but apparent in these comments; Downie and Kaiser's self-congratulatory view of their profession, however, is not shared by much of the public it "serves." Instead, by the start of the twenty-first century, the media were seen more as birds of prey swooping in to pick at the wounded than as protectors or aides. Downie and Kaiser had paid no attention to Lippmann's great rival in this regard, John Dewey, whom journalism scholar Jay Rosen was looking back to when he wrote that the "newspaper of the future will have to rethink its relationship to all the institutions that nourish public life, from libraries to universities to cafes. It will have to do more than 'cover' these institutions when they happen to make news. It will have to do more than print their advertisements. The newspaper must see that its own health is dependent on the health of dozens of other agencies which pull people out of their private worlds."[8]

Rosen expressed that thought in the late 1980s, before the development of the World Wide Web. Yet he was on to something that most in the media could not see. In fact, the rise of the blogs and "citizen journalism," as well as the slightly older "public journalism" (or "civic journalism"), stems directly from public dissatisfaction with the news media—in large part because the media did not follow the path Rosen pointed out. Society had become uncomfortable with media that set themselves apart from the populace, so it cast about until it found alternatives.

Appropriately enough, those alternatives all have a great deal in common with the press of a much earlier time, of the era before commercialization and professionalization began to move the media away from the people and into its own realm, when the press was simply a tool used to further public debate and, one would hope, to help resolve the issues rather than institutionalizing difference.

American public debate of the last two centuries and more has revolved around the question of who governs best—the people or their leaders. It's with us as much at the beginning of the twenty-first century as it clearly was at the end of the eighteenth—and has been discussed ad nauseam without resolution in between. An auxiliary debate, though one without the same clear definition, has paralleled it. Here, too, the question remains unanswered: Are our media responsible *for* the people or *to* the people? As governments sometimes do, the news media have grown to see themselves as separate from the general population, and it is from these separations that debate springs.

In the early days of the republic, public debate stayed close to the people. The press, in fact, was not seen as distinct from the political debates that raged in taverns and coffeehouses, in political meetings both formal and informal. The pamphlet, the magazine, and the newspaper were seen as tools in the debate, not as some entity outside or beyond. That would come later, with the concept of a distinct "fourth estate" appearing almost half a century after establishment of the nation.

Behind the tensions between Thomas Jefferson and John Adams in the years before the turn of the nineteenth century lay the public debate—one that had long been going on in England and in the colonies—over the relationship between the governed and the governing. It had reached its high point, of course, with the Revolutionary War. Afterward, the media's roles in that corollary debate, enshrined in the First Amendment to the Constitution, have grown to be just as problematic as the older issue.

More than fifty years ago, referring specifically to Adams, Jefferson, and the Sedition Act of 1798 (an attempt to bring an unruly press under control), James Morton Smith asked, "Are the people the superiors of the rulers, or are the rulers the superiors of the people? The first view holds that sovereignty resides with the people and not with the government. The so-called rulers are the elected agents and servants of the people . . . . The criminal law of seditious libel . . . emerged . . . when the accepted view made the rulers the superiors of the people. . . . Authority therefore had to be approached with proper decorum."[9] He goes on to describe how, in this second view, words become punishable "because to find fault with the government tended to undermine the respect of the people for it."[10] This dichotomy of viewpoints remains a part of contemporary America, and it is certainly manifest in the tension between the bloggers, who advocate a diffusion of both power and discussion, and the centralized media and political forces, who see themselves as deserving of all the respect that is due to their authority.

When dignity and authority rest with the people and not with the politicians, the words of the people cannot be taken as sedition, as they were by John Adams's administration. On the other hand, a central government does need to wield authority, an authority that can be undermined by determined opposition, even from a minority. It's significant that Smith was writing just as Joe McCarthy reached the pinnacle of his influence, indication of a circling back, at that time, to a situation of greater control over the popular voice by governmental authority than had been seen since the days of the Alien and Sedition Acts of Adams's administration and certainly not since the Sedition Act of 1918's repeal in 1921.

Views of the media have changed since the 1950s, too, but even here things still have a tendency to come full circle. The blogs that have recently grown so important to our political debates have been bringing aspects of the media back under diffused popular control (much as were the newspapers de Tocqueville noted), once again making the media tools within the popular debate. Though new in some respects, what the blogs are doing isn't entirely so.

Imagine reading this passage some fifty years from now: "What emerged from the clutter of verbiage in the . . . [twenty-first-century blogs] was a composite picture of the nation's social and political life, in greater depth than the newspapers could provide, particularly when illustrations appeared. The writing was often atrocious, and much material was borrowed at first, but . . . [blogs] from the beginning held up the mirror to national life, thus becoming a prime source for the social historian."[11] Now let's restore the passage to its original, cutting my bracketed additions and replacing the elided words with the originals: "eighteenth-century magazines" and "magazines." Those words aside, the similarity makes this startlingly clear: the blogs are not an original twenty-first-century phenomenon but, in certain respects, are simply a continuation of an old American tradition in a new technological milieu. They move political (and other) discourse away from the "professionals," putting it once more in the hands of the people—allowing it, once more, to really hold up that "mirror to national life."

The passage above, from John Tebbel and Mary Ellen Zuckerman's *The Magazine in America 1741–1990*, can only be taken so far—it can be used simply to point out those certain similarities. It does little to explain *why* there was no such clamorous media in America in much of the period between the "death" of the partisan press in the 1840s and the blog explosion of the first decade of this new century. And it helps not at all in explaining *why* the resurgence came about.

So just what did happen to our news media in the meantime? Was it really, as some have argued, that it was tamed as it grew in professionalism? What, exactly, were the forces at work that pushed the partisan press to the periphery of American journalism—and why has it come back so strongly today? Changes in technology alone can't be the answer.

Why not?

For one thing, American news media did not manage to keep up with the changing technologies of the last quarter of the twentieth century. Their news-gathering complacency after the fall of the Berlin Wall has become a commonplace in discussions of the failures of the news media. But the news media were also remiss in exploring the possibilities offered by, most particularly, the advent of the World Wide Web in 1994. At most, the Web was seen as a new venue for distributing news, a la *Salon* and *Slate*, the first two significant online newsmagazines. News-gathering and research aspects (outside of database search capabilities) of the Web were ignored, for the most part, by the media until well into the presidency of George W. Bush.

For another thing, the media did not put much effort into examining themselves and their relationships to the general public or the broader public debates. More accurately, even when they did identify their own weaknesses, they did nothing about them. In his 1955 book *The Public Philosophy*, Lippmann wrote,

> the modern media of mass communication do not lend themselves easily to a confrontation of opinions. The dialectical process for finding truth works best when the same audience hears all the sides of the disputation. This is manifestly impossible in the moving pictures: if a film advocates a thesis, the same audience cannot be shown another film designed to answer it. Radio and television broadcasts do permit some debate. But despite the effort of the companies to let opposing views be heard equally, and to organize programs on which there are opposing speakers, the technical conditions of broadcasting do not favor genuine and productive debate. For the audience, tuning on and tuning off here and there, cannot be counted upon to hear, even in summary form, the essential evidence and the main arguments on all the significant sides of a question. Rarely, and on very few public issues, does the mass audience have the benefit of the process by which truth is sifted from error—the dialectic of debate in which there is immediate challenge, reply, cross-examination, and rebuttal. The men who regularly broadcast the news and comment upon the news cannot—like a speaker in the Senate or in the House of Commons—be challenged by one of their listeners and compelled then and there to verify their statements of fact and to re-argue their inferences from the facts.[12]

Unable or unwilling to recognize the dangers in their position vis-à-vis public debate, completely and purposefully ignorant of their own lack of accountability, the news media sailed on, blissfully unaware of the nearing lee shore as the winds of popular frustration with the lack of substantive discussion grew greater with each passing year. While some, like Lippmann, recognized the position, few saw it as genuinely dangerous. Fewer still determined to do anything about it. Instead, most journalists insisted on seeing themselves solely as the watchdogs of others, never willingly turning their eyes on themselves. Just so, Downie and Kaiser, when discussing the role of journalism, turn their vision only outward: "Accountability is an important check on that power [of governments, corporations, and the like]. Our politicians know that informed voters can throw them out of office; corporate CEOs recognize the authority of their boards of directors and the influence of their stockholders; a cop taking bribes knows he doesn't want to get caught. Good journalism is a principal source of the information necessary to make such accountability meaningful. Anyone tempted to abuse power looks over his or her shoulder to see if someone else is watching. Ideally, there should be a reporter in the rearview mirror."[13]

But who is watching the watchers—who is in the reporter's rearview mirror? Notably, there is no mention of oversight of the news media themselves in Downie and Kaiser's list—yet the news media need that knowledge that someone is watching as much as anyone does.

The failure of the news media by the turn of the twenty-first century was much more profound than is generally recognized. Not only did news programming on electronic media (as well as print media) come to be considered a profit center and not in any respect a public service (no longer seen as needed by corporate ownership and no longer forced on the media by government), but coverage had turned parochial and reactive—the news media resting on whatever laurels remained instead of aggressively exploring the incredible possibilities that opened daily (or so it seemed) as the Web grew and evolved.

As with so much else relating to American political society, the shock of 9/11 brought the weaknesses of the media into sharp popular focus. If George Bush can be criticized for reading *My Pet Goat* to school children as the United States experienced its most challenging crisis of a generation, our news media also deserve a great deal of reprobation. They, too, didn't know how to react.

There had been warnings that such attacks could happen: the February 26, 1993, attempt to destroy the World Trade Center through use of a truck bomb; the bombings of United States embassies in Dar es Salaam, Tanzania, and Nairobi, Kenya, on August 7, 1998; and the report by the Hart-Rudman U.S. Commission of National Security/21st Century released earlier in 2001. Yet the complacent and uninformed news media were no more prepared for such a possibility than were the public they had claimed for so long to be serving or than was the government they covered.

Former CBS correspondent Tom Fenton blasts his profession:

We had failed to warn the American public of the storm clouds approaching our shores. And in failing to do so, we betrayed the trust of the public.

"The summer of 2001," says Tom Bettag, executive editor of ABC's *Nightline*, "was the lowest point in American journalism." During those months—a time when at least some members of the Bush administration were considering taking action against al Qaeda—the networks decided that the public was more interested in shark attacks than terrorist attacks. In the three months leading up to September 11, the phrase "al Qaeda" was never mentioned on any of the three evening news broadcasts—*not once*.[14]

After 9/11, the complacency that had grown so prevalent in the media was suddenly apparent to anyone who cared to look. And now, millions were looking.

While many (especially media insiders) have spent much time since 9/11 bemoaning the state of our news media, others have taken initiative, trying to rectify our news structures, mainly through adding to them from the outside. Most of these people have centered their activities on the expanding Internet possibilities for communication and research that the media had effectively ignored, many of them presenting their findings through what had been called "web logs" early on, but that were known, by the time of the twin-towers/Pentagon attacks, simply as "blogs."

As might be expected, given the general news media malaise, the rise of the blogs, too, caught what soon became known as "the mainstream media" (MSM) by surprise. The complacency of the MSM didn't extend solely to themselves, their subject matter, and new technologies, but also to their understanding of the changing news audiences. These audiences, it turned out, *weren't* satisfied with tales of shark attacks—hadn't been, and still aren't. Much of the media still doesn't understand why this is happening (as they continue to focus on "missing girl" stories and similar trivia), allowing the alternative news sources room to continue to grow in importance and even in accuracy, reviving what had been a somewhat moribund journalistic tradition of rambunctious, partisan journalism.

That tradition had been driven into quietude by two forces: corporate centralization, which removed much of journalism from direct contact with its consumers, and the growth of a distinct profession of journalism with its own ethics and standards along with a clear view of itself as a "fourth estate" with unique responsibilities and privileges. Through these forces, the media began to see themselves as part of neither the governed nor the governing, believing themselves somehow removed from the debate. In that vision, too, lay the seeds of their "downfall."

In the 1790s, the press was not yet seen as a distinct "fourth estate." Thus, it wasn't considered to be a distinct part of the debate over governing, but simply as an adjunct either to the people or the leaders, depending on which side a particular publication was on. Only later did the discussion become at all three-way or extend to that second, parallel debate about the news media themselves.

Writing at the end of the 1930s, Bertrand Russell had seen the debate on the people versus their governments as effectively over, at least from a conceptual standpoint. He claimed it "is obvious that publicity for grievances must be possible; agitation must be free provided it does not incite to breaches of the law; there must be ways of impeaching officials who exceed or abuse their powers. The government of the day must not be in a position to secure its own permanence by intimidation, falsification of the register of electors, or any similar method. There must be no penalty, official or unofficial, for any well-grounded criticism of prominent men."[15]

Yet, a mere few years after Russell's words, the other side seemed once again ascendant—in America, at least. Russell's "must" had been rejected—for the moment, at least.

By the time Russell was writing, the press had long since become a profession, one restricted by its own code of ethics and responsibility. Many within still saw it as the bulwark against abuse of governmental authority, however, and felt *that* was the reason for guarding 'freedom of the press' so jealously. Standing supposedly outside the debate, the press could ensure that neither side grew too powerful.

Nostalgia for a press crusading for the people remains alive even today, as the popularity of the film about Edward R. Murrow's decision to take on McCarthy, *Good Night, and Good Luck* (George Clooney, 2005), attests. But that press has disappeared, replaced by corporate media lacking in feelings of responsibility for anything but its profit. In many respects, the debate about the role of the commercial and professional press was over by 2000; the press had become firmly committed to the side of authority and power. Yes, during the time of Adams and Jefferson, the press had been used by those in power, too, but there was as great a journalistic presence on the other side—and that's what had been lost by the end of the twentieth century, a loss the blogs are now attempting to redress.

It is easy enough to see that the rise of this modern mass media as a distinct entity stems from the success of the "penny press" that began appearing in the 1830s. What's more difficult to assess is what was lost as the media grew more powerful and more clearly defined through the nineteenth century. Yet, even though it has taken well more than a century for the American populace to regain what it unconsciously ceded as media grew, it is now doing so. As a result, only today is it possible to really gauge the loss—and assess what is being regained through online "citizen journalism" and the blogs.

To date, few observers of the media have seen clearly what is happening, most seeing the changes in media over the centuries (and even now) as linear rather than, if not circular, at least somewhat more like William Butler Yeats's gyre, a spiraling out that constantly returns to the earlier, though at a higher and broader level. Kurt Anderson, for example, writing in *New York* magazine, tried to throw a bit of cold water on blogger enthusiasm for the new media possibility they espouse:

> Bloggers badly want to believe their time has come. CNN made its reputation by covering the Gulf War, and I am sure someone has declared that the bloggers' recent career-wrecking achievements—discrediting CBS News' National Guard documents, forcing CNN to oust Eason Jordan, outing the weirdo [Jeff] Gannon—amount to their new-media equivalent of Operation Desert Storm.
>
> But just as CNN was never really about to reinvent itself to be indispensable for anything except covering wars and tsunamis, one can imagine the blogs settling forever at their present level of almost wholly media-on-media impact. For now, bloggers are a second-tier journalistic species. They are remoras. The *Times* and CNN and CBS News are the whales and sharks to which Instapundit, Kausfules, and Kos attach themselves for their free rides. . . . If the sharks and whales were to go extinct, what would the blogging remoras *do*? Evolve into actual reporters? . . .
>
> What will take place, I think, is that blogging will be absorbed and then transmuted by larger media entities, something analogous to what happened to theatrical newsreels after their brief heyday in the thirties and forties, when they were subsumed by TV. But in the meantime, until bloggers can commit errors of the Mary Mapes or Eason Jordan kind and then suffer the consequences that Mapes and Jordan did, how seriously can we take the medium?[16]

The inappropriate newsreel/TV analogy aside, Anderson's question is a good one: Just how seriously *can* we take the blogs? Are they, in fact, a reversion or are they simply an anomaly, a curiosity along the way of journalism's development?

This book, in large part, is an attempt to answer that question by placing the blogs within their appropriate historical context, showing them not simply as a new phenomenon nor as a reversion to a type of journalism fortunately long abandoned, but as an outgrowth both of that older journalism *and* the changed media that developed in its place. Unlike Anderson, who sees the changes in contemporary journalism (including the blogs) as a reversion, my argument here is that they are an expansion, taking aspects of both the journalism that was superseded before the Civil War and its replacement—and creating something completely new, but with ties to the very old.

The blogs are also a reaction to one of the most salient facts about journalism. A. J. Liebling puts it quite simply: "The function of the press in society is to inform, but its role is to make money."[17] Over the past half-century, the role has become more and more important and the function less so. Frustration over this, as I have indicated, has been building among the American population for decades. Responding to his own worries about the consolidation of media ownership, Liebling, writing in the early 1960s, was optimistic, believing that change for the better was inevitable, using media reactions to John Kennedy as an example. Interestingly, the picture he paints of how the media wanted to portray Kennedy is completely at odds with how he is remembered today—a fact that, in Liebling's eye, is due almost completely to television. Print journalism wanted to show Kennedy "as a callow gossoon, hiding a low IQ under his father's thumb."[18] But television, which in Liebling's eye had a different agenda (and held a grudge against the newspapers for the way it had been treated during the recent quiz-show scandals), saw in Kennedy the type of candidate it could exhibit to advantage—and did so to the detriment of Nixon, who was not able to come off so well in the new medium. Liebling even goes so far as to insinuate that Kennedy's success was in no small part the result of a desire on the part of the networks to get even with the newspapers—and to show the power they now wielded. The media monolith had fractured. "By such small accidents dissidence survives."[19] Just so, the blogs constituted one of those "small" accidents that have a way of creating lasting change.

How will the "citizen journalism" associated with the blogs manifest itself in the long run? I can't really answer that, of course, but I can, once more, look to the past for possible answers. Liebling describes that past as a nineteenth century of numerous competing newspapers that were without the resources or money of the press of later years. For correspondents, those newspapers often had to make do with letters from people "who were resident in a foreign land or were going abroad, on their own affairs, to write about the countries they had opportunities to study. This was a simple and relatively inexpensive process. The man used his legs, his eyes, his judgment and a pen."[20] Newspapers, grateful to have stories from anywhere they could get them, would take the missives and print them. Sometimes these were detailed and penetrating; at other times they were of somewhat lesser quality.

Either way, it was cheap journalism—and editors of the time were happy to get it.

Something was lost when reporting (especially from abroad) became the province of syndicates, for they tended to look to each other for both style and content, and the individualism of the earlier era started to disappear.

With current technology, though, it would now be possible for the news media to make use of the amateur again, risking getting the bad but taking that chance in order to find the good. Eventually, bloggers may serve the function of the old-fashioned correspondent, melding into the media businesses as stringers of a sort. Tom Fenton, again echoing *Nightline* producer Tom Bettag, suggests something like this (though not with direct regard to the blogs), centered on utilization of small DVD recorders and Internet transmission,[21] though Fenton is not thinking of bloggers, "citizen journalists," or amateur correspondents but of stringers with professional backgrounds.

To make a point about contemporary news media, Fenton divides its frontline workers into two categories: "journalists" and "reporters." His "journalists" read the news on TV or radio or write the actual newspaper stories. His "reporters" are those who go out and do the research, the background investigation. Liebling, writing almost half a century ago, also divided the profession, but into three. First, for him, is the reporter, the recorder of events. Second is the interpretive reporter, who adds a discussion of meaning. And third is the expert, who adds meaning at a distance from the actual events. Over the years since, the expert is the one who has come to dominate the news media, becoming the star—the commentator, the pundit. These are the people who always seem to "know." They have to have that appearance. As Liebling says, to "combat an old human prejudice in favor of eye-witness testimony, . . . the expert must intimate that he has access to some occult source or science not available to either reporter or reader. . . . Once his position is conceded, the expert can put on a better show than the reporter. All is manifest to him, since his conclusions are not limited by his powers of observation."[22]

Fenton's two categories don't really provide room for the bloggers or amateur "citizen journalists" (let alone for pundits) but Liebling's, surprisingly, do. Though many bloggers certainly do fall into the third of his categories (though without the gravitas that the professionals manage), and probably will continue there, many others, one discovers, are functioning in the first two as well.

As this is not a history of journalism but an exploration of the forces and trends that led to the rise in importance of the blogs, a great deal of what would be important to a comprehensive history has been left out. For example, Benjamin Day's *The New York Sun* preceded James Gordon Bennett's *Herald* by two years, both as a penny paper and in utilization of newsboys for distribution; Joseph Pulitzer was at least as significant (if not more so) to the development of American journalism as was William Randolph Hearst; of course, David Sarnoff was a much more important contributor to early electronic media than was William Paley; and Henry Luce with *Time* and *Life* certainly played a role in the development of American news media. There are other examples that could be given, all significant. The careers that I have chosen as touchstones, however, illustrate best the points I wish to make about a contemporary phenomenon, either through their level of success, longevity, or connection with other specific and relevant events and personalities.

Chapter 1

THE CONCEPTION OF A POPULAR AMERICAN PRESS

If any one person deserves the appellation "patron saint of the blogs," it is Benjamin Franklin. From the fact that he had to force his way into the writing field over established opposition (though that opposition consisted of his brother) to his fascination with technology, from his recognition of the positive possibilities inherent in the connection between the press and politics to his understanding of the value of networking, Franklin laid groundwork that, though it percolated slowly, eventually bubbled up to become the blogs.

Given his fascination with the new, Franklin would certainly be at home with the Internet, that method of information transmittal that took hold so quickly at the end of the twentieth century, allowing growth in communications and opening up new media possibilities—much as the telegraph, telephone, and the radio had once done. The Internet has yet to have its Franklin (who transformed an adjunct to the printer's trade into what would eventually be regarded as a new and separate profession, journalism), but that person's day isn't very far off. In the meantime, it is worth looking back to Franklin and his milieu for the additional reason that his position vis-à-vis newspapers and the postal service finds an echo in today's webmasters and internet service providers (ISPs). In fact, the history of the Internet could in many respects be described as the history of Franklin's endeavors writ large and moved forward two and a half centuries.

If there was a first forerunner to the Internet, it was the postal services, first in Persia and finally ubiquitous. The postal services provided an organized method of information transmittal, one that opened up possibilities that hadn't previously been imagined, but that developed quickly in light of the new opportunity: namely, the personal missive, now called the letter—the general news summary that became the newspaper. These means of communication and information dissemination, and more, were made possible by the mails, a means of communication that began (usually) as simply a means for a government to communicate with its parts. With such a system of transmittal in place, however, the wider world quickly became more open to each locality than it had ever been before.

For centuries, the mails formed the primary formal networks that connected diverse communities, really the only stable ones outside the communications that came through commercial trading enterprises. The mails were particularly important to the British colonies in North America, where communication with the outside world was often as rare as it was difficult. Not surprisingly, the nodes of this network, represented by the postmasters, often became associated with the presentation of information as well as with its transmittal. After all, most communication from outside passed through their hands. Eyeing this situation, enterprising printers saw an additional fruitful enterprise for them and seized upon it, becoming postmasters themselves. Because the post was a source of news that could be used for newspapers and broadsheets, increasing the printer's business—to say nothing of the influence that could be generated—the two seemed a natural fit.

In the eighteenth century, little in any newspaper, especially in the colonies, was locally generated. Much of what was printed came from other papers verbatim (often without acknowledgement), and printers obligingly sent on their own papers for the same purpose, so that the origin of a particular article might be several papers removed.

In their symbiosis, the post and the printer proved instrumental in expansion of a new public discursive sphere that went beyond mere local issues. This sphere was itself an important component in the birth of an American identity and of the discussions on civic duties and responsibilities that eventually led to the development of the American political system. Of particular importance (though it may not have been recognized at the time) was the now-obvious intersection of the local and the global, of a local paper but global news, something quite distinct from how local newspapers are utilized in the twenty-first century.

Because towns were few and the villages small, there was little need for the recording of local events in the home newspaper. Everyone knew anything of importance that had happened long before a report of it could ever be set in type. As a result, much of what the printers presented in colonial papers came from distant places—even as far away as Russia. Wars, of course, dominated the news.

Yet sometimes the post was delayed, or there was little of interest in it. So the local printer occasionally had to rely upon items generated either by himself or people close by to fill the empty space. As the laming of Tom Brown's horse was common knowledge, a story on that would not suffice. Without news, commentary on local, colonial, or even overseas controversies was used. The fact of local comment on distant issues provided a certain feeling of local empowerment and involvement, waking people to the intersection of the two worlds, the local and the wider, and eventually even making them aware of the possibility of their own contributions to the distant events shaping their lives.

As we can see, "words," in the political discussion of Franklin's eighteenth century, generally meant either face-to-face discussions or newspapers, though pamphlets also had a great impact on various dialogues. Books other than the Bible were rarer and were much more expensive—and rarely addressed topical subjects. The power of the words in all these places was apparent both to those with political power and to those who wanted to debate them. Naturally, the first group wanted to keep careful track of and authority over the words published, while the second, generally those who wrote and printed, did not want to cede control over their creations.

The tension between these two groups, in terms of what would become the "press" in America, was evident from the start. The first North American newspaper (published in Boston), Benjamin Harris's *Publick Occurrences both Foreign and Domestick* was suppressed after just one issue, for overstepping its license. That is, it went beyond what the authorities felt was appropriate, so they forcibly shut it down. Harris, obviously, had felt that the decision about content was his. The authorities believed otherwise. At that time, they had the power to enforce their opinion.

This was an inauspicious start for a land that came to cherish freedom of the press as one of its basic rights. But that right would be a long time coming: individual liberty and protected expression were not yet cornerstones of governance on the North American continent. Still, it would be nice to imagine that journalism in America began with a triumph. Unfortunately, the real triumph of what eventually came to be called "the press," or the "fourth estate," was slow in building, coming only in the aftermath of the Revolution, nearly a century after Harris's strangled enterprise.

In fact, it can be argued that it was only through the Revolution that the American press, as a distinct entity, came into existence. Before that, there was no discrete newspaper trade or profession; creating a newspaper was nothing more than one among many of the tasks a printer might perform, one meant to keep his press busy (as much as anything else) when other jobs were scarce. Indeed, it wouldn't be until sixty years had passed after the Revolution, when use-specific presses came into common employment, that the job-printing and newspaper trades would have a final parting of the ways.

The second American newspaper, postmaster (a duty he had taken on in 1702) John Campbell's *Boston News-Letter*, appeared in 1704 and carried on its front a clear acceptance of the prerogative of the central power, a "published by authority" statement. As postmaster and editor, Campbell tried to bridge, as much as possible, not only his two professions but also the gap between the two sides of the struggle over words. Having an official position, he was an insider, part of the power structure. As editor, however, he was responsible to his readers. It was a good idea for the time, this pairing of positions, but the tensions of the dual responsibilities could not be sustained forever—as future events proved. Things were changing: censorship, along with other forms of direct government control over publications, was already losing its appeal as a governmental tool, and public debate over policy issues was gaining acceptance. As Jürgen Habermas notes, in England (and the colonies did follow homeland examples) this process, including gradual diminution of censorship, "made the influx of rational-critical arguments into the press possible and allowed the latter to evolve into an instrument with whose aid political decisions could be brought before the new forum of the public."[1]

This process of change was as apparent in the colonies as in the mother country and proved to be, as a means of popular empowerment, one of the forces behind the move toward revolution. Even without resorting to direct censorship, government continued to try to control the printers and their newspapers, for they recognized the shift in power that popular discussion represented. But the now-unlocked door had also been left ajar. Soon the printers were starting to push on it and go through, ultimately winning access and taking much more direct control of the words they published.

In the meantime, the intersection of editor and postmaster did prove most advantageous to Campbell and subsequent colonial newspaper publishers, many of whom also served the postal network. With almost all correspondence coming through their offices, they could ask recipients of mail from distant places to share the information received. In fact, many of the letters were written with such an eventual request in mind. Speaking primarily of England and the Europe of the eighteenth century (again, applicable to the colonies), Habermas writes, "Letters by strangers were not only borrowed and copied; some correspondences were intended from the outset for publication. . . . An idiomatic expression current at the time described the well composed letter as 'pretty enough to print.'"[2]

With privacy not yet the real American fetish it would eventually become, there would have been nothing untoward for a printer/postmaster, alerted to the fact that someone had received something from afar, to ask to share in the reading—and then to share again in print. Like webmasters monitoring the traffic on their sites in the twenty-first century, the postmasters certainly knew what the activity was, where it was from, and where it was going—even when they didn't know the particulars of the missive. Unlike webmasters, who have to be more circumspect, they made it their business to find out.

The printers who produced newspapers but who weren't postmasters themselves also benefited from the postal service. Because there was always a sense that a newspaper was something of a public service in that it disseminated important information, a special relationship developed between the postal service and all newspapers, one that held true for a century—with remnants lasting even longer in the form of special newspaper rates and, now, "media mail."

Without the postal network, the colonial newspapers would have had an even harder time surviving than they actually did. Postmaster and printer corresponded, providing information about distant events (local communities were small enough so that everyone already knew much of the "news"— it didn't have to be printed). In fact, it was partially through this sort of correspondence, along with information brought by sailing-ship captains, that enough information was amassed to make even a four-page paper possible. Even Benjamin Franklin, remembered mainly as a printer, statesman, and writer, was also a postmaster—in fact, in 1753 he was appointed to the position of deputy postmaster general for the entire English colonies.

One of the reasons Franklin was such a success so early in life was that he realized he needed to do more than simply be a printer or a writer, given the needs and possibilities of his community. As biographer Walter Isaacson writes, Franklin succeeded "by building a media conglomerate that included production capacity (printing operations, franchised printers in other cities), products (a newspaper, magazine, almanac), content (his own writings, his alter ego Poor Richard's, and those of his Junto [club]), and distribution (eventually the whole of the colonial postal system)."[3] Most successful printers in America, until the 1830s, did somewhat the same, though rarely to the extent of Franklin. No single pursuit was sufficient for sustained success. Even in the larger cities, there wasn't a concentration of demand sufficient for division of the trade into stand-alone parts. The breadth of a printer's trade (especially Franklin's) could be even greater than Isaacson suggests, for it also included the profitable service to the government (printing government documents, often in return for political support), a mainstay of printers' incomes up to the 1840s. Also, Isaccson's mention of "products" is somewhat misleading in that he neglects the very real (and sustaining, for most printers) job-printing business: printers produced handbills on demand, printed sermons and sheet music, and produced a variety of other documents and items for the general public.

Everything was decentralized in a colonial printer's world; all decisions about the news, for example, were made locally in each shop, never coming from a central authority. Naturally so: looked at in simple geographic terms, those arguing for central control, either before the Revolution or in the decades after, were faced with a losing proposition. Even had people in distant locations been willing to bow to the "metropole" (in the sense of the deciding economic entity), there was no effective way for the central power to enforce its control, either from London or, later, from New York, Philadelphia, or even Washington. Because those in the political center of the colonies (and, later, the United States) had to rely on the willingness of the governed, movement was inexorable toward diffusion of power—in media as in government.

What is the relationship of this fact to the blogs of the twenty-first century? Quite simply, the development of a diffused power structure led not only to a federal framework for the United States of America but to a decentralized communications network outside of control by any single authority, even of the authority nominally in control. This network defied attempts at centralization in the early years of the nation just as the Internet defies attempts at control today.

Even with the rise of the blogs, which, themselves, can be seen as a throwback to the type of press not really seen since the Civil War, the conception and place of the newspaper in colonial American and early antebellum America was quite different from what is standard in the early twenty-first century. Then, the press, even when dealing with national issues, was absolutely local. Today, the press—like most of the new media—is seen by most Americans as representative of the rich and powerful, of the center and not of the people. The blogs are often considered by their promoters as a reversion, as a means of taking power back from the corporations, the representations of the rich, and returning conversation to the people. When Benjamin Franklin's brother James went to work for one of the colonies' earliest newspapers, the *Boston Gazette*, in 1719 and then founded his own a few years later, there was a similar place of unfettered conversation by the people: the coffeehouses. There the real conversational ferment was happening, and James Franklin, a habitué, was simply to extend the conversations he participated in and heard to the newspaper—again something seen today as the older news media begin to incorporate blogs into both their reporting and their operations.

The coffeehouses of the time were much more central, and much more important, to informal political debate than might initially be assumed today, when our image is one of coffee bars offering quiet places for reading and intimate talk. Coffeehouses began appearing in American during the early decades of the eighteenth century and followed the pattern that had been established in England, where there were already "3,000 of them, each with a core group of regulars. Just as Dryden, surrounded by the new generation of writers, joined the battle of the 'ancients and moderns' at Will's, Addison and Steele a little later convened their 'little senate' at Button's; so too in the Rotary Club, presided over by Milton's secretary, Marvell and Pepys met with Harrington who here probably presented the republican ideas of his *Oceana*."[4] The coffeehouses of Boston couldn't claim the luminaries of those in London, but the concept was the same and discussion was certainly as heated—and as politically edgy.

So volatile was coffeehouse discussion that British authorities kept a sharp eye on them, for they were where new ideas were bandied about, shouted down, and greeted with applause. Though the political thinkers who frequented the coffeehouses ranged from those on the cutting edge to quite reactionary ones, the new phenomenon wasn't trusted by anyone in power. In fact, the reaction to them was much like that to the blogs: uneasiness coupled with feeble condemnation. Authorities in the colonies were as leery of these new places for new types of discussion as were those in England. And they had reason to be so.

Out of the coffeehouses grew a new type of publication, the political/cultural journal. Habermas sees these journals as a natural outgrowth of the growing movement, one that had become so popular that the coffeehouses themselves could not sustain it. He sees the *Tatler*, which began publication in 1709, as a response to a discussion circle that had grown too large for face-to-face discussion—much as the blogs are meeting a need for greater discussion today: "The periodical articles were not only made the object of discussion by the public of the coffee houses but were viewed as integral parts of this discussion; this was demonstrated by the flood of letters from which the editor each week published a selection."[5] Just as the blogs do today, the journals amplified talk that had been ongoing, but on a level not quite so public.

Because of technological limitations, however, the journals couldn't have gone far beyond the local discussions even if they had wanted to—keeping them attached to localities and even to particular coffeehouses. As Paul Starr says, "the limits of newspaper sales prevented those who ran the papers from acquiring the power and autonomy that their successors would be able to achieve on the basis of larger circulations and greater revenue from both readers and advertisers."[6] The coffeehouses used the newspapers as sources and were sources for them, much as blogs use the news media of today and are used by them, but the coffeehouses were really more important than the papers, which often got their most important dissemination by being read aloud there. Unlike the coffeehouses, however, the blogs *are* publications, though they also serve the same function as the coffeehouses, discussion. In going into the printing business, James Franklin, who had spent considerable time in England, would have recognized that aspect of the coffeehouses of Boston that was missing: the periodical, where the coffeehouse declamations could be given more permanent form.

In Bernard Faÿ's biography of Benjamin Franklin, published in 1929, well after the first major change in the American press but before the explosion of electronic media and the final twentieth-century consolidation of media power, the author describes the possibilities and conceptions of the press facing James Franklin: "A newspaper was what he needed. He had seen enough of them in London to realize how powerful a gazette was in the hands of the dissatisfied. Thanks to it, one could organize a party."[7] It wasn't a completely rosy picture, as Faÿ admits. An editor could easily be thrown in jail and had to write in baldly inflammatory terms in order to gain notice—something that resulted in negative reaction as often as positive. "Such insults as 'Calumniator' or 'Vile Pamphleteer' were to be accepted as commonplace and a good deal of audacity was needed. . . . No one could hope to be a popular leader or to have a lively newspaper if he could not succeed in over-exciting his readers."[8]

Writing long before the advent of the blogs, Faÿ nevertheless outlines a situation very similar to that of these early days of the blogs. With a few simple changes, this passage could be describing the rationale and situation of contemporary bloggers, though they don't—in the United States, at least—face jail and injury as a result of their activities.

The parallel continues. In 1717, though the population was diffused through small rural communities, power in the colonies was concentrated. This made the elites who controlled such hub cities as Boston even more powerful than one might imagine, given the small populations even of such a "major" urban center. James Franklin, by becoming a focus of rural and dissatisfied sentiment through his newspaper, was able to act as an outlet for the people who did not care much for the clergy and the wealthy, who wielded disproportionate power.

Faÿ writes that a "newspaper in 1717 didn't amount to much."[9] But, in James Franklin's imagination, a newspaper could. Few contemporary blogs amount to much either; but they could, also—and in exactly the same way as those early newspapers did. The blogs are raising the hopes of the politically dissatisfied today by giving them a means for finding each other and uniting.

The most important point to be made through this, aside from the parallels, is that newspapers of the colonial period served a popular discursive purpose in the public sphere quite distinct from the major American media of the early twenty-first century—a purpose that has remained unfulfilled for quite some time but one that the blogs, perhaps, are beginning to fulfill.

James Franklin had already established a print shop of his own when he founded his newspaper, the *New-England Courant*, in 1721. He quickly joined in the ongoing battle between the "liberals" (who could not accept the "unscientific" concept of using a disease to fight a disease) and Cotton Mather over, ostensibly, smallpox inoculation. The fracas, at least as bitter as any blog-war today, climaxed with the tossing of a "grenado" through Mather's window. Fortunately, it did not explode.

Though the papers in the colonies did begin to get involved in controversies such as the one over inoculations, most of what they published consisted of economic reports (often supplied by shippers) and letters from distant places and reprints from English papers. After all, the colonies looked with avid interest to affairs in Europe, seeing the old world as the center of life and knowledge. But the seeds of a more local, more activist journalism were being sown through local controversies such as the smallpox debate.

In addition, ships, post offices, and printers combined (in the years before the Revolution) to form a network of information transmittal that became increasingly important at the local level as resistance to rule from London grew. The network they formed created links among a dispersed, increasingly rural population. The coffeehouses and taverns became places where the information managed and transmitted was then discussed and, in some cases, sent on again with a new twist. Because most lives were lived within walking distance of home, these places also served for the transmittal of local news by word of mouth, information that would not leave the neighborhood, interest in it being strictly personal.

In fact, one reason that newspapers did not try to cover local news is that, for the most part, doing so would have been redundant. When even the population of the larger towns numbered only in the thousands, the backfence/tavern network could move information from one end to the other in minutes. The newspapers, most of which came out weekly, could rarely match that speed.

Newspapers, back fences, taverns, ships, and the postal service: these and similar means of communication made up an efficient, if jury-rigged, system. Especially since it lacked any sort of central control, this network is even *more* akin to today's Internet than it might seem at first. This was no rudimentary version of the Associated Press wire with a central clearing house, but an extensive and diffuse system that grew on its own rather than through plan. One newspaper might be muted, a tavern could be closed down: it wouldn't matter. The system would keep on operating, ships and postal services providing the connections while coffee houses and taverns served as the Web sites.

At the same time, certain individuals (many of them in the combined role of postmaster and printer) started acting as "correspondents" (a word whose use in this context started to gain currency in the first decades of the eighteenth century—the earliest use in this fashion may be by Richard Steele in *The Spectator* in 1711)[10] for newspapers in other locations, exchanging local news for news from elsewhere. These weren't reporters or journalists as we use the terms today, going out and finding news stories, but simply collators of what came to them. Still, as "correspondents," they were writing more than had printers of the past, a step toward the concept of "newspaperman" as writer and not simply as printer. In the colonies, Benjamin Franklin, once he had established himself as a Philadelphia printer, became the most important of these. In fact, he did more, becoming, in some respects, an active seeker of news—one of the first to do so.

For the most part, however, the "correspondents" of the day were performing something of the same function as contemporary bloggers. That is, they weren't generally finding the news but were more often reading the news themselves in the local papers wherever they happened to be and, as time went on, commenting upon it. This function of the bloggers is often disparaged by twenty-first-century journalists, who see it as only a secondary journalistic occupation, one riding on the backs of the "real" journalists. But, like the "correspondents" of the eighteenth century, who presaged that very type of journalism, the bloggers may be heralds of another entirely new sort.

Before removing to Philadelphia, one of those who wanted to get involved in the newer, developing, and therefore more exciting form of journalism was, of course, the younger Benjamin Franklin. In 1722, he started on his own career as more than just a printer, anonymously submitting "letters" from one Silence Dogood to his brother's newspaper. Even though Franklin had reason for hiding his identity from a relative who would not countenance such activity, pseudonyms were nothing unusual. They were, in fact, the rule of the day for such letters—just as they are, today, for many bloggers.

Like the early blogs, the fledgling press in the colonies was small and relatively weak, so it was not likely an explicit target of a Crown attempting to control colonial opinion. If anything, the press was seen more as an annoyance than as a threat. Even though the infamous Stamp Act, passed in 1765, attempted to place a tax on the newspapers of the time, along with all other printed items, this wasn't simply an attempt to muzzle the press. In fact, its primary purpose was the raising of money for colonial defense. The reaction against the Stamp Act came fast and furious in the colonies—not out of defense of the newspapers, but because of the nature of a law of taxation coming from England without American input. Though the Stamp Act was repealed the next year, its importance vis-à-vis the press grew in memory over the years until it came to be viewed as a seminal event in the growth of freedom of the press in America rather than what it really had been: part of a fight over a different issue. The concern over taxation of a necessary component of news media production remains, however, with ISPs and others concerned with maintaining the Internet watching anxiously as governmental authorities eye their businesses as sources of revenue.

Also like the blogs of today, the press in Colonial America and the early years of the Republic was quite vituperative. In trying to explain this, Eric Burns, a Fox News commentator, contends that the problem was a lack of a tradition of journalistic ethics, particularly one containing the concept of impartiality: "If you told a man he had a civic duty to report the news objectively, he would have asked what duty the artisan had, or the ironworker or the shipbuilder or the farmer. These were men who did their jobs, nothing more; so was he."[11] The concept of "reporting the news" as an end in itself had not yet appeared. Like blogs today, eighteenth-century newspapers were more involved in commenting on the news and in furthering specific political agendas than they were in informing the public.

To understand the power of the blogs today, it is helpful to recognize that there wasn't even a "press" or "journalism" in the eighteenth century, not as we understand the words today. What they did have served a function more like that of the blogs than that of the journalism of the intervening years—a function that has been somewhat repressed over that time, one of unvarnished public opinion. The contemporary vision of the press as a "fourth estate" was a concept that gained currency only in the middle of the nineteenth century. Some scholars, Habermas for example, do find at least a proto-"fourth estate" in the eighteenth century (starting with the appearance of the *Craftsman* in 1726) in England,[12] but I think it would be hard to sustain any argument that there was a distinct institution of the press in America before the nineteenth century. The newspaper was simply one product of a printer's trade—which makes Burns's statement accurate in that sense, at least.

Though I have been pointing out similarities between the press of the colonial era in America and the blogs, there's a danger in doing so too glibly.

It's often easy, looking back, to impose the systems of our time on a different era. Burns, for example, claims that James Franklin's *New England Courant* "was the first American paper to employ a staff of reporters—or rather, since it did not pay them, the first paper to allow young men to volunteer their time and their pens in the hope of making a name for themselves in the new and growing field of event retailing."[13] But these were no more reporters than they were part of the "new and growing field of event retailing," which would not appear for more than a century. The earliest reference in the *Oxford English Dictionary* to the word "reporter" in the sense of a newspaper employee is 1798.[14] What the wits were doing was merely an extension of what they did in taverns and coffee houses. The idea that the newspaper was "selling" information on events in the way a merchant sells goods would not have occurred to them at all.

In 1731, Benjamin Franklin, again after he had established himself in Philadelphia, published a piece in his newspaper that shows his view of the position of the printer in society. It came in response to criticism he had received for a handbill he had printed, one that had signaled the sailing of a ship and that had been soliciting passengers and freight, except that "no Sea Hens nor Black Gowns will be admitted on any Terms"—thereby barring women of shady character and Anglican clergy. In response to criticism over that line, Franklin wrote what he titled "Apology for Printers."

It's understandable that someone from a later time might mistake his apology for one having to do with newspapers, for Franklin begins by writing "Being frequently censur'd and condemn'd by different Persons for printing Things which they say ought not to be printed, I have sometimes thought it might be necessary to make a standing Apology for my self, and publish it once a Year, to be read upon all Occasions of that Nature."[15] This does remind us of the problems newspapers have had concerning what they publish—but Franklin was not writing of a situation where he had to accept ownership of the words printed, as newspapers of later eras (for the most part) had to do. As a printer, he claims, he was not responsible for the content of what he printed at the request of someone else (and for payment). In the "Apology," he lists ten "Particulars" that he wanted his readers to consider:

1. That the Opinions of Men are almost as various as their Faces. . . .
2. That the Business of Printing has chiefly to do with Mens Opinions. . . .
3. That hence arises the peculiar Unhappiness of that Business, which other Callings are no way liable to; they who follow Printing being scarce able to do any thing in their way of getting a Living, which shall not probably give Offence to some, and perhaps to many. . . .

4. That it is as unreasonable in any one Man or Set of Men to expect to be pleas'd with every thing that is printed. . . .

5. Printers are educated in the Belief, that when Men differ in Opinion, both Sides ought equally to have the Advantage of being heard by the Publick. . . : Hence they chearfully serve all contending Writers that pay them well, without regarding on which side they are of the Question in Dispute.

6. Being thus continually employ'd in serving all Parties, Printers naturally acquire a vast Unconcernedness as to the right or wrong Opinions contain'd in what they print. . . .

7. That it is unreasonable to imagine Printers approve of every thing they print. . . . It is likewise as unreasonable what some assert, *That Printers ought not to print any Thing but what they approve.* . . .

8. That if all Printers were determin'd not to print any thing till they were sure it would offend no body, there would be very little printed.

9. That if they sometimes print vicious or silly things not worth reading, it may not be because they approve such things themselves, but because the People are so viciously and corruptly educated that good things are not encouraged. . . .

10. That notwithstanding what might be urg'd in behalf of a Man's being allow'd to do in the Way of his Business whatever he is paid for, yet Printers do continually discourage the Printing of great Numbers of bad things, and stifle them in the Birth. . . . I have also always refus'd to print such things as might do real Injury to any Person, how much soever I have been solicited, and tempted with Offers of great Pay; and how much soever I have by refusing got the Ill-will of those who would have employ'd me. [*The Pennsylvania Gazette*, June 10, 1731][16]

It is easy to see why many contemporary writers mistake this for a statement on the press, forgetting that the press did not then exist as an enterprise separate from the printing trade and ignoring the fact that Franklin constantly refers to his role as printer, not as writer, editor, or publisher. Burns, for example, sees it as Franklin's means "to explain the problems of journalism to his readers,"[17] and Isaacson calls it "one of the best and most forceful defenses of a free press."[18] The relevance, however, is simply to printers, as is indicated most forcefully in point #5, where Franklin writes that printers "chearfully serve all contending Writers that pay them well." This a defense of a craft in practical terms, not of an institution (especially not of an institution that did not even exist in a codifiable form at that time).

The printer, as presented by Franklin in this piece, serves the function of a twenty-first-century webmaster more than that of a journalist or publisher. In fact, the problems that Franklin was encountering are just those faced by contemporary ISPs and webmasters. In point #10, he admits that the printer does have a certain responsibility for what is transmitted, but he avoids having to explain or justify those limits by turning to a complaint that the public just doesn't understand the problems of printers. This thorny issue remains for ISPs, for webmasters, and even for search-engine providers today (look at the criticism Google received on conforming to Chinese censorship demands in 2006). This was not, however, a problem faced by the journalism profession as it developed in the nineteenth century, where the publication became responsible for its contents—even the advertisements (to some extent).[19] In the modern press, most of the words actually *are* the responsibility of the issuing entity—something far from the case with Franklin's handbill.

As revolution neared, the need to rally the colonists to resistance to the Crown led to a growth in political publications of all sorts, from pamphlets on up. John Dickinson's series of articles, collected and called *Letters from an American Farmer in Pennsylvania to the Inhabitants of the British Colonies*, were perhaps the most famous of these. Published in the *Pennsylvania Chronicle* in late 1767 and early 1768, they set a standard for much of the agitation against the British Crown of the next few years. Like all of the propaganda of the time, these articles were the work of an individual in support of a cause he believed in, not of a professional writer. Certainly, they were not works of professional journalism.

In fact, the word "journalism" itself did not come into common usage until the next century. The oldest citation in the *Oxford English Dictionary* comes from the *Westminster Review* in 1833: "Journalism is a good name for the thing meant. A word was sadly wanted"[20]—though "journalist" goes back to the late seventeenth century (as more of a descriptor of an activity than of a profession). Yet, if Dickinson's essays weren't journalism, neither were they letters. That was merely a convenient form, a fiction for political purposes.

Letters, both real and fictitious, did play a role in the agitation leading up to the Revolution, and sometimes they were not even meant for publication. Burns recounts an incident in which Samuel Adams managed to get hold of letters by one of Massachusetts's Crown officials, one Thomas Hutchinson, "in one of which he stated that 'there must be an abridgement of what is called English liberty' in Massachusetts. It was a sentiment guaranteed to incense the citizenry if it became known. . . . Adams printed the letters out of context. . ., putting words into Hutchinson's mouth that he had never uttered and passing them off as the historical record."[21]

Adams's purpose, though, was never to report news, but to influence opinion, as general reaction to the newspaper he published in clearly establishes. The *Boston Gazette* was loved by those who shared its viewpoints, and hated with passion by just about everyone else. To British officialdom, it was nothing more than "a vehicle through which Americans could 'spit their venom' at royal officials."[22]

A newspaper of this sort wouldn't have seemed particularly unusual at the time, and hatred of it wouldn't have bothered Adams any more than similar criticism bothers contemporary bloggers. After all, as Michael Warner points out, "print had come to be seen as indispensable to political life, and could appear to men such as Adams to be the primary agent of world emancipation"[23]—just as many bloggers see their vehicle of communication today. Even Benjamin Franklin, the man moving most clearly toward a distinct journalism profession, rarely saw what he was doing simply as news transmittal. Yet, as the best and most successful printer of the colonies, Franklin was beginning to set standards for "news" presentation, standards that would remain in place until population growth and technological change made it possible for the parts of his trade to start splitting off from each other. That is, even in his writing, he saw no boundaries. As Isaacson writes, Franklin "was graced—and afflicted—with the trait so common to journalists . . . of wanting to participate in the world while also remaining a detached observer. As a journalist he could step out of a scene, even one that passionately engaged him, and comment on it, or on himself, with a droll irony."[24] Franklin, of course, would not have defined himself as a journalist, but that's not the point here. Franklin saw himself as part of the world, as an actor in it, not merely an observer of it. Following his example, participation in the world (of politics, at least) would be the hallmark of American newspapers for a full half-century after the Revolution, in part because of Franklin and his attitude, but also in part because of another man, an immigrant to the colonies just before the Revolution who took up the cause in print, and with great passion: Thomas Paine.

Chapter 2

THE RISE OF
ADVOCACY
JOURNALISM

A change in what was considered appropriate for debate within the public sphere, the change that had started in the coffeehouses and newspapers of the early years of the century, came to fruition in the American colonies during the 1760s as a part of the rise toward revolution. This was a radical transformation, one that wrecked almost all boundaries previously staked around political discourse. John Dickinson and Samuel Adams were just two of the hundreds of writers pushing to expand both political discourse and political rights. A better writer than either—and perhaps the most radical and the most important of them all—was latecomer (both to the colonies and to writing) Thomas Paine.

In part because they could read each other in print (their words achieving a certain permanence and, thereby, importance) and then respond, the people in the colonies had begun to feel empowered—and to take power, finding themselves even able to influence those debates that had once happened behind high walls, debates most people previously had known of only through their results. Jürgen Habermas, who has chronicled the rise and fall of the public sphere, claims that this empowerment came about through appropriation by the public of what had previously been a state-controlled public sphere, allowing that public to establish the bases of discourse through utilization of the mechanisms—the press, the coffeehouses, and the like—that had already begun to be used in that sphere, though for somewhat different purposes.[1] In other words, people were starting to use the technologies (printing, in this respect) and institutions (public gathering places such as coffeehouses and taverns) available to them to horn in on discussions that had once been exclusively the purview of the elites, who wielded real societal power. Next, the people started to demand that their voice in the discussion be considered in the decision making. And, finally, they were insisting that their voices be part of that process itself. The practice is echoed today in the growing influence and power being exhibited through blogs, which offer twenty-first-century amateur writers the same staying power that print offered their ancestors on the eve of the Revolution. Whether it will move these people, too, into positions of real influence and power remains to be seen.

Though the public sphere may have shrunk as commercial forces have encroached upon it (with the blogs maybe acting as a counterforce today), the progression toward a genuine public sphere in the English colonies during the eighteenth century did not stop with the Revolution but continued for several generations. The movement had its roots in both English and earlier colonial discourse and was abetted by the evolving political possibilities resulting from the difficulty of control over the colonies from across the ocean and the colonies' burgeoning economic might (not to mention the power of a growing population). When James Franklin and Cotton Mather argued about inoculation, they did so because they believed they could have an impact on the world—on what people actually did. This was a major step beyond powerless griping over beer or coffee, for it was a recognition that people, and not authorities, could be the decision makers.

As time passed and the writers began to realize that they could actually affect what governments did as well, discussion got bolder and (if possible) even more raucous. Though they might not have recognized it, the pre–Revolutionary War writers, through their arguments in print, were molding both a people and an ethos and were creating a new public space, one that would eventually provide room for the development of the "fourth estate." Only in this new arena, claims Habermas, could the real truths of the political world be revealed to all people: "In the discussion among citizens issues were made topical and took on shape. In the competition among equals the best excelled and gained their essence— the immortality of fame."[2] In this passage, Habermas was writing specifically about the ancient Greeks, but his words apply equally to the American colonies from the time before the Revolution on through Jacksonian America, where the best writers, such as Thomas Paine, in spite of humble background, could excel and gain immortality through participation in the public sphere as writers and political activists. Just as enthusiasm for development of a new nation had begun to grow from the dream of a disgruntled few to the desire of a large-enough percentage of the colonials for revolution, it was possible for new debate and political construction to also grow.

By the 1770s, newspapers and pamphlets in the colonies had exceeded all bounds of taste and decorum (much as the blogs have, in this respect the newspapers' spiritual inheritors). Looking back from the twentieth century, Americans who read the works of that earlier time were sometimes a bit perturbed. The colonial writers, some of them seen as "founding fathers," certainly hadn't respected the journalistic ethics that had developed by the twentieth century. As Samuel Adams had, these writers thought nothing of twisting the words of others to suit their own purposes or of making private missives public without permission. Even temperate readers of that colonial time must have despaired at this, wondering if any good could ever come of it.

But, of course, good things did come. All the writing wasn't simply ranting against the power of the Crown and local political opponents. Of all the thoughtful writing of the time (and there was much, even among the acrimony), perhaps the best and most important of the essays produced before the Revolution (or in its early days) was *Common Sense*, written by that former English excise officer, Paine. He had arrived in Philadelphia at close to forty years of age, with no real experience as a writer and only a recommendation from Benjamin Franklin as an entrée into the publishing business. Surprisingly, though almost unnoticed, he did manage to do quite well during his first months, writing for a variety of periodicals and working for a time as editor for *The Pennsylvania Magazine*, which grew under his leadership.

Though a latecomer to both the colonies (he had been in Philadelphia little more than a year when *Common Sense* appeared) and the burgeoning discussion and activism in print, Paine almost immediately joined the fractious political arguments, both in his role as editor and as an essayist. Most everything he wrote was unsigned, however, so he personally did not build much of a reputation— until, of course, the outbreak of the clamor surrounding *Common Sense*.

The impact of *Common Sense*, probably even to Paine's surprise, was immediate and widespread—and that was its greatest significance. Paine biographer Harvey Kaye writes, "Arguably, Paine's greatest mischief . . . was to democratize ideas that had been previously circulated only among the higher social ranks by making them understandable and accessible to laboring folks."[3] Paine, perhaps the greatest popularizer of his time, may have been as directly responsible for the growth of the public sphere as any man in history— simply by writing in a style accessible to almost anyone. His introduction to the third edition of *Common Sense* shows that Paine was quite aware of what he was doing (beyond simply stirring up revolutionary sentiment):

Perhaps the sentiments contained in the following pages, are not YET sufficiently fashionable to procure them general favour; a long habit of not thinking a thing WRONG, gives it a superficial appearance of being

RIGHT, and raises at first a formidable outcry in defense of custom. But the tumult soon subsides. Time makes more converts than reason. As a long and violent abuse of power, is generally the Means of calling the right of it in question (and in Matters too which might never have been thought of, had not the Sufferers been aggravated into the inquiry) and as the King of England hath undertaken in his OWN RIGHT, to support the Parliament in what he calls THEIRS, and as the good people of this country are grievously oppressed by the combination, they have an undoubted privilege to inquire into the pretensions of both, and equally to reject the usurpation of either. In the following sheets, the author hath studiously avoided every thing which is personal among ourselves. Compliments as well as censure to individuals make no part thereof. The wise, and the worthy, need not the triumph of a pamphlet; and those whose sentiments are injudicious, or unfriendly, will cease of themselves unless too much pains are bestowed upon their conversion. The cause of America is in a great measure the cause of all mankind. Many circumstances hath [*sic*], and will arise, which are not local, but universal, and through which the principles of all Lovers of Mankind are affected, and in the Event of which, their Affections are interested.[4]

To Paine, the public sphere needed to be universal in content, geography, and class—and needed to be spoken to directly. This was the opposite of how those allied with the monarchy, or even the Whig elite in opposition, would have viewed the world. In their view, everything started from the top and worked down. And it didn't really matter if anything trickled the whole way down or not. After all, the only people who mattered in decision making were the educated people and those above them in class. The class of educated people was growing in importance and power, providing the basis (along with the merchant class) for the birth of the bourgeoisie. Jurists tended to be the most politically active, though pastors, scholars, and teachers also contributed significantly to the new public sphere, as did doctors, postmasters, and even printers.

Though the myth that has grown up around the "founding fathers" might have us believe otherwise, the impetus for revolution in America came from this class, moving down the scale as time went on. The American Revolution did not start from the bottom, as did the revolution in France a short time later. Paine was an anomaly, not only coming from a lower stratum of society, but also writing to it. In America, the divide between the rich and the rest of the people, though it was not as wide as in Europe, was still quite significant. George Washington, of course, was never really a man of the people, even though he came to be adored by them, but was a patrician who saw his position as, in part, his due. Even Jefferson, who proclaimed egalitarian beliefs, lived an elite lifestyle. The true revolutionary Paine, however, would have none of it, and the radical nature of his stance was not lost on the elite classes, even at the beginning of his career when they had to accept him, for the most part, for the sake of the Revolution. Later, his views would force him to flee England (where he had returned) and even receive an uncertain American welcome when, after a sojourn in France, he was able to make his way back to the United States.

The growing conflict in the colonies did not calm discussion or slake thirst for news—and Paine did not put aside his pen. In fact, the public sphere continued to expand even as fighting progressed. At the start of the Revolutionary War, more than twenty newspapers were actively publishing in the colonies; more than forty were doing so when the war ended. More and more, the writers for the papers and the pamphleteers were following Paine's example and addressing the common people, not just the educated elite. It was here, clearly, that Paine was a leader and not just another agitator. He "took the polemical style of earlier pamphleteers, stripped it of its pretense, and rendered it accessible to those readers and unlettered listeners who gathered in the plebian taverns and debating clubs that he himself habituated."[5] A true man of the people, he wrote for them only.

Men like Paine weren't necessarily printers or editors (though Paine, as we have seen, had worked as one). Instead, they were among the first to take effective advantage of printing technology without actively participating in the trade. To them, the newspaper and pamphlet were simply tools for their activism, not their means of sustenance (not yet).

One of the ironies surrounding *Common Sense* was that speculation as to the identity of its (at first) anonymous author focused on the famous, with few imagining that a "nobody" could be its author:

> Though only a few actually knew the name of the author [of *Common Sense*], many imagined they did. General Horatio Gates wrote his comrade General Charles Lee: "*Common Sense*—it is an excellent performance—I think our friend Franklin has been principally concern'd in the Composition." Others nominated the likes of John Adams, Thomas Jefferson, and Samuel Adams. In spite of how the pamphlet differed fundamentally in content, language, and tone from all hitherto published pieces, almost everyone assumed a leading figure of the American political elite had written it, presumably a radical member of Congress.[6]

There was a reason that speculation about authorship of this particular essay was rife: it was *selling*.

> *Common Sense* would go through twenty-five editions, selling an estimated 150,000 copies and reaching an audience several times that large in a single year. It was "the greatest sale that any performance ever had since the use of letters," according to its author. . . and he may have been right if that is understood as short-term penetration of a society, not to mention long-term impact on it.[7]

Never has a single book or pamphlet achieved the kind of penetration that *Common Sense* did. Even with the many pirated editions that quickly appeared, supply was constantly outstripped by demand. Everyone wanted to read it or hear it, and quite soon, everyone had. According to Harvey Kaye, hundreds of pamphlets were printed in the colonies in the decade or so before the start of hostilities, but "whereas the most notable of these was read by tens of thousands, *Common Sense* was read by hundreds of thousands. . . . The equivalent sales today would be fifteen million, making it, proportionally, the nation's greatest best-seller ever. By one estimation, half a million copies were sold in the course of the Revolution. Plus, copies were shared, and those who could not read it heard it read aloud in homes, taverns, workshops, and fields."[8]

Nothing with the astonishing success of *Common Sense* has yet to arise from the blogs. Not only have they not seen their Benjamin Franklin, but they also are far from producing their Thomas Paine, the writer coming from the blogs, the writer to whom everyone turns. But they will. Paine united the rebellious faction of the colonies as no one else had and expanded the universe of political discourse to include even the unlettered. What he was able to do resulted from both technological and cultural changes that offered new possibilities—which he took advantage of. Eventually, someone will take advantage of twenty-first-century possibilities in a similar way, though maybe with not quite the "revolutionary" impact.

One of the most immediate consequences of *Common Sense* was the Pennsylvania Constitution of 1776, a document composed, in part, by men influenced by Paine's thoughts on how government should be constructed. Though the convention that devised it met the same summer and in the same town as the Second Continental Congress that ratified the Declaration of Independence, the two groups were, as Sean Wilentz describes them, at opposite ends of the revolutionary spectrum: "The planters, merchants, and professional men who signed the Declaration of Independence—including

John Hancock, John Adams, and Edward Rutledge, as well as Franklin and Jefferson—were notables of wealth and standing, with reputations of high degree, at least in their respective provinces. . . . The leaders of the Pennsylvania Convention were very different. Most were Philadelphia artisans and intellectuals of a radical democratic bent, many of them disciples of Thomas Paine. . . The majority of the delegates were humble farmers from the rural interior, chosen by the radical leadership because of their adherence to democratic political ideals."[9] The unicameral legislature established by the convention certainly reflected Paine's suggestions in *Common Sense*, as did other aspects of the new state constitution, one of the most truly democratic ever enacted (though it only lasted until 1790).

Unlike most other pamphleteers, Paine actually did present a plan for the future and not just complaints about contemporary injustice. His plan was clear and logical, and it stemmed from a precise political philosophy. He recognized that no constitution that would fit his beliefs could be a compact between distinct entities (the crown and the parliament, for example), but had to be *from* the people and *for* the people alone. For liberty to exist, wrote Paine, there could be no king:

> Yet that we may not appear to be defective even in earthly honors, let a day be solemnly set apart for proclaiming the charter; let it be brought forth placed on the divine law, the word of God; let a crown be placed thereon, by which the world may know, that so far as we approve of monarchy, that in America THE LAW IS KING. For as in absolute governments the King is law, so in free countries the law OUGHT to be King; and there ought to be no other. But lest any ill use should afterwards arise, let the crown at the conclusion of the ceremony, be demolished, and scattered among the people whose right it is.[10]

By necessity, only the law could have precedence over the people—and only then so long as the people didn't change it. The genesis of the law, in other words, must lie in the people. Michael Warner describes Paine's pamphlet *Four Letters on Interesting Subjects* as an early argument for a written constitution:

> We read that "All constitutions should be contained in some written Charter but *that* Charter should be the act of *all* and not of *one man*." The specific negative reference here is Pennsylvania's proprietary charter, granted by the Crown. Such charters are inappropriate models, the pamphlet suggests, because they emanate from the authority of persons and are thus "a species of tyranny, because they substitute the will of ONE as the law of ALL."[11]

The degree of originality in *Common Sense* has often been called into question, starting with John Adams, who claimed it was nothing more than a reworking of what Adams and others had already said. Whether this is true or not, Paine certainly touched a nerve, and in a manner clearly more attractive to a wider number of readers than anything published before *Common Sense*. Yet, even if he was not an original thinker (and there are many who believe he was), his example is still just as important to the bloggers of more than two centuries later. Though often criticized for it, too, the bloggers rarely claim originality. Instead, they rework information obtained elsewhere, making it their own—just as Paine may have done.

The responses to Paine also presage the responses to bloggers, especially those from the professional news media, where standards and order have often been the rule of the day (and where reaction to the blogs has been negative, from both the right and the left). As Kaye comments,

> *Common Sense* made many a moderate and conservative Whig feverish. Elias Boudinot of New Jersey, who would serve as a colonel in Washington's army, referred to its author as a "Crack Brain Zealot for Democracy." Virginia plantation owner Colonel Landon Carter recorded that "*Common Sense. . .* is quite scandalous & disgraces the American cause much," for it advanced "new and dangerous doctrines to the peace and happiness of every society."[12]

Just as the bloggers are stepping around the professional and commercial news media, Paine was sidestepping the colonial elite, who saw it as their right and duty to be America's guides. In neither case was or is it simply fear of a specific movement; entire institutions were or are being threatened. Of course, the professional news media is in no way the contemporary equivalent of the whole of the upper classes of colonial America, but the perceived threat to cherished power is just as real.

Even John Adams himself got into the fray, writing *Thoughts on Government* in an attempt to provide an alternative model for government to the one Paine presented. Paine responded with the pamphlet *Four Letters on Interesting Subjects*, where he argued, again, that governments come from the people, and not the other way around. Perhaps more than elsewhere at that time, this discourse (according to Kaye) presaged one later but central American debate: "In the Adams–Paine exchange we see the beginnings of the perennial contest in American political culture between those who would try to set limits to the expansion of democracy and those who would seek to extend and deepen it."[13]

Completely the idealist and passionate activist, Paine never made money off of *Common Sense*, having directed that all royalties go to the revolutionary army to help purchase winter uniforms (he also gave up royalties to the *American Crisis* series that ran through the war). Though he never promoted himself as the author, Paine quickly became known for having written *Common Sense*. His role as a writer throughout the Revolution made him one of the most beloved of all the figures associated with the war. It is easy to see why. His first of the *American Crisis* series, containing one of the most famous passages in all of American literature, gave the rebellion a confidence it sorely needed at one of its lowest moments:

THESE are the times that try men's souls. The summer soldier and the sunshine patriot will, in this crisis, shrink from the service of their country; but he that stands by it now, deserves the love and thanks of man and woman. Tyranny, like hell, is not easily conquered; yet we have this consolation with us, that the harder the conflict, the more glorious the triumph. What we obtain too cheap, we esteem too lightly: it is dearness only that gives every thing its value. Heaven knows how to put a proper price upon its goods; and it would be strange indeed if so celestial an article as FREEDOM should not be highly rated. Britain, with an army to enforce her tyranny, has declared that she has a right (not only to TAX) but "to BIND us in ALL CASES WHATSOEVER" and if being bound in that manner, is not slavery, then is there not such a thing as slavery upon earth. Even the expression is impious; for so unlimited a power can belong only to God.[14]

Little has ever *stirred* American souls the way this, just the start of that essay, did.

Even so, even with his great popularity, Paine never did manage to win over the colonial elite, not even those who shared with him the championing of independence. For many, particularly the Southerners, his forthright opposition to slavery was a bit too much to stomach. Also, he clearly saw the Revolution as a struggle for democracy that was much more important (and international) than simple independence from England.

In the last of the *American Crisis* essays, Paine reflected back on his first awakening to the cause:

It was the cause of America that made me an author. The force with which it struck my mind and the dangerous condition the country appeared to me in, by courting an impossible and an unnatural reconciliation with those who were determined to reduce her, instead of striking out into the

only line that could cement and save her, A DECLARATION OF INDE-
PENDENCE, made it impossible for me, feeling as I did, to be silent: and
if, in the course of more than seven years, I have rendered her any service,
I have likewise added something to the reputation of literature, by freely
and disinterestedly employing it in the great cause of mankind, and showing that there may be genius without prostitution.[15]

There have been few like Paine since his time and fewer still since the
commercialization of the news media along with the rise of a professional
punditry.

Again, to date, no one of impact remotely akin to that of Paine has arisen
from the blogs. It is possible that no one ever will (though, always an opti-
mist, I believe such a person is just around the corner). However, when one
remembers that it was *societal* demand for change along with *technological*
change that set the stage for Paine's entrance, it is hard to imagine that the
social needs of the twenty-first century, on top of the technological advances
of the late twentieth century, will not force Paine's modern-day equivalent to
step from the wings.

Chapter 3

DEBATE IN THE EARLY AMERICAN PRESS

On the eve of the Revolution, Alexander Hamilton—like Thomas Paine, a young, new American upstart (though an immigrant from the West Indies, not England)—began taking on New York's loyalists in the local press with an authority and vigor belying his age and short tenure in the country. He would soon become what his biographer, Ron Chernow, calls a "human word machine,"[1] writing for public consumption for more than a quarter of a century—until laid down in a duel with Aaron Burr.

Hamilton's writing career (one of at least four careers, including lawyer, military man, and Treasury Secretary) began in 1774, even before Thomas Paine's, when a loyalist named Samuel Seabury, a clergyman from Westchester, attempted to debunk John Dickinson's *Letters from a Farmer in Pennsylvania* with Seabury's own newspaper pieces and pamphlets signed "A Westchester Farmer." Before the end of the year, a pamphlet entitled *A Full Vindication of the Measures of the Congress* had appeared in response. Though published anonymously, it had been written by Hamilton.

The battle went back and forth, through response and attack in print, with Seabury responding quickly to Hamilton and then Hamilton coming back with *The Farmer Refuted*, which was printed, strangely enough, by Tory printer James Rivington (who had also printed Hamilton's first pamphlet). Seabury clearly had no idea what he had come up against, and this was not surprising: Hamilton was little more than a kid. Chernow describes the rather low debate, using Hamilton's own words:

> "Such is my opinion of your abilities as a critic," Hamilton addressed him directly, "that I very much prefer your disapprobation to your applause." As if Seabury were the young upstart and not vice versa. Hamilton taunted his riposte as "puerile and fallacious" and stated that "I will venture to pronounce it one of the most ludicrous performances which has been exhibited to public view during all the present controversy."[2]

Given this sort of exchange (which was already common) at the birth of the nation, it should not have been surprising when, two centuries and a quarter later, such invectives rose to a high level again in public American political discussion (though one hopes that the modern-day results will not resemble the kidnappings and destruction that were the immediate upshot of the Seabury/Hamilton debate). Debate such as this not only helped found the United States of America but was, for generations, part of its tradition. It was only sidetracked when commerce gained control of the public sector—as the quick rise of the blogs has shown, the desire for public political debate remained, unabated.

For the past century and a half, there often has been an idealization of the public sphere that imagines it as a place of reasoned discourse somehow stripped of passion. What it always has been when not limited by commercial encroachment and professional containment, however, is a free-for-all that can devolve into violence and even revolution as easily and often as it leads to peaceful evolution. It is as dangerous as it is necessary.

Though the loss of the public sphere through commercial and profession incursion has had a negative impact on contemporary culture, it has also had a calming effect—at least temporarily. However, as John Kennedy said when speaking of his Alliance for Progress, "Those who make peaceful revolution impossible, make violent revolution inevitable." If the narrowing of the public sphere reduces violence in the short run, it also keeps new and dynamic cultural movements from arising—and raises the specter of horrific future violence.

There is a balancing act in public discourse, and many participants seem unable to keep the board still. This failure was particularly apparent in the early years of the republic, before there was an editorial apparatus acting to bring things back to the center. Then, many public figures regularly teetered back and forth between the honorable and the horrific—with Hamilton being one of the foremost of these public figures, most certainly. He knew the differences between the two worlds—one of discourse toward establishing a foundation for a nation's future and the other of the often overwrought realm of immediate political strife—but saw no reason he could not participate in both. Where readers in the twentieth century, looking back on his writing, might see schizophrenia, Hamilton would have simply seen two distinct arenas calling for different weapons. It is certainly possible to call Hamilton's time, as Chernow does, "both the apex and the nadir of American political expression."[3] But that's not enough. We must do more than simply brush aside attempts to understand why so many writer–politicians of the time saw no problem with participating in both the high debate and the low.

Given a contemporary perspective that includes the blogs, it is apparent that the emotions behind both kinds of debate, and the desire for both, have always been present in American discourse. It is apparent as well that the base side too often has been suppressed or relegated to an unworthy sensationalist, tabloid bastard child of the "real" press rather than recognized as a necessary part of national discussion (one needing a certain societal containment, it is true, but not complete approbation). The twin demands of professionalism and commercialism, as they grew through the nineteenth century, separated the debates, leaving only one as culturally acceptable. Together, they stabilized the teeter-totter by narrowing the group who had access to the means of discourse and by replacing the political and public-affairs emphasis of the press with a monetary one. By excluding passion in favor of commerce, however, the emasculated debate has drawn fewer and fewer people to it.

Though there were others who followed Dickinson's and, later, Thomas Paine's lead or who had already thrown themselves into the verbal fray (Samuel Adams comes to mind), none of these proto-bloggers became as much of a force in the development of the young nation over the next decades as Hamilton. Paine was the closest, but he was never directly involved in government in America. Hamilton quickly became a regular contributor to the debates, eventually for printer John Holt's *New-York Journal*, contributing more than a dozen essays to that paper over three months at the end of 1775 and beginning of 1776. Unlike Paine's, Hamilton's activity wasn't all simply for the public good: though he clearly believed fervently in the cause of the colonists, Hamilton was also aware (as are many contemporary bloggers) that this could be an avenue to real notice for a youth of quick mind and confident pen. As Chernow writes, "For an ambitious young man of a broadly literary bent, polemical broadsides fired at the British ministry presented the surest road to fame."[4] Hamilton's penchant for self-promotion eventually allowed his critics to easily and ceaselessly question his motives (generally, it must be said, on spurious grounds).

But it was not these articles, of course, that brought Hamilton his greatest renown—or that are even his most important contribution as an exemplar for twenty-first century bloggers. Outside of his groundbreaking work at the Treasury Department and as George Washington's closest presidential advisor, Hamilton's fame rests on *The Federalist Papers*, his defense, beginning in 1787, of the proposed new Constitution.

Ratification of the Constitution was no foregone conclusion at the time. Though no longer the Whigs and Tories of the pre-Revolution period, Americans were once again dividing into factions. Those who favored the new proposed Constitution, including Hamilton, soon came to be known as "federalists," that is, people in favor of the proposed federal governmental structure. Their opponents came to be called, for lack of a better term, "antifederalists." Hamilton, who had been much involved in contesting almost every paragraph of the evolving document during the Constitutional Convention, was now one of the most fervent of the federalists. As a New Yorker, his primary concern was that his state would not join him—that it would refuse to ratify. Argument was certainly fierce and heated, but of great significance, so much so that the "rancor ushered in a golden age of literary assassination in America politics. No etiquette had yet evolved to define the legitimate boundaries of dissent. Poison-pen artists on both sides wrote vitriolic essays that were overtly partisan, often paid scant heed to accuracy, and sought a visceral impact. The inflamed rhetoric once directed against Britain was now turned inward against domestic adversaries."[5]

Though it might not seem possible, the rancor was even worse than it had been *before* the Revolution. As previously mentioned, the common understanding of the past century has been that the culture of the United States eventually tamed those passions, redirecting them into a more decorous debate through a professional press and, later, other news media. The recent impact of blogs on national discourse, however, has exploded that myth, showing that an underlying need for much more raucous debate has probably existed unnoticed through the years, only looking for a means of escaping from the cage that had been built for it. What happened wasn't a diminution of desire, but of outlet.

Significantly, Hamilton, seen today as a serious and austere "founder," never could get off that teeter-totter of "high" and then "low" debate—or stabilize it in his own interest. Even as Secretary of the Treasury, he took active part in the most vituperative of the public "discussions." From his earliest days, he aroused such rancor through his own attacks that sometimes the ones against him turned especially vicious, not surprisingly. Early on, Hamilton was called "Tom S**t" in the press in response to his own stories and was attacked as a foreigner, as a bastard, and even as having African ancestry, a grave insult in that time of commonplace racism. But Hamilton was never one to back down from a fight (as his tragic end at the hands of Aaron Burr in a duel later aptly showed). Out of a dung heap can come the most vibrant of flowers—which may be the lesson Hamilton provides for both today's bloggers and those critics who disparage them as simply attack animals. Hamilton, as surely as he was attacked, could attack—but he was also a great deal more than that.

Watching the debate over the Constitution (and participating, even before the start of the *Federalist* project) during the early fall of 1787, Hamilton came to the conclusion that another type of debate needed to be added to the mix if the Constitution were to be ratified by New York. He recruited John Jay and James Madison (and William Duer, whose work was never used in the project) to collaborate with him in producing a series of essays explaining the Constitution to the public—the public of New York, in particular—in such a way that debate would lead to ratification. The original idea was that each writer would handle his own area of expertise and that all would contribute equally. Jay took sick, however, and produced only a few of the eighty-five final essays. Madison contributed a good number, but the bulk of the work (which finally amounted to more than 170,000 words) fell to Hamilton.

The essays were published in as many as four New York newspapers at once and were quickly picked up by out-of-town papers. The use of the pseudonym "Publius" not only hid the fact that this was a group effort (saving time from unnecessary explanations), but also was in the tradition of public debate of that era, where the words said were supposed to transcend the identity of the sayer (and where the sayer could thereby have a little protection at least from physical attack). In addition, the authors were bound by the confidentiality agreement of the Constitutional Convention in which they had participated, so they wanted to avoid being accused to breaching that.

The debate over the Constitution had already grown quite hot. Not surprisingly, no debate since the days before the Revolution had engendered such an amount of printing and shouting. Publications of all types took up the issue, as did people from all levels of society. Here again, the use of pseudonyms, often taken from classical times, was the order of the day, with the identity of the authors providing subject for hot debate.

In later years, of course, once journalism had developed into a profession separate from other activities with its own set of ethical standards, the use of pseudonyms came into disfavor. Though people did still write under them, they disguised their aliases as "real" sounding names, hiding the fact that they weren't willing to disclose their identity. During the debate over the Constitution, however, most writers had to earn their livings apart from writing and could not sacrifice their incomes for the sake of their political pursuits. The situation, of course, is much the same today for many bloggers—and the identities of many of the early writers (especially the best known) did become common knowledge then, just as the names of prominent bloggers are common knowledge now.

Significant to how we should be considering the blogs today is the fact that the collection of federalist essays published by Hamilton, Madison, and Jay (not much different, in many respects outside of content and period style, from the best of the blogs—and also produced by amateur writers, talented and experienced though the writers were) has become one of the most important sets of documents in American history, one that continues to have an impact on the political debates of the nation. For two hundred years, *The Federalist Papers* has remained both in print and in influence. Few other books can say the same. Yet it was written under a great deal of pressure—and not just from printers demanding more material.

The real pressure came from the looming ratifying conventions, the first scheduled to start just a month after the first essay appeared. Hamilton and Madison wrote as fast as any blogger. At one point, Hamilton produced more than two essays a week over a two-month stretch. How did he manage it? As Chernow says, "It is important to note that virtually all of his important work was journalism, prompted by topical issues and written in the midst of controversy. He never wrote as a solitary philosopher for the ages."[6] Like a blogger, Hamilton was energized by conversation and opposition. It was the dynamic of debate that kept him going, not the ideas themselves.

It is important to remember that the press of Hamilton's time wasn't "journalism" as it has come to be known since—that is, a profession with its own ethical guidelines—but was a raucous press that had not yet been removed from the public sphere by the forces of commercialism and professionalism. The fact that Hamilton was working in a milieu with many more similarities to the twenty-first-century blogs than to journalism as it has been practiced for most of the intervening time is significant to any attempt to evaluate the blogs and their own possibilities for contribution to American political life. On the other hand, Hamilton's own attitude was not the egalitarian one behind the blogs, where each voice contributes to the debate, the conclusions appearing through the debate. This Jeffersonian ideal (and one in keeping with Habermas's idea of the public sphere) would not have sat well with Hamilton, who would have been more in agreement with Walter Lippmann, who wrote that it "is not necessary. . . to invent a collective intelligence in order to explain why the judgments of a group are usually more coherent, and often more true to form than the remarks of the man in the street. One mind, or a few can pursue a train of thought, but a group trying to think in concert can as a group do little more than assent or dissent."[7] Ideas, in this view, do not originate with the masses, but are presented to them by the few. This fits well with the reasoning that led to creation of *The Federalist Papers*.

The inspiration for that series of essays was, of course, Hamilton's. New York Governor George Clinton was a formidable opponent, and Hamilton recognized that it would take more than simple attacks to defeat him. By this time a skilled propagandist who had been forged by the fire of revolutionary debate and shaped on the anvil of the needs of a new country (and through his participation in the Constitutional Convention), Hamilton knew that it was time to turn the debate away from personalities and to the issues directly. The debate was already framed as an either–or, up-or-down discussion, so it was necessary to give reason to vote *for* a particular candidate, rather than against another one. Attack, in such an environment, would not do. Even so, "his new plan called for a kind of 'saturation bombing' of the electorate, a sustained barrage of arguments appearing in the newspapers four times a week."[8] In perhaps one of the first example of massive "cross-posting" (the term bloggers use for entries or posts that appear on a number of different blogs), the resulting essays appeared in numerous periodicals (the first ones appeared in three separate newspapers), even in New York, and soon came out in book form, giving them even wider distribution.

The Federalist Papers have more parallels to contemporary blogs than simply pseudonyms and cross-posting. Though there were three writers contributing—Hamilton, Madison, and Jay (who wrote only five)—or perhaps, because of this factor, "Publius" was able to produce up to four new entries a week. Such frequent publication of commentary on political topics under one name was rarely seen again for over two centuries—not really until the advent of blogs. Also like blogs, these were not stories resulting from active news gathering (though the writers had participated in the process leading to the document under discussion), but were "about" something that had already appeared—something that was, in fact, already well known.

There was no pretense of impartiality, no assumption of the mantle of a seeker, in these essays. In fact, in the first of the papers, "Publius," the pseudonym Hamilton had selected for what he had hoped would be even more of a group project than it finally proved, wrote,

> I effect not reserves, which I do not feel. I will not amuse you with an appearance of deliberation, when I have decided. I frankly acknowledge to you my convictions, and I will freely lay before you the reasons on which they are founded. The consciousness of good intentions disdains ambiguity. I shall not however multiply professions on this head. My motives must remain in the depository of my own breast: My arguments will be open to all, and may be judged of by all. They shall at least be offered in a spirit, which will not disgrace the cause of truth.[9]

This could be taken as a statement of principle by many of today's political bloggers, no matter their political leanings. Like Publius, they wear their convictions on their sleeves and expect to be respected for that candor. However, then as now, even the purest motivations did not necessarily lead to unmanipulated views of the subject matter. Bias and truth, in the eyes of both Publius and contemporary bloggers, are not mutually exclusive.

Though the ascension of the rule of law over the rule of rulers may have been emblemized by the United States Constitution that was ratified in part because of Hamilton's efforts, this did not mean that debate was over. However, many of the American political elite, including the new president, were uncomfortable with the unhampered (and often vicious) debates that were now raging outside of the new political institutions. The fact of governmental structure, in place and in process, did not stop the arguments—they simply moved to a new sphere and, in part out of deference to Washington, often continued to be anonymous. Certainly, Hamilton, now Secretary of the Treasury and George Washington's top advisor, did not manage to keep his disagreements with Secretary of State Thomas Jefferson from spilling into the press.

Even before that famous contest and the resulting birth of American political parties, Hamilton had continued to use the press as his primary political battleground. Not surprisingly, his first major conflict after ratification was over the choice for New York's second Senate seat (in those days, senators were not expected to be elected by popular vote), Hamilton's old foe, Governor Clinton. In a series of sixteen letters published anonymously in *The Daily Advertiser* in 1789, Hamilton, reports Chernow, "questioned Clinton's bravery as a brigadier general during the Revolution: 'After diligent enquiry, I have not been able to learn that he was ever more than once in actual combat.' In one letter, Hamilton differentiated between two types drawn to revolutions: those sincerely interested in the public good and 'restless and turbulent spirits,' such as Clinton, who sought to exploit unrest to become despots."[10] Hamilton even accused Clinton of electoral shenanigans, something common to today's political blogs as well.

Though he was angling for a top spot in Washington's administration at the very time these letters were published, Hamilton, who clearly did not share Washington's feelings about the importance of decorum in political debate, also did not seem to believe the letters would hurt his chances. After all, what he was doing was not very far out of the ordinary.

Hamilton wasn't the only one to see the opportunities the press offered in the new milieu. Because of the role they played directly before and during the Revolutionary War, newspaper editors (printers, essentially) also felt emboldened to continue and increase their involvement in politics once the war had been won and the Constitution ratified. In fact, through those years, newspapers were in the process of taking their place as an integral part of the American political scene. They were more than willing to work directly with a Hamilton or, later, a Jefferson toward political ends. Soon, it was almost impossible to get any momentum going for any political movement without association with a newspaper.

Something similar may be happening with the blogs of the twenty-first century. In the years after the revolution, newspapers played an integral role in the development of political parties by providing clear rallying points. Today, the blogs may be reshaping the parties through a similar grassroots means. Like contemporary bloggers, who are constantly attentive to any move to infringe upon their rights to post, newspapers also grew more and more protective of what they began to feel were their prerogatives and rights. Like the bloggers, newspapers were also quite aware of their growing numbers and power. Significantly, with their growth also came a shift in overall political orientation (again like the blogs, which started out with a decidedly right-wing orientation, but which have been shifting left as the numbers grow).

The number of American newspapers, which had grown rapidly throughout the Revolution, continued upward in the post-Revolution years. By 1800, there were more than two hundred, many times what there had been on the eve of the Revolution. In the early years after the Revolution, most of the papers leaned toward what became the Federalist Party. The number of Federalist newspapers didn't increase much in the 1790s, most of the new papers being of a more republican bent. Similarly, the early political blogs were predominantly conservative. After the 2004 election, however, the trend was toward the liberal perspective.

One of the hundred or so papers already established in the new country in 1790 was the Hamiltonian *Gazette of the United States* (edited by John Fenno), whose motto was "He that is not for us, is against us"—exactly the feelings of many political bloggers. Such a sentiment surprised no one. Newspapers were inextricably (or so it seemed at the time) caught up in the political parties and were critical components in each new political movement.

When it came to establishing the Bill of Rights, which had been clamored for during ratification debate, freedom of the press was strongly pushed. Looking through the lens created by two hundred years of history and inter-pretation, it is easy to assume that the "freedom of the press" established by the First Amendment was meant as a protection for a distinct and independ-ent entity, one of whose roles was that of watchdog over the government. That, however, is not how it was seen at the time. James Madison's draft (based on a resolution adopted by the ratifying convention of Virginia) for what was finally adopted after much change, read, "The people shall not be deprived or abridged of their right to speak, to write, or to publish their sen-timents; and the freedom of the press, as one of the great bulwarks of liberty, shall be inviolable." [11] The press, clearly, was seen by the Virginians as a tool of the people, not as an institution with its own rights. For there to be polit-ical debate (something, then as now, considered quite necessary), a press unencumbered by government was essential. But the press was a vehicle of the people, not an independent entity with its own inherent rights.

In addition, because the idea of political parties was close to anathema among the founding fathers, it was the press that was seen as providing the focal point for political debate, not factions (it was not yet clear that the press would also be the focal point for establishment of those very parties). In fact, the press may well have been seen as an alternative to parties, though this view certainly couldn't have lasted too long, for parties quite quickly became a prominent feature of the political landscape of the new republic.

As was becoming his habit, Hamilton was at the center of the controversies that led to the coalescing of opposing forces into political parties. His tendency to see things in a black-and-white perspective of "either you are for us, or you are against us" placed him as a natural leader for the nascent Federalists. His policies as Treasury Secretary secured the backing of northeast banking and mer-cantile concerns, providing a secure financial underpinning for the new party.

Of course, Hamilton could never draw some people to him without push-ing others away. Madison, who once had been Hamilton's ally, found himself estranged and paired with rival Thomas Jefferson. Seeing the Federalists organizing, the opposition began to do the same, becoming the first opposi-tion party of the United States.

Anticipating divisions—divisions that would last into the twenty-first century (though the parties did change)—the Federalists (speaking broadly) placed more faith in the rulers than in the people, looking upon the rabble as, like as not, eventual destroyers of what the nation was trying to build. Given what was then happening in France, their fears are understandable. Jefferson's Republicans saw things quite differently, suspecting that the Federalists were monarchists at heart and proponents of an oligarchy. Despite the names, the Federalists were the spiritual ancestors of today's Republicans, whereas the early Republicans evolved into the modern Democratic Party.

The leaders of the nascent parties were also the two most contentious of Washington's advisors, Hamilton at the Treasury and Jefferson, who was serving as Secretary of State. Jefferson was ever suspicious of the energetic Hamilton and felt he tilted too much toward England as a trading partner and more. Having spent the preceding years in France, Jefferson had become something of a Francophile—even more so once the Jacobins dominated. Washington tried to force peace on the two men, but was unable to succeed. The battle lasted through the first Washington administration and did not even end after Jefferson had left government and returned to Monticello.

While still in office, and seeing the way Hamilton was able to operate through the *Gazette of the United States*, Jefferson worked out a way of subsidizing Philip Freneau, whom he wanted to see editing a Republican paper. Though Freneau was not really conversant in any language other than English, Jefferson had him hired as a translator so that he could be guaranteed an income while the *National Gazette* got on its feet. Because Fenno, the editor of the *Gazette of the United States*, was also subsidized (through government contracts), Jefferson saw nothing wrong with his move, starting a tradition of close interaction between governing personalities and the press, one that would last into the 1840s.

After Jefferson's retreat to Monticello early in Washington's second administration, Hamilton must have felt quite victorious. But the battle between the two was not over. In some respects, it had hardly even started.

Chapter 4

THE VICTORY FOR RIGHTS OF THE PRESS

Though Thomas Jefferson and Alexander Hamilton took opposite sides in almost any debate either put forward, they were equal masters in manipulation of the political machinery of their time, though in different ways. Hamilton was more of a frontline general, leading his troops by example of his obvious skill and courage. Jefferson worked as the master strategist well behind the lines, devising grand strategies and then sending his lieutenants to do the work in the trenches. They each bested the other at different times, neither ever giving up the war at the loss of a battle.

They were well matched, for each was astute enough to examine and develop new tools of battle, to do more than simply pick up what was near at hand and use it to try and clobber the enemy. They also each studied the other and learned from him. If one subsidized a newspaper, the other found a way to do the same. If one saw that a political base could be constructed through the use of the press as a focus for developing a cohesive political party, the other wasn't far behind.

Not surprisingly, many of the other politicians of the new American republic followed the lead of these two political geniuses. And many of the most prominent politicians who followed had been (or were still) involved, to some degree or other, with the press, whether by writing, by acting as an editor, or by promoting a certain newspaper because of its political slant.

Like the press of the 1790s, the blogs are becoming an organizing entity for what may prove to be a new manifestation of major American political parties. The news media have long blocked themselves off from such a function, forcing the parties and candidates to buy space and time, to act *through* the media rather than with it, as once had been the case. The blogs, though, have no ethical or professional considerations keeping them from acting as direct participants in the political process, opening them up to a role much like that of the press in the development of both Hamilton's Federalist and Jefferson's Republican parties.

If the blogs have yet to produce their Benjamin Franklin and Thomas Paine, they also lack their Hamiltons and Jeffersons. As of 2006, the most influential political blogger (in terms of party politics) was arguably Markos Moulitsas, whose The Daily Kos, receiving two million visits on election day in November, 2006,[1] had become one of the most popular of the liberal blogs. Yet even Moulitsas was a long way from reaching either the level of skill or the sophistication of political thought (not to mention political success) that marked his early predecessors. Though the blogs have begun to show strength in the political discourse of the nation, they have a long way to go before they become even nearly as influential as the newspapers were little more than two centuries earlier.

The symbiosis of government and press had grown even before the Revolution, in part because of the connection between printing and the post. A printer who was also a postmaster had ready access to the news people wanted to read (that from faraway places) and could keep in touch cheaply and efficiently with "correspondents." Because the decision of who would serve as postmaster generally rested with the local or state government, it was unlikely that a printer–postmaster would dare to alienate those in power locally (distant power, of course, was another matter). As time passed, and particularly as the new republic began to take shape, the needs of governments on all levels for printed documents grew dramatically—and so did the lucrative contracts that were meted out to fill those needs. This gave the government a great deal of power over the press and made the editors fierce supporters of the side that, among other things, would give them contracts if in power, cementing relationships that would have been strong in the first place. None of this was thought untoward, and all was common practice. Therefore, Jefferson certainly would have seen nothing wrong with using government printing contracts or even jobs, as he did, as an inducement toward the creation of a newspaper of the sort he imagined. After all, Hamilton had been doing the same thing.

In 1791, with the help of James Madison, Jefferson induced the poet Philip Freneau to take a position with the State Department as a translator, something of a no-show job (Freneau knew French, but not as well as such a position would require). It wasn't much of a job, paying only $250 a year (compared with Jefferson's own meager—in terms of his needs—$3500), but it was enough of an added perk for Freneau to agree to edit what would become the *National Gazette*, the flagship paper for the growing republican movement and the opposition to *The Gazette of the United States*, edited by John Fenno and the primary voice for the Federalists.

In urging Freneau to take on this task, Jefferson was quite aware of the power of the press—but it was a power different from that wielded by the press in later generations. At that time, when the population was primarily rural or village—and transportation (and communication) was tedious at best—the newspapers were vehicles, like the blogs are today, for bringing the like-minded together in spirit when they could not meet in person (as those in the few large cities could do more easily, in coffeehouses and taverns). Because the political parties were organizations of the like-minded, it is not surprising that the newspapers paralleled them in sentiment (again, much as the political blogs do, today)—even when the newspapers weren't directly party organs. Highly literate Americans certainly wanted the pleasures both of reading and of being part of something greater than the events of their localities, and the newspapers gave them both, flourishing in America to a degree unseen in the rest of the world.

By today's standards, the papers were small and graphically uninteresting (only rarely did an illustration appear), and they contained little that could be considered news—except for the accounts of battles and other events in far-away places that had taken place in previous months. Instead, the papers concentrated on opinion. In this sense, they really do have more in common with the political blogs of today (and with the opinion journals of the period in-between) than they do with the newspapers that succeeded them in the middle part of the nineteenth century. Not hemmed in by any sense of professional ethics (or even by a sense of being part of a profession at all), they were quite willing to print rumors and wild accusations, going well beyond what anyone in the professional news media of the late twentieth century would have found acceptable.

Still, a national newspaper could bring scattered viewpoints into one cohesive vision, even for a party that was, technically, out of power (though the group in question was yet to be something that could even really be considered a party—and Jefferson, at least, was still a part of the administration). So, Jefferson put his quite considerable energy behind establishment of the *National Gazette*. A national newspaper, perhaps, was something of an insurance policy against the straying of the rabble. In addition, it (and the stories reprinted from it) would carry a weight with readers that would be impossible for any single local paper.

Certainly, though he suspected the verity of the press, Jefferson was never constrained from using it for his own ends, even if his own side was no more truthful than the other. He certainly knew that he needed the press if he were going to organize any sort of effective response to the Federalists, who seemed to have a strong grasp (through Hamilton) on the administration. Bowing to reality, Jefferson and Madison knew that they needed something better than their portrayal in the Federalist press. They justified their promotion of a Republican press by claiming that it was needed to counterbalance the points of view in the "Tory" press, where the opinions of bankers, merchants, and even monarchists (in the eyes of Jefferson) dominated.

Not surprisingly, one of the first of America's many newspaper wars followed the establishment of the *National Gazette*, as vicious as any since, as vicious as any of the blog wars of today. The conflict reached the point where even George Washington was concerned that it had gone too far. He spoke to both Jefferson and Hamilton, hoping to calm the feud. But though they agreed, the sparring continued unabated, deepening the national divide and assuring that party politics would become the way of American government.

The battles in the press continued through Washington's first term, as Jefferson and Hamilton angled for influence. Hamilton, who was quite willing to participate himself and even to see his name associated with even the most scurrilous attacks (although he continued to use pseudonyms, it was often clear who the author was), kept close to the battle while Jefferson fought from a remove, encouraging aides and friends to do the writing for him. Knowing that Jefferson was behind these "Whig" attacks, Hamilton derided Jefferson for keeping up an image as the philosopher above the fray.

By the end of 1792, Jefferson knew he was in danger of losing the war. He resigned his post for the second Washington administration but, under pressure from Washington, agreed to stay on temporarily, eventually returning to Monticello only in the fall of 1793. He probably regretted staying so long, for he had to suffer through the antics of "Citizen" Genêt, the French envoy who tried to arm and man privateers in American ports for use against English shipping during the new continental war. The Francophile Jefferson wanted to keep good relations with France, but Genêt was making that difficult, much to the Anglophile Hamilton's delight. Here again, the divide between the two new parties grew.

In fact, the divide came to resemble a mile-wide canyon. Writing as "Pacificus," Hamilton defended neutrality in the press as passionately as he did in the halls of government. Jefferson, still unwilling to enter into the battle of the press himself, convinced Madison to respond. Madison did, with a series of five articles signed "Hevidius." But this proved to be too little too late. Jefferson, already hard-pressed by Hamilton and his forces, now had no real choice but to make good on his resignation, retreating to Monticello and regrouping, beginning to plan not for the present conflict (which he knew he had lost), but for 1796 and what looked to be a most grueling presidential campaign.

Without Jefferson in Philadelphia to provide direct support, the *Gazette* floundered, lasting only a total of two years. But the number of Republican newspapers was growing at such a pace that the *Gazette*'s place in the national debate was quickly filled by new, though local, publications. One of these, Benjamin Franklin Bache's *Aurora* (not technically new, but renamed), did manage to garner something of a national reputation, staking out a position for itself that would resonate with the press of a later era. As Eric Burns writes, "William Duane, who would eventually succeed Bache [who died in the yellow fever epidemic of 1799] as the *Aurora*'s editor, claimed that the paper provided 'the most formidable check upon ambition and false policy, which this nation has possessed for five years past.'"[2] The vision of the press as an independent entity with a clearly defined function within democracy was beginning to appear.

To a twenty-first-century American, the motivations of Jefferson, Hamilton, and the editors who supported them may not seem to have been very pure. But they were creatures of their time and did not see the press as we do, as an entity separate from politics, as a "fourth estate" with its own prerogatives and responsibilities. The role of the press had been no more codified than the relation between the government and the governed—and the two were quite mixed together and in flux. As media historian Paul Starr writes, "Popular sovereignty implied a change in the cognitive relationship between the state and the people. Traditionally, the state obtained knowledge about its individual subjects but disclosed little about itself, except what served the interest of those in power. But if the people were to be sovereign, they had to have the means of understanding their government, keeping up to date about distant events, and communicating with each other."[3] That a free press would be a necessary part of the new system was evident. How else could the public sphere be kept informed? But what did that mean, this phrase "free press?" No one yet knew.

At this time, the press certainly was considered an avenue of popular expression separate from the ballot box. That is, it really was considered the "voice of the people"—a notion that would be only metaphorically true once commercialism and professionalism had effectively separated the newspapers from direct popular expression. Through the papers, a lot could be learned of popular feelings (giving the papers a function something akin to the opinion polls that developed in the twentieth century). Anyone wanting to keep informed of popular opinion had to read papers from all along the political spectrum. This was also true in England, where, as Habermas writes, the results were the same. Election results were recognized as quite different from "the sense of the people." "'The common voice,' 'the general cry of the people,' and finally 'the public spirit' denoted from this time onward an entity to which the opposition could appeal."[4] In this way, the press became a check upon whatever elected government was in place, providing a natural voice for the opposition. It was not, however, as the press later became, a check through an independent entity outside of the political process.

The perceived value of the press as a part of the political process was illustrated by the Postal Act of 1792, which allowed every newspaper to send single copies to other papers without postage. By allowing easy communication between papers, Congress effectively put away any continuing conversation concerning establishment of a national newspaper. The distribution of stories through this system would be just as effective, but would not run the risk of encouraging centralized control.

The situation during Washington's first term, however, with both Jefferson and Hamilton within the government, was somewhat different. To many at the time, the whole conflict in the press just seemed exasperating— or worse, for it was leading to what was considered one of the evils of the English system, political parties.

In one of the more rancorous incidents of 1791, Jefferson gave what he may have thought of as a private endorsement of Thomas Paine's *The Rights of Man*, at the same time criticizing what he saw as anti-republican positions. Though never meant for public consumption, Jefferson's comments ended up the press (through carelessness on his part), leading to debate on the nature of republican politics. One of the writers responding to Jefferson styled himself "Publicola," an ingenious choice of name, for it was taken from the same early Roman republican leader, Publius Valorius Publicola, whose name Hamilton used for his *Federalist Papers*, giving the author (possibly John Quincy Adams) a firm connection (in his own mind, at least) to both the earlier American debate and the struggle to establish a republic in Rome. The debate led to an even clearer taking of sides by the various newspapers, solidifying their connections to the forming political parties.

In his note on *The Rights of Man*, Jefferson wrote that he expected Americans to rally once more to Paine and that he was pleased at the idea that they would. But he had imagined his note as private (here, again, he wanted to stay away from direct participation in the wars of the printed word). Not surprisingly, he was shocked and dismayed when he learned that his note was heading the American reprint of Paine's work.

One result was a bit of necessary fence-mending, especially with Vice President John Adams, with whom Jefferson was not yet ready to break.

Another result for Jefferson was that the subsequent controversy cemented him to Paine and to the growing opposition movement, making him its de facto spokesman without his ever having intended to take on that role publicly.

Clearly, it would be a mistake to consider the newspapers of the 1790s simply as creatures of the new political parties, for the parties had yet to develop structure of their own. Their leaders were leaders only because their followers imagined them there—no method of defining leadership had arisen. If anything (and because of the lack of any other structure), the papers did serve as something like party structures themselves, even before the parties really existed, for they provided that connection between like-minded people in distant places, allowing them to develop means of direct communication that did lead to creation of real party apparatuses.

While the newspapers were beginning to provide a nationwide network, new political societies began to appear throughout the states, generally including either the word "Democratic" or the word "Republican" in their names, most all of them extolling the virtues of the recent French Revolution. In many ways, these were formalized extensions of groups that had been gathering in taverns and coffee houses to discuss political issues and actions. By the mid-1790s, dozens of these societies had come into being. Their debates led to resolutions and appeals to the government. These, in turn, demanded some sort of structure (or a name, at least) for the originating body. With the establishment of such entities came desire to contact other, similar groups—and correspondence was begun. Through this, the groups began to energize each other, swapping ideas and complaints and, in an extremely blog-like manner, building into an informal network of opposition groups.

Not surprisingly, those in power viewed these new societies with concern. Some even saw them as potentially subversive, as a loose cannon on the deck of an orderly postrevolutionary ship. What was really developing, in addition to what would be American political parties, was the concept of the rule of law arising from the people, not from the political elite—and there were many who found this objectionable. Yet these societies were a critical part of what Habermas calls a "political consciousness [that] developed in the public sphere of civil society,"[5] a consciousness that led to the expression of the popular will and that, in the Jeffersonian vision, became the only source of legitimate law. Without the societies, American political discourse would have developed in entirely different directions.

Still, uncontrolled by any central party power or by government, the new societies made many of the insiders of the young republic nervous, just as bloggers do, today, for they were claiming for themselves what the elites had seen as their own. So worrying were these societies that, in his annual message to Congress in 1794, Washington singled them out for condemnation, accusing them of being negative forces only—just as many now see the blogs. Others, however, saw them differently. Sean Wilentz writes that, by "puncturing the pretension and defying the ridicule and noblesse, the societies showed that the science of government fell well within the comprehension of ordinary citizens."[6] They saw real democracy as coming from them and other representatives of the general populace—which, of course, is exactly how many bloggers see the world and place of real "democracy" in the early twenty-first century.

These societies, however, continued to cause alarm in the federal government even after Washington's presidency, especially given that most of them were in opposition to the new party of the Federalists that was headed by John Adams once he had succeeded Washington—and more and more of the newspapers associated with the societies, with Jefferson's quiet help, were drifting more overtly toward the opposition.

Once he was back in Virginia and out of government service, Jefferson began to plan how to get back in—but not as a member of the cabinet. Having seen what the press could do in conjunction with the new societies (not to mention what it had done for his own position as leader of the opposition), he began to develop a network for the coming campaign. Now fully aware of the importance of the press in the political arena (something Hamilton had understood quite a bit earlier), he developed and put into action a carefully conceived strategy based on the newspapers that were providing a great deal of the fodder for the societies that were now supporting him. Though Jefferson pulled the strings, little was heard from him directly. He operated through Bache and John Beckley in Philadelphia and through writers such as James Thomson Callender, whose work was reprinted extensively throughout the country. Speaking about him and (almost clandestinely) for him, these and other writers kept Jefferson's name before the public in a manner that would be reproduced successfully by Andrew Jackson's supporters a generation later. With an innate understanding of grassroots operations, Jefferson knew not to rush things, but to build his campaign through local affiliates, much as successful national politicians (including Jackson) have been doing ever since. By 1798, Jefferson had written "hundreds of letters and political pamphlets that would circulate among Republican newspapers and supporters to become an underground campaign."[7]

Generally a private correspondent—unlike Hamilton, who usually wrote for public consumption—Jefferson never overcame the carelessness that is the "right" of personal communications. Though he should have learned a lesson from the *Rights of Man* affair, he did not, and he was often a little careless, writing things that he did not believe would appear in print.

In 1797, once he was vice president, a letter he had sent to Philip Mazzei suddenly surfaced in *Minerva*, a New York City newspaper edited by Noah Webster. It had reached the American press through a circuitous route, first having appeared in an Italian paper and then showing up in France, translated from the Italian. The version that appeared in *Minerva* was a translation from the French. In what he had thought would remain a private missive, Jefferson had complained about the elite running the government, which he saw as having monarchist and aristocratic pretensions.

Having gone through two translations, the version presented by *Minerva*, not surprisingly, wasn't exactly as Jefferson had written it. Whereas he had meant to criticize the trappings of Washington's administration that sometimes seemed like those of a king, it now sounded like he was criticizing the very structure of the new American government. There was also an added sentence that had Jefferson criticizing his government for not being appropriately thankful to the French and for trying to bring about closer ties to England. Unlike Hamilton, who would have come up slugging and would have tried to turn this to his own advantage, Jefferson, never much of a street fighter, did not respond himself, but left his defense to others.

The vituperative quality of the opposition press began to worry even the Federalists more and more, especially President Adams (even though the Federalist press was doing pretty much the same thing). A touchy and proud man at the best of times, Adams couldn't see the attacks on him as simply part of the political debate, but instead felt that they were attacks on the nation that he, as president, represented. Adams, therefore, was not averse to proposed laws that would control the press.

Getting wind of the bills that were under consideration for reigning in the press, Jefferson, who was by now thoroughly convinced of the importance of the press in the evolving American political process—and who, quite correctly, assumed that enforcement would be against that part of the press that supported him—took the already partisan issue and made it part of what would grow into his 1800 campaign for the presidency. He saw what would come to be called the Alien and Sedition Acts as a direct attack not only on his supporters but even on the Bill of Rights itself.

He was right to be concerned. By 1798, with renewed possibilities of war with France as the excuse, the government felt it had the support necessary for doing something about opposition papers and other entities that it felt were undermining the new republic. In June and July of 1798, Congress did pass a series of acts calling for, among other things, the imprisonment or deportation of enemy aliens as well as limits on what could be said in the press. The final Sedition Act contained a sunset clause coinciding with the end of Adam's administration, making its political element quite clear even to the most naïve. The act reads, in part, as follows:

> That if any person shall write, print, utter or publish, or shall cause or procure to be written, printed, uttered or publishing, or shall knowingly and willingly assist or aid in writing, printing, uttering or publishing any false, scandalous and malicious writing or writings against the government of the United States, or either house of the Congress of the United States, or the President of the United States, with intent to defame the said government, or either house of the said Congress, or the said President, or to bring them, or either of them, into contempt or disrepute; or to excite against them, or either or any of them, the hatred of the good people of the United States, or to excite any unlawful combinations therein, for opposing or resisting any law of the United States, or any act of the President of the United States, done in pursuance of any such law, or of the powers in him vested by the constitution of the United States, or to resist, oppose, or defeat any such law or act, or to aid, encourage or abet any hostile designs of any foreign nation against the United States, their people or government, then such person, being thereof convicted before any court of the United States having jurisdiction thereof, shall be punished by a fine not exceeding two thousand dollars, and by imprisonment not exceeding two years. . . .
>
> That if any person shall be prosecuted under this act, for the writing or publishing any libel aforesaid, it shall be lawful for the defendant, upon the trial of the cause, to give in evidence in his defence, the truth of the matter contained in the publication charged as a libel. And the jury who shall try the cause, shall have a right to determine the law and the fact, under the direction of the court, as in other cases.[8]

In part because of the opposition of Jefferson and his allies, this first and most famous attempt to muzzle opposition expression ultimately did more to confirm the First Amendment's protection of freedom of the press than to undermine it. Yet, during the eighteen months that the Sedition Act was on the books, twenty-five writers and editors were prosecuted, and ten were convicted. They included even a politician collecting signatures for a petition supporting repeal of the acts, whose "martyrdom" turned him into a local hero. Benjamin Franklin Bache, certainly one of the targets of those who wrote the acts, escaped only by dying during the yellow fever epidemic in Philadelphia in 1799.

The act backfired right from the start, improving rather than tarnishing the reputations of those who were prosecuted. Enforcement soon, and quietly, ceased. In the meantime, the rights of the press, which would soon be known as an independent entity in its own right, were being expanded amidst the hoopla—not by law, but by popular will in opposition to a law, an insistence on an extended and well-protected public sphere. Only in the aftermath of the Alien and Sedition Acts did our contemporary conception of the First Amendment begin to become clear. Before that, the press had been seen as an extension of political debate and protection of freedom of the press simply as a protection for the opposition. Now, with editors and writers (only politicians secondarily) being targeted, the press was beginning to win a conception of itself as something of the independent entity it would later become. By the time the laws lapsed in 1801, the press was no longer seen as simply the extension of debate (and protected as debate is protected) but was beginning to be considered as a thing in itself. With the election of Jefferson, the institutionalization of the concept of "freedom of the press" began to be real, with the rights of the press becoming recognized as distinct from the personal and religious freedoms also delineated in the First Amendment.

The debate over the Alien and Sedition Acts wasn't solely shouting and fist-shaking, the low debate now so much associated with that time. Like the blogs today, where debate ranges from the most venal to the most thoughtful, discussion included serious thinking and writing on the role of the press in the new American political system. These efforts, more that the more high-profile debates, more than the rantings, more than the crowds at sedition trials cheering for the defendants, were what let to the new conception of the press. One of the major publications against the Sedition Act was George Hay's (writing as "Hortensius") *An Essay on the Liberty of the Press*. In it, he listed the following principles as presumed:

I. That all power originally belongs to the people.

II. That the powers of government are powers granted by the people.

III. That the individuals selected from the mass of the people, to administer the government, possess no powers, general or special, but those which are either expressly delegated or are *necessary* to carry a power expressly delegated into effect.

IV. That it has frequently happened in the source of human affairs, and may again happen, that the individuals thus selected may abuse the power entrusted to them, and may usurp more power than was meant to be entrusted to them.

V. That one abuse does not justify another, and that the usurpations of Congress cannot be vindicated by the encroachments of the State Legislatures.

VI. That the decision of a constitutional question, ought not, in any manner, to be affected by the conduct of France, or the opinions of Mr. Jefferson, or any other man, or men, in the world, but should rest on the immutable principles of reason and of truth.[9]

Hay expands upon these points throughout, ending with a rejection of the idea that the press comes under English common-law provisions:

The common law knows nothing of printing or the liberty of the press. The art of printing was not discovered, until towards the close of the close of the 15th century. It was at first in England, a subject of star-chamber jurisdiction, and afterwards put under a licencer by statute. This statute expired just before the commencement of the present century. Before this event, the rights of the press, were at the mercy of a single individual. There can be no common law, no immemorial usage or custom concerning a thing of so modern a date.

The freedom of the press, therefore, means the total exemption of the press from any kind of legislative control, and consequently the sedition bill, which is an act of legislative control, is an abridgment of its liberty, and expressly forbidden by the constitution.[10]

Hay's argument, "if it wasn't around when the law was created, the law can't cover it," is one heard today in terms of regulation of the Internet as legislators scramble to integrate it into the panoply of media regulations. But it was also one of the many arguments that were used to fight the Alien and Sedition Acts and, almost unwittingly, to give the press an expanded and independent role in the conception of the American political process.

In addition, the uproar over the Alien and Sedition Acts certainly led to a more contentious press than otherwise, completely the opposite of the intended effect. "By the election campaign of 1800, the country had eighty-five Republican papers, up from fifty-one in the spring of 1798."[11] After the election of 1800, "Jefferson and his lieutenants credited the press with his victory, while Federalist chiefs and journals alike berated opposition newspapers for sweeping that party from office."[12]

Just as today's blogs show both the best and the worst of what the news media can do, the election of 1800 showed a similar range, for much of the press was filled with mud-slinging and downright falsehoods, setting the stage (in a most unfortunate manner) for the next thirty-five years of newspaper "discussion" and even, in some ways, for the entire political history of the nation. There has not been a national election since that did not contain elements of slander against one candidate or another (generally against both), coupled with sly innuendo and outright derision. Though Jefferson himself was uncomfortable with the rancor of the 1800 campaign, he did participate in it, as have even our greatest presidents since.

Mudslinging has been part of the American public sphere since the nation's beginnings. Though many may decry it and ask the press to remove itself from it, "dirty politics" may be as necessary to the process as elevated debate. After all, a politician who has never learned to defend herself or himself from the lowest of attacks will be helpless when such an onslaught comes—and come it will, for the temptation will prove too strong for the opposition to withstand.

Though the campaign of 1800 lowered the standard of political debate in America, it also had positive results. The press was now firmly a part of the electoral process, and political censorship was (for the most part) a thing of the past. The importance of this development, for good and ill, cannot be overestimated. For the next two hundred years, for the most part, the American press operated unfettered by governmental control of its content. As Habermas states, this "made the influx of rational-critical arguments into the press possible and allowed the latter to evolve into an instrument with whose aid political decisions could be brought before the new forum of the public."[13]

In some respects, the uproar caused by the Alien and Sedition Acts opened a Pandora's box, releasing a sense of vigor and entitlement in the press that hadn't existed even in the contentious (in terms of the press) 1790s. Certainly, the newly vigorous American press was different from anything found in Europe and was much more extensive. The desire to participate in the public debate was manifest in the newspapers, which were still close to the people they served. The American need to be part of the public sphere has reasserted itself, of course, in the blogs, which have become a more important phenomenon in the United States than anywhere else in the world (though that could easily change through the American example). Jefferson, who was instrumental in unleashing this power, probably had little idea of what would result.

Chapter 5

THE HEYDAY OF THE PARTISAN PRESS

Today, Francis Preston Blair, if he is known at all, is remembered primarily as the namesake of Blair House, the U.S. President's official guest house. From 1830 until 1845, however, as editor of the Washington, D.C., newspaper *Globe*, he was one of the most powerful men in America, included as part of President Andrew Jackson's "kitchen cabinet" (the informal group of advisors the president relied on), and the most politically influential newspaper editor in the country. Later, he was a confidant of Abraham Lincoln through the Civil War. Though he had not been a Jackson supporter initially, Blair's early career and success in Washington were tied closely to Jackson's, whose own political triumphs were based on recognition of the power that the press (especially as it was constituted at the time) can have in the building of a political movement—hence his interest in Blair.

Blair's career arc, however, had begun almost a decade earlier, when, as a protégé of Amos Kendall, editor of the *Argus of Western America*, he began writing for that Frankfort, Kentucky, newspaper. Like almost all of the papers of the time, the *Argus* was an extremely political paper, and Blair eagerly joined the fray in support of Henry Clay. After Andrew Jackson's loss of the presidency to John Quincy Adams (despite winning a plurality of the popular vote), the *Argus* became even more political, with Blair taking a greater and greater role and still supporting Clay. By 1827, however, the paper had switched sides, joining the Jacksonian movement it had earlier opposed. Latecomers though they were, Kendall and Blair quickly became leading voices for Jackson in Kentucky.

By the time he moved to Washington to become the chief Jacksonian editor there, Blair had become the exemplar of the partisan editor of the time. Press historian Gerald Baldasty describes men of his profession during that period as filling

> their newspapers with partisan essays, argument and counterargument. These newspapers were a vibrant part of the political process. Editors did not debate in some idealistic desire to create a vast marketplace of ideas. Rather, they argued with one another because they wanted power. They were highly opinionated and interpreted events within their partisan ideology. Through all this they defined their readers as voters. Despite their bias, their intolerance of their opponents, and their subservience to political parties, they produced fervent and wide-ranging debate about political issues.[1]

Blair was perhaps the most successful of these editors of his time and certainly was the most politically influential. More important to the twenty-first century, he was also the prototype for the political bloggers of today (and not for the modern newspaper editor), for people like Glenn Reynolds of Instapundit and Josh Marshall, who founded Talking Points Memo. These, and the dozens upon dozens of other prominent political bloggers, have found in the blogs an avenue to political influence quite similar to what the newspapers of the 1820s and 1830s provided. Though the newspaper business changed in the 1840s (when editors started to see readers as consumers and not as voters) and began to leave Blair and those like him behind, the role they played has never completely disappeared, as its resurgence today confirms.

If any gulf between the American press and its political parties had been spanned in the 1790s, it was during the 1820s that the bridge was most effective, and Blair was at the apex of what might even be called a revitalization of the connection (coinciding, not surprisingly, with a revitalization of party politics). Politics, after 1824, was fast becoming one of America's favorite pastimes, and the newspapers were quick to make sure they had a role.

After touring America, the Frenchman Alexis de Tocqueville was struck by the newspapers' ubiquity, by the breadth of opinion they expressed, and by the weaknesses that resulted. He observed that almost every town in the United States had its own newspaper (something unheard of, at the time, in Europe), leading to a cacophony of opinion and extreme diversity of viewpoints. "Newspapers in the United States, therefore, cannot establish great currents of opinion that sweep away or overflow the most powerful dikes."[2] He saw three other significant results from this, and the first was that newspapers, being commonplace, did not instill awe or fear in the populace, who could feel perfectly free and able to take them on in debate. Second, the fact of great numbers, in de Tocqueville's eyes, precluded great profits. Therefore, business tended to keep its hands off, allowing the newspapers to remain vehicles for the people. And, finally, because newspapers were so common and published so much, few of the writers could be expected to be particularly skilled in the arts of writing and editing, resulting in the perception of the newspaperman as someone no different from his fellows, not elevated in any way, as might be a member of the traditional professions.

Alexis de Tocqueville was right in many ways, though he could not have imagined what technology would do to the newspaper trade just a few years hence, taking something that had been of low profitability and making it into an avenue for producing immense wealth. What de Tocqueville describes could also pass as a description of the blogs today, right down to their lack of real profitability—which can make one wonder if they, too, will one day be the basis of economic empires, as newspapers were later in the nineteenth century.

Blair and other increasingly sophisticated and educated editors and writers started to change the situation that de Tocqueville had observed, to alter the impression of the newspaper business as a generally untalented and vulgar trade. Blair himself grew more sophisticated and certainly wealthier as he grew in influence and importance, taking on the trappings of the American elite. But for the time being (roughly 1825 to 1835), the newspapers were also the prime forum for a rough and tumble political debate of exactly the sort going on today through the blogs.

If Jackson was the first politician to rise through this contentious milieu, Blair was its first activist writer of sustained national reputation. We have yet to see politicians harness the blogs as successfully as Jackson did the newspapers, but that is probably coming. Contenders for Blair's mantle, however, are already making their appearance—the one with the highest profile so far being Markos Moulitsas, founder of the liberal blog The Daily Kos. Like Blair, Moulitsas broke no ground when he founded his blog, but, again like Blair, he has risen above the others in terms of impact and recognition. It remains to be seen, of course, whether he will match Blair in terms of ultimate influence.

Like the contentious 2000 election, the election of 1824 was directly responsible for a renewed interest in politics throughout the nation. Not only were the results not based (ultimately) on the popular vote, but it also was the first election since 1800 whose results were not a forgone conclusion, with the successor having been named by the incumbent. Monroe, breaking with that tradition, had refused to name anyone at all, leading to a rollicking campaign and its unsatisfying conclusion in the House or Representatives.

It probably wasn't Jackson himself who developed the strategy that would eventually lead him to the White House four years later—any more than it was Howard Dean himself who, in 2004, first recognized the power that blogs could have in sparking enthusiasm for a campaign (not to mention in raising money). In fact, it was the partisan press that led Jackson; newspapers were part of the campaign even before his *first* campaign had really started. As early as the start of 1822, Jackson was being mentioned as a potential candidate, pushed by papers such as the *Aurora* of Philadelphia. Putting forward Jackson's name was one of *Aurora* editor William Duane's last acts as editor, for the successor to Benjamin Franklin Bache was soon to retire. Though other established papers did begin to push the idea of a Jackson candidacy, it was newer papers, such as Stephen Simpson's *Columbian Observer*, that began to carry the torch for Jackson, sparking what had become, by 1828, a conflagration. Senator John Eaton of Tennessee, writing as "Wyoming," composed a series of letters for the *Observer* that presented Jackson as the protector of the heritage of the Revolution against the onslaught of the privileged and as the one person who could represent the entire nation and not just a single region.[3]

The campaign, however, was not organized well enough in 1824 to ensure its success that year, even though Jackson ended up polling ten points better than Adams with about a 42 percent plurality—with William Crawford and Henry Clay splitting the rest of the vote. Adams and his supporters were able to win Clay's support (Clay had never liked Jackson) when the election was thrown to the House of Representatives, ensuring Adams's ultimate success. Clay soon joined the new administration as Secretary of State, causing cries of outrage from the opposition press, suspicious that this had been part of a deal with Adams for Clay's support.

The loss spurred Jackson's supporters (yet to include Kendall and Blair, who were then still backers of Clay) to feverish activity over the next four years, activity that included establishment of a wide network of Jacksonian newspapers. Adams inadvertently gave them an assist through his first annual message to Congress, which they heard as an attempt to amass power in the presidency without regard for the fact that Adams was a minority president and as a plan to support the will of the elite over the broader populace. In part because of the anger at the perceived arrogance of this president "elected" by the House of Representatives, a new and primarily Western and Southern populism was able to grow in strength.

As in 1824, the loser of the popular vote was elected in 2000 (it also happened in 1876 and 1888), though it was the Supreme Court, not the House of Representatives, that ultimately decided that more recent election. Four years after the 1824 election, the candidate who had won the popular vote, Andrew Jackson, did manage to win the White House. The same thing did not happen 176 years later, of course; Al Gore did not run again, and George Bush was reelected, this time winning the popular vote. Whatever the reasons Gore did not run, he certainly did not take advantage of (or shape, as the Jackson forces did) the populist media tool of his time, the blogs, whose ancestor, the partisan press, was so critical to Jackson's eventual success. This may have delayed popular recognition of the potential power of the blogs.

Almost as soon as the 1824 vote was over, Jackson began that campaign in the press that would bring him to power during the next cycle—but it was a press significantly different from the one Al Gore later faced, for Jackson and his party controlled a large part of the press and could work to build more. Gore would have had to build an alternative, and in 2001, that alternative (which is proving to be the blogs) was not easily recognized, but its power has since begun to show. Defeated, in part, by more adroit use of a mainstream media that he had found he could not manipulate in the same manner, Gore was not able to see that there was, in fact, a way similar to Jackson's of keeping his campaign alive and vibrant for the four intervening years.

By the 2004 election, however, the power of the blogs was becoming clear. Trent Lott, after all, had lost his position as Senate Majority Leader in 2002 in part because the political blogs had refused to ignore the racist undertones of statements he had made concerning the political career of Strom Thurmond. Yet the moves were assumed to be only stunts when both parties invited bloggers to their 2004 conventions, and the mainstream news media did try to make fun of them in a condescending way. The politicians, though, were a bit more cognizant than the news media of the growing importance of this new phenomenon and were right to invite them: the blogs were coming of age. Openly partisan and, in a growing number of cases, directly connected to political campaigns and candidates, the blogs had started to make themselves a part of the American political process—in terms of both issues and fundraising.

Perhaps, had Al Gore been as forward-looking in terms of the blogs as he had been years earlier in terms of the Internet itself, recognizing the new power that was being born, he might have considered keeping his campaign alive, as Jackson did so many years earlier. A student of political history (and with a background in journalism), Gore would have been able to grasp the parallel with 1824 and might not have decided to abandon his presidential ambitions—had the blogs exploded onto the political scene just a couple of years earlier. The power of the Jacksonian press was extraordinary in political terms and was unlike anything that was to be seen in America after the Civil War. Not even the Hearst empire, with its (somewhat mythical) ability to create wars, had quite the same punch. This was due, simply, to the fact that the press of the time was primarily a creature of politics—newspapers having clear political purposes and affiliations, with no commercial considerations eroding their power. Advertising had yet to become their economic driver, making maximum circulation the goal and replacing maximum influence over the political process and maximum voter turnout of the like-minded.

Complementing the invigorated press, Jackson initiated a new type of campaigning, taking part in it personally in a manner that candidates of previous eras had felt was unseemly, beneath the dignity of a presidential contender. He talked to anyone who wanted a word with him—including newspaper editors who wanted to interview him—and wrote letters for publication elsewhere. From the start, it was clear that he hadn't given up his presidential ambitions, that his campaign had not ended with the inauguration of Adams. Gore, on the other hand, withdrew from political life (at least for the time being) and then turned to issue advocacy instead of direct political involvement.

In the 1820s, as had been the case in the 1790s, newspapers weren't as much tools of political parties as they were the very entities that made political parties viable. Together, the papers could form a decentralized network with strength far beyond anything emanating from Washington. The blogs may be beginning to serve the same purpose today, taking the political parties away from their centralized focus and back to more local control (though the Republicans have been using church-based groups for essentially this same purpose for several decades already).

As public identification coalesced around Whig and Democrat, their networks of newspapers became more and more important—and it was the Jacksonian forces that understood this first and utilized it best. In addition, the Jackson editors were, with Jackson himself, perhaps the first people ever to understand the importance of continual campaigning and the necessity of alliances with constituent groups and single-issue movements. It was during this period, after all, that other types of publications were beginning to establish themselves, the most prominent being the abolition journals, though publications for workingmen and advocating temperance (among other things) also arrived on the scene. A good editor would make alliances with the editors of other periodicals, expanding the influence of each. If they could ally these papers to their own populist cause, Jackson's people could, of course, make his political movement even stronger.

Like editors all over the country were doing in their regions, Blair was honing his political skills in Kentucky. Once the *Argus* (upon emerging from a debt that editor Kendall had owed to Clay, a debt likely paid by Jackson supporters) switched its support to Jackson, its pages, with Blair doing much of the writing, quickly started presenting "evidence" of malfeasance on the part of the Adams administration, accusing the leaders of turning a blind eye to corruption and never letting its readers forget that Adams had not won the popular election. Blair Biographer Elbert Smith catalogs some of the sins Blair found in Adams:

> He had opposed Tom Paine's *Rights of Man*. . . . He had abused Jefferson, opposed the Louisiana Purchase, tried to betray the West at the peace conference and Ghent, and finally abandoned the Federalist party without, however, abandoning its principles. . . . And last but not least, the *Argus* complained, Adams had persecuted "faithful, well-tried, and patriotic republican printers," while rewarding those who were "subservient": The *New Hampshire Patriot*, the *Eastern Argus*, and the Frankfort *Argus* had been "deprived of government patronage for exposing fearlessly the abuses committed by Mr. Adams." [*Argus* March 5, 1829][4]

This last, though not exactly a burning public issue, was extremely important to the newspaper editors of the time. Unable to rely on subscriptions (it was extremely hard to collect) and existing before the development of networks of news vendors, printers were often dependent on government contracts for survival (newspapers, remember, were still but one part of a printer's trade). Granting of these contracts was always politically contentious, and such decisions were sometimes meant to send a message to other branches of government. For example, in 1825 the Senate made General Duff Green, whose *United States Telegraph* was a constant thorn in the side of the Adams administration, its official printer at the behest of Senator John Calhoun, another opponent of Adams.

The extent and impact of the Jacksonian network of newspapers is hard to understand in the twenty-first century, when the size and population of the United States is so much greater, for the growth, in raw terms, seems small. But for the time and population, it was extraordinary. It is worth reiterating, also, that this growth was not accidental. Soon after the defeat by Adams, Jackson's supporters in Congress decided to back the establishment of as many newspapers as possible, blanketing the entire nation. They succeeded in spectacular style. The number of Jacksonian papers in Ohio grew from five to twenty-three. Nine new newspapers appeared in 1827—in

North Carolina alone. "In each state, the Jackson forces arranged for one newspaper to serve as the official organ of their respective state committees, refining the broadcast of an authoritative message."[5] The editors soon began to find it worth their while to stick closely to the Jacksonian line, for new and bigger ways of providing support for them were being created by backers of the growing network (both in Congress and elsewhere). This was politics of a new sort and on a new level, and it caught politicians of the older style, like Adams, by surprise. Today, the blogs are beginning to have similar impact, though the politicians have been quickly catching on—perhaps faster than anyone else. It is the older news media that, this time, are being caught flat-footed, a reversal of the situation in the 1820s.

Jackson was only the first politician who understood the importance of this developing network of newspapers and supporters. He showed his appreciation soon after the 1828 election, handing out postmasterships (among other patronage positions) to newspaper editors, in particular, all over the country. "Especially outrageous to his foes was Jackson's propensity to appoint loyal newspaper editors, among them Amos Kendall. . . mere 'printers' one Virginian sneered—to conspicuous public office."[6] Furthermore, a majority of the contracts for the printing of federal laws were soon moved to the shops of printers who also produced Jacksonian newspapers. These editors, Jackson knew, were the people who had made his presidency possible. Once in power, he could not—and did not—ignore them, especially in the atmosphere of patronage that was still the order of the day.

Though the blogs have yet to reach any comparable level of influence, the newspapers of Jacksonian America, once again, are the closest the United States has experienced to this newer media phenomenon. Since the time of Jackson, however, American newspapers have evolved into something completely different from those driven by Jackson loyalists, into a professional news media that tries to keep a distance from direct political activity, a news media that reached its current form only during the last decades of the twentieth century.

The reasons for the change, as we will see, have a lot to do with the growth of a professional journalist class, the move of news media into the commercial sphere, the diminishment of the public sphere, and the concentration of media ownership. Here, it suffices simply to point out the remarkable parallels between a type of newspaper that has long been seen as a peculiarity of its time—indeed, an aberration or dead end—and a developing set of online "news" outlets that have revived not only the practices but also the precepts of the newspapers of that earlier time.

The newspapers of the Jacksonian era were often seen by viewers from the twentieth century as an unruly rabble only waiting for professional journalism to arise and impose order. Yet they really did have an order of their own and even ethical standards—in fact, much like the blogs of today, they often touted a clear moral stance, a way of looking at the world that brooked no opposition, that was based on principles enunciated almost continually through daily or weekly stories (depending on the frequency of publication). They were the descendents of Tom Paine, strident and motivated—though often beset by devils of their own making.

The concept of impartiality or neutrality that became such a hallmark of American journalism starting in the years just before World War II was almost completely absent from the Jacksonian newspapers. A claim of neutrality, in fact, might have raised the specter of a hidden agenda, for it was not considered possible for someone to be actually neutral.

As political entities, the newspapers provided a connection between people and party that has deteriorated in the years since. Here again, though, the link may be in the process of being reforged through the blogs. Like bloggers are trying to do today, the newspapers worked to bring out the vote, especially in areas that were not easily reached by the political foot soldiers of the cities and towns. Like blogs, the newspapers were easily accessible to just about anyone anywhere and served as the basis of heated political debate. In addition, the parties needed them, as Gerald Baldasty writes, "because they weren't as ephemeral as rallies and speeches. Newspaper essays could be read, discussed, and debated a week, a month, or more after publication. And people read these papers."[7] They felt a personal connection with them, much as do the readers, diarists, and responders of today's blogs with their medium.

As I have said, if twentieth- and twenty-first-century editors see (and saw) their readers as consumers, their predecessors in Jacksonian America, like twenty-first-century bloggers, considered their readers only

as *voters* and provided content that would woo them to a particular party and then mobilize them to vote. There was no room for indecision or neutrality in the press. The *Louisville Public Advertiser* condemned a purportedly neutral Indiana paper: "We do not know how it is in Indiana, but, in this State, people have more respect for an open, independent adversary than for dumb partisans or shuttlecock politicians, who are considered too imbecile to form an opinion, or too servile to express an opinion when formed." [July 9, 1828] The Washington D.C., *U.S. Telegraph* condemned a purportedly neutral Baltimore paper, noting that the neutrality was probably indicative of a complete lack of principle and an abundance of opportunism. [October 7, 1828][8]

The significance of that distinction—voter instead of consumer—should not be underestimated. When the point isn't to sell papers or (by extension) advertised goods as much as it is to convince readers to vote in a certain way, the ethics of the newspaper business are necessarily different—and they were. It also leads to a milieu in which editors "did not try to be all things to all people, and they did not seek to cater to every interest."[9] Certainly, when an editor desired, first and foremost, to effect certain political ends, questions of neutrality must have seemed both bizarre and irrelevant. Politics, after all, were extremely personal. Journalistic distancing brought on by "objectivity" had not yet been born.

Blair, though he had tied his fortunes to Jackson's success, could not have expected, when still writing for the *Argus*, to end up as the most important editor in Washington and a political participant in governmental business. This happened in part because of Duff Green, the protégé of Calhoun (soon to be Jackson's running mate) who was funded to some extent by Jackson supporters and who repaid the favor with huge politically oriented newspaper editions distributed throughout much of the nation in the run-up to the 1828 election.

With Jackson in power, Green's piece of the government contract pie only increased, as did his influence. The magnitude of government printing needs was staggering even then—and there was not yet any federal printing service to meet them. Therefore, it is not at all surprising that contracts to fill printing needs were a financial mainstay of the press, which, after all, was still attached to the job-printing industry. The needs were legitimate, from recordings of governmental activity to the stationery used in correspondence with constituents. And most printers were competent to meet the needs. How, then, to decide which one?

The answer was simple and obvious: use the one that had supported the decision makers in its newspapers. Each house of Congress made its own decisions concerning printers, as did the executive branch and the courts. Then there were the state administrations and the local ones, all with continual need of printed product. For a politically connected printer, there was bound to be work. Even when his party was out of power in one venue, given the fact of a predominantly two-party system, there were other entities where his party was still dominant. Most lucrative, however, were the contracts with Congress. "From 1819 to 1846, each house of Congress elected a printer to publish its proceedings, debates, and laws. These lucrative contracts ran for two years with profit margins running from 20 to 55 percent. Editors used the profits to maintain their political papers and to undertake other partisan activities, such as publishing campaign newspapers."[10]

Though Blair was certainly aware of the possibilities open to a Washington political printer and editor (including an income well beyond even the dreams of a regional editor) and even had friends who were rapidly rising in the Jacksonian patronage hierarchy, he would have seen his future as lying elsewhere. Though he must have been aware of his skill and talent, it is not likely that he would have been angling for a move to Washington himself.

As noted already, the patronage system was not monolithic, as the appointment of Duff Green as Senate printer, even though he was an opponent of the administration, showed. In fact, because of the plethora of government entities, the patronage system had exactly the opposite effect of what one might expect. Instead of encouraging a press that simply pandered to (or provided the base for—depending on point of view) those in power, the patronage of the time actually served diversity. This system of backdoor subsidy of a contentious press, then, could be seen as a boon to the public sphere, encouraging debate, as long as no one political party took control of all branches of government on all levels.

Blair's big chance came as the result of a miscalculation on the part of Green, who had hitched his wagon too firmly to Calhoun's star, not imagining that the old and infirm Jackson could effectively manage the government and his political party—let alone run for reelection in 1832. Seeing the growing division between president and vice president, Green jumped ship in 1830, "spreading the word that Calhoun's pretensions could not wait another six years."[11] Jackson, he was saying, should not run for reelection but should step aside in favor of Calhoun.

Calhoun, certainly, was ambitious and was no real fan of Jackson. But like his editor Green, he underestimated the man. So strained were relations that, well before the midway mark in Jackson's first term, the president and vice president had become enemies much more than allies—and Calhoun's immediate presidential ambitions were made all the more clear. The upshot was that this gave Jackson both the chance and the reason to start looking around for someone to replace Green as the Washington spokesperson for the administration. Blair was not Jackson's first choice as founding editor of the new newspaper he had in mind (Simpson of the *Columbian Observer* turned the president down), but Kendall kept pushing for him, and eventually Blair was given the chance.

Kendall had left the *Argus* in Blair's hands at the beginning of the Jackson administration in favor of political patronage positions in Washington. He had confidence in Blair, and having finally sold his stake in the *Argus*, he no longer had a personal concern about the future of that paper (which, he felt, might not survive without Blair). Green's paper was still a problem in the plan, but Kendall managed to convince Green that there was governmental printing enough to take care of two Democratic papers. By the end of 1829, a deal had been reached, and Blair had set out for Washington to produce his newspaper.

Green couldn't have been fooled for long, but he was firmly in Calhoun's camp and still saw that as the wave of the future. Unfortunately for him, he was wrong and was soon bypassed in influence (both in Washington and nationally) by the new paper, the Washington *Globe*.

Though from the wilds of the West (Kentucky was no eastern state), Blair seems to have fit in with power and society in Washington, D.C., quite quickly, making himself a real presence at the White House and even across the country, where his work was widely reprinted. "By 1835 it [the *Globe*] had 17,000 subscribers, and its influence went far beyond its numbers. . . . As the Jacksonians used the patronage to build up their grass-roots organizations, subscriptions to the *Globe* became the responsibility of local politicians everywhere."[12] Blair rode this cresting wave to a position far above anything any editor (aside from Benjamin Franklin) had yet to achieve.

So close were the ties between the administration and the new paper that, if anyone wanted him, Blair would be found, like as not, in Jackson's presence. He quickly became a part of the patronage system, to the extent of often being the one who would decide if, and what, patronage job an applicant would get. At the same time, Blair continued the populist clamor that had been the hallmark of the Democratic party since the time of Jefferson: "America's greatest danger, said the *Globe* in editorial after editorial, was the possibility that wealthy aristocrats might use the government's great power to increase their own privileges, thwart the ambitions of the less fortunate, and create a permanent native aristocracy."[13]

As a political organizer who worked through the newspaper he edited, Blair never stopped what really had now become a perennial campaign, constantly networking with other newspapers and with party leaders throughout the nation, printing reports of political activities in far corners of the country and sending out stories from Washington in return. "Blair's editorials and lead stories were the fountain of wisdom and inspiration for some 400 other papers, and no other single agency did so much to create the national image of Andrew Jackson."[14] In this respect, Blair can even seem, as Elbert Smith sees him, to have been the creator of the first truly national press service.[15] Certainly, his portrait should command a spot of honor on the wall of every successful political blogger today.

It should be reiterated that, though he was every bit the partisan editor pushing a political agenda through his newspaper, Blair was not contravening journalistic ethics as he saw them—or as they were seen in general at the time—and neither were the other editors like him. Blair did see that he had a duty to convey important information, but that did not preclude doing so with an overt political bias. In addition, because they were able to gain subsidies, as it were, through government patronage and by providing government printing services, these printer–editors were able to prevent the narrowing of the public sphere that followed inexorably on the commercialization of the press. Blair and the editors of his time managed to place their newspaper enterprises within a larger framework of interwoven activities, which kept at bay the necessity of commercializing the newspapers themselves. Thereby, they were able to remain a "press that had evolved out of the public's use of its reason and that had merely been an extension of its debate remained thoroughly an institution of this very public: effective in the mode of a transmitter and amplifier, no longer a mere vehicle for the transportation of information but not yet a medium for culture as an object of consumption."[16] In this, they were different from contemporary bloggers, who have found that they don't need substantial funding to manage to find audiences, though bloggers may suffer the same fate, disappearing into commercial enterprises as such possibilities arise.

Even so, this group of antebellum editors, often seen in later decades as having been an aberration, as an unprofessional sidetrack on the line to a real professional journalism, in fact played an important role in the public debate of the time, a role that has atrophied since and that, perhaps, has regained strength only with the rise of the blogs.

Chapter 6

THE RISE OF
PROFESSIONAL
JOURNALISM

By the start of the Civil War, three related forces had begun to have substantial impact on American journalism, combining to move it away from the overtly political (and much more blog-like) nature of the Jacksonian antebellum press to a form still recognizable to newspaper readers even as late as the start of the twenty-first century. This was also the first period in which technological changes (along with cultural forces) had tremendous impact on journalism, changing its very nature, creating the profession as we still know it today. The second period of great technological impact is the one we are experiencing right now, one that is, paradoxically, helping us reclaim what those earlier changes removed from the public sphere.

The changes that had the greatest impact in that earlier age were (1) developments in printing technology leading to high-speed single-use newspaper presses, (2) the birth of a journalism profession apart from that of the printer, and (3) the rise of a distinctly commercial (and particularly urban) press. The second and third of these changes were related to the activities of James Gordon Bennett—a man who also was one of the earliest to explore the possibilities of the first change, the technology developments.

By 1835, when Bennett founded his *New York Herald*, a new, real mass-market press was already developing, one that would change the public sphere, ultimately (and ironically) reducing it even though seeming to broaden it by taking politics out of the news. The first example of this, of what came to be called the "penny press," had appeared two years earlier in the guise of Benjamin Day's *New York Sun*. The changes were almost immediate and quite obvious. Jürgen Habermas has described some of the implications of what was going on, writing that the success of the newly expanding news media rested on commercialization of public-sphere participation through use of a vehicle that had originally served simply as a means of access to the public sphere. Commercial needs soon began to trump public needs. Soon, the public sphere had become less a place for political discussion than one for sowing the seeds for commercial enterprise. "In the case of the early penny press it could already be observed how it paid for the maximization of its sales with the depoliticization of its content—by eliminating political news and political editorials on such moral topics as intemperance and gambling."[1]

It was commercial consideration, and not any sense of ethics within the growing profession of journalism, that caused the separation of the press and politics. In other words, this was no maturing of the press, but a move into a completely separate arena from where it had operated before. It was also the result of the fact that more papers could be printed faster and more cheaply, making it financially advantageous to concentrate on circulation above all other considerations.

Though his wasn't the first of the penny presses, it is certainly true, as John Steele Gordon puts it, that Bennett, "more than any single individual, [invented] the mass media and made it the major player in the game of public affairs that it has been ever since. This changed the rules of politics completely and made the modern political world possible."[2] It was also that change in focus from politics to commerce that made the modern media world possible. After all, it was only the fact that the press was now financially separate from government and politics that allowed its real establishment as a "fourth estate" with its own ethics and standards.

One reason that Gordon can claim Bennett as the inventor of mass media is that it was Bennett himself, more than Day or any other editor of the time, who was responsible for those changes in the antebellum press (outside of the technological) that moved American journalism from its advocacy state to one of an independent profession—that necessary first step in the creation of truly independent mass media. Ignoring politics, for the most part, Bennett was an active seeker of other news, items that would draw enough interest so that people would shell out that coin for his paper. Sensationalism sells papers, Bennett discovered, starting a trend that still dominates the media.

When Gordon calls the mass media a "major player" in public affairs, he is referring to something quite different from the roles played by newspapers such as Francis Preston Blair's *Globe*, newspapers that were direct participants in politics, as almost (and, in some cases, really) extensions of political parties or bases for establishing parties. He is referring to the press instead as a separate and independent entity, as what came to be known as "the fourth estate." In other words, Gordon's very conception of the media is tempered by the changes in it associated with Bennett.

It is significant that Gordon was writing about Bennett in 1996, in the days before the rise of the blogs, for the blogs are, in some respects, now attempting a reversal of the trend Gordon associates with Bennett. This change may prove to alter politics, political participation, and the news media as significantly as that earlier change did. It is even possible that the American political situation is actually moving *back* to something similar to what Bennett had seen at the start of his career, something his activities implicitly rejected, but that had long been a major part of American participatory democracy. If the blogs are successful in what they are attempting—reasserting citizen presence in the public sphere, shoving the professionals at least somewhat aside—a part of what Bennett represents may even come to be seen as having been an aberration, a dead end off the road toward a genuine and effective public sphere. If nothing else, the role of the press, as established in Bennett's time, is changing again in response to technological changes allowing any person to be actively involved in public discussion of the news instead of simply being an observer of debate by professionals in the news media.

So, today, in light of a decade of developments in the Internet and in its political usage, Gordon's statement should be amended. Bennett made possible the position of the media as a major player in public affairs, yes, but he also set off a chain of events that eventually would leave millions of Americans of all political stripes feeling powerless in the face of media sway in the public sphere. In that sense, however, he is also responsible for one of the reactions to the perceived power of corporate media: the very personal and individual blog.

These changes, though, would be a long time coming—and are the subject of later chapters of this book. Here, the focus is on the forces that moved the press away from its earlier, blog-like aspects and toward the mass media that dominated so much of the twentieth century.

Perhaps the first of these was the development of cheap, readily available paper. Though pulp paper had been introduced around the turn of the century (greatly speeding up paper production and reducing costs), it wasn't until papermaking machinery was introduced a couple of decades later that cheap paper was available in bulk. Steam-powered cylinder presses came into use in England (and then America) not too many years later, greatly increasing the speed of any press run, but it wasn't until the advent of the rotary press in the 1840s that technology drastically changed the essential nature of the newspaper business. Prior to the 1840s, running a newspaper was just once aspect of a larger printing industry, one that included books, broadsides, government documents, and small, private jobs—and one that often left time for such things as postal duties and political activity. By the 1840s, because of technological forces, population growth, and increased urbanization, the industry had begun to split apart, these activities and more becoming things of the past as far as the newspapers were concerned.

Richard Hoe's innovative rotary press, the "Lightning," was put into commercial use for the first time in 1847, just at the time when the newspaper business was poised for a jump into larger distribution. In part because of Bennett, newspapers had already moved toward greater diversity in coverage—almost as though in preparation for the new presses.

The Lightning and later huge rotary presses, with their continuous paper feeds, could serve only one function efficiently—printing newspapers. They could not be easily used for other types of jobs and were certainly not cost-effective for small runs. The introduction of the rotary press, therefore, effectively divided the urban newspaper business (the only place where demand was extensive enough to justify the huge press runs) from the rest of the printing industry and even from the book industry (which, by this time, had its own single-use presses too).

Most job printing requires a flexibility that cannot be found through the large, fast rotary presses. Different papers need to be used for different jobs, for example, and sizes are not standard in such operations. In addition, a wider variety of fonts is required than for a newspaper, which tries to be true to its design model. For book publishing, too, the required technology was becoming increasingly distinct from newspaper needs. Here, the huge presses were not generally cost-effective (press runs for books being much smaller than for newspapers) and did not produce a product of the quality required by most book purchasers. However, a new aspect of book publishing did develop as a result of the new presses, the "dime novel," cheaply printed sensationalist books for the "masses," but for the most part, book publishing, as an industry, continued to separate from the newspaper world.

Other factors, as well, separated the industries, starting in the 1840s. Newspapers, with their insatiable demand for paper and ink (among other things) needed warehouse space for raw materials. Book publishers, on the other hand, did not need to keep such items close at hand in large quantities, but did need space for warehousing of finished products—something a newspaper business did not require. In the same vein, newspapers would immediately melt down stereotype plates (another new technology) from the day's run to reuse the lead whereas book publishers would store them for possible reprinting.

Another spin-off of the printer's trade that was to become extremely important to the American news media was the magazine. Here, it wasn't only technological changes that led to the growth and popularity of the magazine, but also the other changes that were going on in the newspaper world. The growth of magazines was as great as the growth of newspapers, the number of them increasing sixfold from 1825 to 1860.[3] Why? As John Tebbel and Mary Ellen Zuckerman point out, the changing nature of newspapers was largely to blame. After "1835, with the advent of James Gordon Bennett and his New York *Herald*, newspapers devoted themselves more and more to coverage of the news."[4] Earlier papers had concentrated on opinion and politics, often serving as outreach vehicles for political parties, but now the magazines were beginning to take over those functions, though often without the direct political ties.

The need for the type of argumentation that the newspapers had previously provided did not disappear simply because the newspapers had changed. Certainly, the magazines did take up some of the slack. They were, however, generally national (or regional) in distribution, so they did not provide a venue for participatory discussion within local communities in the way that local newspapers had. Readers had to be satisfied as observers or, at best, as composers of letters to distant editors, letters that might not see print until long after the passions that sparked them had subsided. Still, the weekly magazines and the increasingly popular monthlies focused extensively on the issues of the day, including emancipation, and were particularly important in a churning public arena that kept the magazine world growing. The extreme turmoil of the years directly before the Civil War was a bonanza for the magazine industry, the number of publications nearly doubling in just the years from 1859 to 1860.[5] One fallout of the changes in newspapers was this increase, this chance for magazines to step into a niche that the newly commercialized newspapers had vacated.

The changes in the publishing business were possible because, by 1850, what had been one industry—printing—had now split into at least four: the newspaper trade, the book trade, the magazine trade, and the job printing trade. Each was becoming so distinct from the others that movement back and forth between them was becoming increasingly rare, at least in the large cities. Along with the technological changes in printing had come new delineation of jobs. No longer were "printers" responsible for books, magazines, newspapers, broadsides, pamphlets, and various job printing, but different people, and then different firms, began to take responsibility for each area. Earlier editors had known how to hold a composing stick and lock a chase. No longer was that necessary or even useful.

Even within the newspaper field, specialization began to appear, with distinct roles for publisher, editor, and reporter—none of them any longer directly involved with the presses themselves. Only in the smaller towns where newspapers could not really be supported on their own, and where magazines and books were rarely produced, did the job-printing and newspaper trades stay coupled, often remaining together until late in the twentieth century. It was only in these few cases that a newspaper editor could really still claim to literally have "ink in his veins."

For every trend, there is a countertrend, of course, and the one here was movement toward gathering all of these new trades (except for job printing) under umbrella organizations—but not to combine production, as had been the case of the old-fashioned printers. Here, the symbiosis was between products that could be used to promote each other, and such amalgamation became the basis for the media conglomerates that grew after the Civil War and through the twentieth century. The production facilities, however, were generally kept separate.

Operating on a different economic model from daily newspapers, and often supported by issue-advocacy groups, the magazines took up the political debate that newspapers, edited by people now emulating Bennett's success, were increasingly abandoning. America's insatiable appetite for political debate needed an outlet somewhere, and the magazines at the time were providing at least an approximation of it, just as the blogs would do 150 years later. Rather than focusing on news, the magazines could focus on debate, on discussion that could attain a depth newspapers never had the ability to reach—a depth that had been the purview of the pamphlets that magazines had, in some senses, replaced. Indeed, it may have been the huge debates of the time (as much as the newspapers moving away from political advocacy) that made the magazines of the time so successful. The slavery issue drove a large number of magazines, allowing people to align with the magazines much as many do today with their favorite blogs: one's reading was a clear indication of one's stands.

One of the possibilities today is that technology once again will help bring about a split from one industry into many, as it did when it spun off newspapers, magazines, and books from the job printing trade. It is even possible that the expanding opinion sections of daily newspapers, broadcast and cable news channels, radio stations, and even magazines will start to disappear as the blogs take over the activities of issue discussion in the public sphere, leaving the traditional news media to news gathering only. The older media may then begin to develop in other directions.

Just as politicians have been quick to add their voices to the blogs (even former president Jimmy Carter has done so, as has losing 2004 presidential candidate John Kerry), recognizing the importance of the new vehicle for both rallying the troops and getting opinions placed publicly and quickly, politicians and political activists of the late antebellum period abandoned the newspapers (which were no longer providing them the support they once had) for the magazines, where they could still find platforms and could continue to be directly involved. Certainly, "*Harper's* was political from the first, since the brothers themselves were much interested in politics; one of them, James, was later to become mayor of New York."[6] Other politicians were involved in journalism too, of course, including *New York Times* and *Harper's* editor Henry Jarvis Raymond, who also served in the House of Representatives.

One other fallout of the attempt by the new type of newspaper to reach the widest number of readers was the growth of magazines targeted to specific audiences, in addition to the general-audience publications. The Harper brothers, for example, moved into the magazine business not only for political reasons but also because they felt they could use it to augment their extant book business. They had developed a clear business plan, one that called for their magazines to appear on the tables of the professionals of the time, the physicians, lawyers, clerics, and teachers—as well upon those of the rich. "This was the audience that had the money to buy Harper books and the leisure time to read them. It was also the audience that would later be called 'opinion makers.'"[7] The Harpers understood synergy in the same way that William Randolph Hearst would a generation later. They could review their own books in their own magazines, ensuring that the reviews would be seen by exactly the target audience for their books. By deliberately setting apart the more educated and monied section of the population for their publications, however, the Harpers may have been taking the first step down the path toward development of a professional punditry, a path that would lead to a clearly defined elite in the world of public opinion by the end of the twentieth century and an abrogation of the place of the general public in the discussions of the public sphere.

When Bennett founded the *New York Herald* in 1835, he could do so with relatively little financial backing, for he could rely on the flatbed cylinder press, a type of press developed decades earlier by Frederick Koenig and in widespread use by the 1830s. But though the flatbed cylinder press had more than tripled the possible hourly output from a press, it had nothing like the capacity of those much more expensive Hoe rotary presses that soon came into use, presses that could produce up to twenty times as many copies in a comparable period. Given the limited number of papers he could actually produce at the start with his press, Bennett (though he did struggle financially at first) did not initially need funding for the much more extensive distribution apparatus that, among other things, the new presses would soon demand. The newsboy system provided distribution at little cost, for the papers sold bundles to the newsboys, who essentially acted as independent contractors.

The first real reporters, people going out and actually gathering news as a distinct profession, also began to be hired in high numbers with the advent of the penny presses. Not surprisingly, the founder of the *Herald* himself had been one of the earliest professional "correspondents," writing for the *New York Enquirer* from Washington as early as 1827; Bennett knew from experience the value of searching for news rather than waiting for it to come to the newsroom.

The *Herald* was Bennett's fourth attempt to establish his own newspaper. His first three were more traditional Jacksonian papers, but Bennett came late to that game and found it difficult to gain the patronage and government contracts that would provide the necessary financing allowing survival according to the "traditional" model. At some point, Bennett realized he needed a different model, one that wasn't dependent on political affiliation, if he were to succeed in this field. What he developed was an exclusively commercial model with no dependence on (or direct financial ties to) political entities, a model that would be the base for all American news media of the future. In many ways, he turned out to be the right man at the right time, for the forces for such a change were all in place, simply waiting for a catalyst. A capitalist economy, a stable political state (though the Civil War would soon put that to the test), and a hands-off attitude on the part of the political establishment towards toward press (in terms of control) made a commercially oriented press not just possible, but inevitable. As Habermas writes, only "with the establishment of the bourgeois constitutional state and the legalization of a political public sphere was the press as a forum of rational-critical debate released from the pressure to take sides ideologically; now it could abandon its polemical stance and concentrate on the profit opportunities for a commercial business."[8]

Given the combination of cultural changes, technological possibilities, and urban demand, then, it isn't surprising that someone was able to successfully combine them, providing a new type of newspaper that was cheap (a result of the new technologies), that was readily available (the newsboy system of distribution, developed in England and first used in the United States by Day's *New York Sun* two years before the founding of the *Herald*, helped with this), and that crossed political boundaries (providing a much larger potential readership).

Bennett, knowing he had to replace politics with something else that would motivate people to buy the papers, quickly turned to sensational stories of murder and prostitutes. The dedicated news hound that he was, Bennett also expanded coverage into every possible area, from Wall Street to the theater, broadening the scope of the newspaper business forever. His primary focus, however, was on the salacious. In looking back from the vantage point of 1872, *The New York Tribune* published an obituary of Bennett that described the *Herald* as a paper that "immediately became disreputable and soon became popular. If offended all parties and all creeds."[9]

Certainly, Bennett had discovered that he didn't need to present a newspaper in the terms of the past, not even in the style of presentation. In fact, he learned that his customers preferred what was, by contrast to the style of newspaper writing of earlier days, a succinct and informal presentation. One of the first real salesmen of the news business, Bennett realized that if increased readership was the goal, it was more important to entertain his readers than to inform them. This simple concept irrevocably changed the news business, though not without a great deal of controversy and pain within the profession. William Cullen Bryant, for example, "characterized this trend in American journalism when he. . . said that Bennett was not an editor in the model of Horace Greeley [a contemporary of Bennett and editor of the *New York Tribune*] or others from earlier in the century, but a news *vendor*. Earlier in the nineteenth century, editors and politicians shaped news with an eye to politics. By century's end, advertisers, publishers, and editors joined to shape news with an eye to revenues and profits."[10] The commercial press had come to dominate and would continue to do so for at least another century.

It was during the Civil War that the news-gathering abilities of Bennett's *Herald* and the others of the new style of journalism, including Greeley, really started to show their possibilities (commercialization of the press, they certainly proved, wasn't all bad). Because of the telegraph, another technological development of the earlier two decades, news could now be transmitted quickly across the country, making the importance of the reporter much greater than it had ever been, with his or her impact being much more immediate. In addition, the Associated Press, just a little more than a decade old when the war started, began providing details of the war with a speed unimaginable to previous generations. Reporters, still generally referred to as "correspondents," covered every aspect of the war, from the personal and local to the great movements of armies.

Paradoxically, the magazines, which had been growing at an incredible rate, partly as a result of the changing focus of newspaper coverage, were hurt by the war while the newspapers thrived. The magazines, so well-suited for the debates that led up to—and heralded—the Civil War, were not able to provide the quick news from the battlefields that Americans now thirsted for. Newspapers, in conjunction with the telegraph, most certainly could. This, coupled with the rising costs and shortages of war, squeezed magazines greatly, reducing their numbers for the last time until the advent of electronic media. Newspapers, on the other hand, were growing like never before, and journalism as it has come to be known in the years since was first practiced on a massive scale during this time.

Soon after the Civil War ended, the magazines began to recover, and recover quickly, but it would be decades before they once again took the position in American culture that they had had before the outbreak of hostilities at Fort Sumter. Newspapers, on the other hand, enjoyed a heyday during the Civil War that they may never again match. During the war, millions of Americans got into the habit of turning to newspapers, often twice a day, taking both a morning and an afternoon paper, to keep up with the latest from the battlefronts. They were the only way the civilian population had of keeping abreast of what might be happening to sons, husbands, and brothers. Letters from the fronts could take weeks and sometimes didn't arrive at all. Newspapers also kept people informed of the fast-changing political aspects of the war, dispatches from Washington becoming the central part of the American news media, as they have been ever since.

Instead of being *participants* in politics, however, the papers now saw themselves as *reporters* of politics, leaving advocacy to the magazines and to editorials deliberately set off from the news aspects of the papers. Finally defined as a profession, they had begun, for the first time, to really see themselves as somehow aside from the events they covered and no longer as part of the stories.

They had begun to set themselves off from the population they served and the stories they covered, setting the seeds for an ethical stance that would serve them well in the twentieth century, but that would start to come unglued just as the century was ending. Until that time, they could watch the battles, safe on the sidelines (for the most part). Like the cameras carried by the photographers who were becoming their colleagues, they were simply recorders—in their minds, at least.

Chapter 7

THE CREATION OF
PRESS EMPIRES

As with most things associated with him, William Randolph Hearst sits in an unusual position in regard to the growth of American journalism—especially in relation to the developments that would eventually lead to the success of the blogs. First of all, he was, in one sense, a throwback to the editor-politicians of an earlier day (though he came to politics through journalism, rather than the other way around), but he is also the exemplar of the two of the most important trends in the maturing journalism profession. First, his "yellow" journalism actually helped push other parts of the profession toward an ethic of "impartiality" in response to what were seen as his transgressions. And, second, by bringing money *into* journalism (rather than first making that money *through* journalism), he showed the way for later conglomerates to turn to journalism in their quest for new profit centers.

Just how successful was Hearst? As successful, certainly, as Rupert Murdoch would be, a century later. At its height, Hearst's empire reached every corner of the United States. No other entity could touch so many people and certainly not so efficiently. Not even Murdoch or Time Warner today, though their outlets may be available in a larger percentage of homes, can match the effective reach of Hearst and his empire in its heyday. Never satisfied, Hearst went even beyond the printed word to the birthing movie industry as soon as he could. Even before World War I, his companies were taking work from his papers and magazines and transferring it to film, and not simply for personal reasons. People today often remember Hearst's unceasing promotion of his paramour Marion Davies (in part because of the fictionalized version of this promotion presented in Orson Welles's 1941 film *Citizen Kane*) when they think of his connection to film, but his purposes went far beyond that. He had discovered the interconnectedness of media and took it several steps further than the Harper brothers had decades earlier. As Hearst biographer David Nasaw writes, Hearst's "news stories were recycled in newsreel form—and vice versa; his Sunday comics were turned into animated cartoons; each episode of his serial films was 'novelized,' run serially as a Sunday newspaper feature, and then published in hardcover. The next step was to adapt the fiction he bought for his magazines for feature films and publicize those films in his newspapers and magazines."[1] Like an Iowa farmer who could find a use for every part of a pig except its squeal, Hearst discovered ways of making everything—even his girlfriend—work to his advantage. By moving into the movie business, Hearst was doing as much to cross-pollinate his businesses as have any media moguls in recent years, with their much greater technological possibilities.

The Hearsts of today, of course, continue to try to do the same thing, using different media in synergistic relationships to create wholes larger than the sums of their parts. Some of them are working on ways to profit from the blogs, fitting them into their networks not simply because the blogs have proven so popular, but because a way of making real money from them is certain to be established.

Hearst was not aware of, and probably would not have cared about, the consequences of his new (though he did not create it—he just practiced it best) type of journalism business. Yet he has become the exemplar of a change that, according to Jürgen Habermas, moved the press into a new realm of public manipulation in the process of its own extensive commercialization. "Ever since the marketing of the editorial section became interdependent with that of the advertising section, the press. . . became the gate through which privileged private interests invaded the public sphere."[2] And Hearst invaded with a vengeance. This new manipulation, however, was quite different from the Jacksonian papers' attempts at political persuasion and from what the blogs are trying to do today. It became an attempt to alter public perceptions, not through persuasion or argument or by encouraging discussion, but through careful manipulation of the presentation of information—through, in fact, corrupting information and purposely narrowing public discourse to a consideration of issues only through "either–or" possibilities.

Of course, Hearst wasn't the only rich man to see the possibilities for business expansion during the post–Civil War years or whose impact went far beyond the immediate results of greed and power-mongering. In fact, the decades of the second half of the nineteenth century were to be defined by the growth of corporations, many controlled by tycoons even more avaricious than Hearst. Consolidation of ownership was the theme of the day—at least until the time of Theodore Roosevelt and his attacks on the trusts. Not surprisingly, the newspapers (and not just Hearst's) became a part of this broad big-business expansion. Even the owners of smaller newspapers started to dream that they could be something quite different from their forbearers for, by the end of the century, they had become businessmen and not political activists. As a result, they had expanded both the reach and extent of their coverage, adding cultural coverage and even humor and sections for children, creating publications with little similarity to those de Tocqueville had examined in the 1830s.

Hearst understood from the beginning that in the bright new business milieu of the gilded age, it would take deep pockets to compete in any enterprise, especially one that was in the process of expanding its brief in the way newspapers were. No longer could papers be started on a shoestring, as had been the case in the 1830s. Now it took real money and a willingness to take risks, to take what could amount to huge losses in the hopes of gigantic future profits. As David Nasaw points out, Hearst succeeded because he was willing to pay up front for "a bigger, better looking, better written, better printed and illustrated paper than his competitors could offer."[3] He understood the changes in the business while they were happening in much the way Walter Lippmann described them from the vantage point of the 1920s:

> What was the precise nature of the changes in nineteenth-century newspapers? In many ways, what figures most prominently in all the newspapers is the growth of news as a commodity, as a commercial product, to be shaped, packaged, and marketed with a constant eye to profit. Early in the century, the paper and its editor existed to win power, to contest elections, to argue about politics and programs. Certainly profits were part of the economic calculus of editors then, but the *raison d'être*—so clear from content and from discussion about the press in that era—was political. By century's end, although many editors and publishers retained links to party, the newspaper had emerged as a business, dedicated to presenting information within the parameters of profitability.[4]

When Hearst took over the San Francisco *Examiner* (which his father already owned) in 1887, it was the third-ranked newspaper in town in terms of circulation. One of the others, the *San Francisco Call*, was on a downslide, but the third, the *San Francisco Chronicle*, was robust and growing. To compete with the *Chronicle*, Hearst immediately started hiring those he saw as the top-flight writers of the area, regardless of expense, in addition to arranging an exclusive San Francisco contract with the *New York Herald* for reprint rights from that paper. Hearst knew that the paper would see no immediate return from these expensive arrangements, but he understood that he could not compete successfully with the *Chronicle* unless he was willing to outspend it.

In the tradition of James Gordon Bennett, who, of course, had founded the same *Herald* that was now feeding East Coast and European news to the *Examiner*, Hearst wanted to produce a paper that would appeal to readers across the board, creating a newspaper far removed from the political sheets of the era before the Civil War: "Hearst wanted every resident of San Francisco—baseball cranks and horse-racing enthusiasts, yachting aficionados and Sarah Bernhardt fans, recent immigrants anxious for news from abroad, businessmen concerned with international commerce, readers with a literary bent, even those with interests on the salacious side—to find something to read in his newspaper. While sending his sob sisters out on 'stunts,' publishing international news cables from the *New York Herald*, beefing up his sports coverage, and giving Ambrose Bierce and Arthur McEwen, his chief editorial writer, forums to insult whomever they pleased, he added new higher-class literary features."[5]

"Something for everyone" became an underlying rule for early Hearst papers as well as the philosophy behind the later extensive Hearst media empire—it could even be argued that this line of thinking was the basis for the synergistic relationships between the parts of that empire. This is an approach directly opposite to much of earlier journalism, but it became the standard for news media for a century. Only small publications (generally magazines) could aim at niche audiences, and these were relatively unprofitable, though remaining expensive to establish, let alone produce. (It wasn't until the advent of the blogs that a venue both powerful and inexpensive appeared to replace a venue for expression that was then being lost to all but the rich.)

Hearst also came to a conclusion that would eventually split the news media into two almost incompatible strains, a conclusion at which Bennett had arrived as well. News, Hearst came to realize, "is not a phenomenon that exists in the real world, waiting to be discovered."[6] News is a creation of the newsroom from what its agents (the reporters and correspondents) can gather, from what its editors can craft, from what its headline writers can push. Most of what happens in the world never becomes news simply because it doesn't fit the particular needs of the news media on a particular day. On the other hand, "non-events" can be made into news by an enterprising news media staff. I remember sitting in Wenceslas Square on the day that Czechoslovakia split into the Czech Republic and Slovakia, listening to the BBC (normally a fine news organization) tell me that a disturbance was taking place around me—when only a couple of students were asking people to sign petitions. Someone at the BBC wanted a more exciting story, so they created one—following squarely in the Hearst tradition.

One fallout of the ability to find (and create) news on what was soon a global level was the start of the decline of the small newspaper, which had neither the resources nor the varied skill sets necessary for the new type of paper. When story becomes more important than the news itself, making entertainment the center of the trade, the businesses that do not know how to change to meet the newly created entertainment demands begin to fade. Without the resources to attract those skilled in the newer newspaper arts, the smaller papers began to disappear, though the process was gradual, eventually taking more than a century (and not quite finished yet). The same thing happened later with television and radio stations. Those with vast resources could offer so much more, in terms of entertainment, than the poorer ones; certainly, those who relied simply on the less attractive reporting (often cheaper than entertaining) were rarely able to compete.

The consequence? As Habermas writes, it was the development of a mass culture through adapting to a desire for the easy in order to facilitate sales, through looking to the lowest, rather than the higher, levels of society for the lead. It was a culture that no longer sought "the guidance of an enlarged public toward the appreciation of a culture undamaged in its substance."[7] And this, of course, has led to a loss of discourse, a shrinking of the public sphere.

Though Hearst, at least at first, did try to provide something for everyone (even the intellectual), the logic of his moves had an irreversible culturally downward trend. After all, no matter how it might be justified, what he was doing was pandering to the audience rather than providing an offering to it in the spirit of public discussion for the public good. For a democracy dependent for survival on the strength of its public sphere, this is extremely dangerous. For, as A. J. Liebling claims, it "is an anomaly that information, the one thing most necessary to our survival as choosers of our own way, should be a commodity subject to the same merchandizing rules as chewing gum, while armament, a secondary instrument of liberty, is a Government concern. A man is not free if he cannot see where he is going, even if he has a gun to help him get there."[8] When information becomes a commodity, it soon stops being information at all, serving as nothing more than confirmation of the biases of the audience. It is at that point, as Liebling implies, that the "man" becomes blind.

Fortunately for the survival of public discourse in the United States, not all newspapers and news media organizations reacted as Hearst's did. In fact, some large news organizations did manage to survive, and even prosper, by sticking to what they saw as an older tradition of informing instead of entertaining, and this is the other side of a split in attitudes toward the news business that would dominate the business for most of the next century. Chief among the papers that emphasized informing rather than entertaining was *The New York Times*. Unlike Hearst's papers, the *Times* never tried to cater to every taste, never (in the most famous example) even providing a page of cartoons or the lonely-hearts columns that were ubiquitous elsewhere. Feeling that it was their mission to inform, not entertain, the owners of the *Times* never presented news on the basis of story—as Hearst did, almost plotting out his stories as carefully as a novelist, making sure all the requisite parts were present.

Times editor Adolph Ochs, making a virtue out of what really was a necessity (in the face of the successes of Hearst and Joseph Pulitzer—neither of whom would he have been able to best at their own game), published something of a manifesto for the *Times* on taking it over in 1896, issuing it under cover of a simple change-of-ownership statement:

Business Announcement

The New-York Times Publishing Company, proprietor of THE NEW-YORK TIMES, has been reorganized. The new organization assumes the ownership today. Mr. ADOLPH S. OCHS of Chattanooga, Tenn., in the interest of the new owners, becomes the publisher and general manager. Mr. CHARLES R. MILLER will continue to be the editor.

New-York, Aug. 18, 1896.

———

To Undertake the management of THE NEW-YORK TIMES, with its great history for right doing, and to attempt to keep bright the lustre which HENRY J. RAYMOND and GEORGE JONES have given it is an extraordinary task. But if a sincere desire to conduct a high-standard newspaper, clean, dignified, and trustworthy, requires honesty, watchfulness, earnestness, industry, and practical knowledge applied with common sense, I entertain the hope that I can succeed in maintaining the high estimate that thoughtful, pure-minded people have ever had of THE NEW-YORK TIMES.

It will be my earnest aim that THE NEW-YORK TIMES give the news, all the news, in concise and attractive form, in language that is parliamentary in good society, and give it as early, if not earlier, than it can be learned through any other reliable medium; to give the news impartially, without fear or favor, regardless of party, sect, or interests involved; to make of the columns of THE NEW-YORK TIMES a form for the consideration of all questions of public importance, and to that end to invite intelligent discussion from all shades of opinion.

There will be no radical changes in the personnel of the present efficient staff. Mr. CHARLES R. MILLER, who has so ably for many years presided over the editorial pages, will continue to be the editor; nor will there be a departure from the general tone and character and policies pursued with relation to public questions that have distinguished THE NEW-YORK TIMES as a non-partisan newspaper—unless it be, if possible, to intensify its devotion to the cause of sound money and tariff reform, opposition to wastefulness and peculation in administering public affairs, and in its advocacy of the lowest tax consistent with good government, and no more government than is absolutely necessary to protect society, maintain individual and vested rights, and assure the free exercise of a sound conscience.

—ADOLPH S. OCHS[9]

For the next century, then, there would be these two strains within the news media, one of them dedicated to information and the other to entertainment. By the 1990s, however, the information strain had begun to atrophy, practically leaving the field open for the uncontested spread of the other.

Unlike its contemporary manifestation, the *Times* felt that it could survive, and even thrive, by positioning itself as the one outlet where information trumped entertainment every time. But even it was caught in a circulation trap magnified by the needs of advertisers. This reality of the news business, then as now, is described by Lippmann, who argues that the "real problem is that the readers of a newspaper, unaccustomed to paying the cost of newsgathering, can be capitalized only by turning them into circulation that can be sold to manufacturers and merchants. And those whom it is most important to capitalize are those who have the most money to spend. Such a press is bound to respect the point of view of the buying public. It is for this buying public that newspapers are edited and published, for without that support the newspaper cannot live. A newspaper can flout an advertiser, it can attack a powerful banking or traction interest, but if it alienates the buying public, it loses the one indispensable asset of its existence."[10]

In Jacksonian days, buying a paper was often seen as also supporting a cause, making people more willing to shell out the cash. Even the *Times*, in this new milieu of accent on numbers and de-emphasis of political affiliation, had to start taking a new kind of care with what it printed, though it did try to keep the newsroom separate from the business end of the paper (a tradition that became an important part of that segment of the news media represented by the *Times*, only really dying as the twenty-first century approached). Yet this never meant that newspapers stopped taking stands on political issues or putting great effort into political coverage. Though the lines between politicians and people in the news media were never as well-defined as people on both sides have often claimed, newspapers did try to stay away from overt political advocacy. Caution, more and more, became the watchword of the news media. Soon, its new timidity was being justified as "objectivity" and "balance."

The Hearst story is, however, much more complex than simply his having been part of a change in newspaper journalism toward a greater business model and part of a split between entertainment journalism and informational journalism. It's also a story of the loss of control of the media by local communities, of consolidation of media ownership beyond simply the newspaper business, and of an evolving relationship between politics and the media. In addition, it's a story of the development of other media forms (Hearst started buying magazines around the turn of the century and was among the first to move aggressively into the film business) and even of the growth of "muckraking" or investigative journalism.

Long before Hearst became involved in American media, magazines had begun reasserting themselves as an important part of the public sphere (after a downturn during the Civil War, one that allowed daily newspapers to gain relatively more influence). They weren't often immediately profitable, but many journalistic entrepreneurs saw possibilities in them, especially as newspapers became relatively more expensive to establish. The popularity of magazines can be seen in their growing numbers after the war, when their numbers grew dramatically (nearly doubling in the five years after the close of hostilities—and doubling again in the next decade). By 1885, there were over three thousand magazines in America, up from some seven hundred only twenty years earlier. Given the short life span of magazines of the time, probably thousands more had been started and abandoned.[11] In comparison with the number of newspapers in the country (more than 11,000 in existence in 1880 alone), these numbers aren't large, but they are still significant, especially considering that a magazine covered much more physical ground than a newspaper. Though chances of success were slim, the rewards—as possibilities for advertising revenues grew—could be quite high.

In earlier days, writers for magazines, even more than those for newspapers, had generally been unpaid, seeking livelihood through other ventures. Soon after the Civil War, however, magazine writing, like reporting, began to become a profession. New accessible writing styles, among other things, began to be demanded, and these were not something the amateur could easily master. As the profession grew, it began to develop its own informal version of apprenticeship, further removing the creators of magazines (and newspapers, which were going through a parallel process) from their audiences.

By 1900, a clear delineation had developed between the professionals of the magazine business and the amateurs who were still occasionally writing for the publications. Instead of coming to the business from other enterprises (having been successful writers in other venues, for example), more and more magazine professionals rose through the ranks of that single business, though often with an eye toward greater ends: "More and more, too, writers thought of magazines as stepping stones to book publication. Writing itself had become a popular occupation. An estimate in 1900 concluded that 20,000 Americans were writing, or trying to write, for publication, most of them unsuccessfully."[12] In this way, "writing" became something other than an exercise in participation in the public sphere, as it had been for most of the history of the nation (and even before). In fact, perception of writing moved almost completely into the commercial sphere, where it stayed (in terms of news media, at least) until the advent of the blogs.

Significantly, one aspect of public-sphere discussion, the acceptance of anonymity as a protection for participants, began to fall away as professionalism grew. Someone wanting to make a career out of writing, after all, would rarely want to separate the writings from the person. So, not surprisingly, the frequency of anonymous magazine articles declined as professionalism in the business grew, "although the *Nation* continued to carry unsigned articles into the late 1870s. But the *North American Review* had begun publishing authors' names in 1868, and the practice spread rapidly."[13] In most cases, however, the professional writers demanded recognition for their work because it was no longer work done for the love of it or for public purposes, but for advancement—and one could not advance if one were not known. The blogs, of course, have reversed this trend (even the news magazines such as *Time* and *Newsweek* that used anonymity when they first appeared between the wars now place bylines on almost all of their articles), bringing an acceptability back to anonymity that had almost disappeared by the end of the twentieth century.

With renewed emphasis on writing, much greater concentration on political and intellectual events, and a breadth of in-depth analysis a daily newspaper could not match, magazines soon rivaled newspapers for impact once more, becoming one of the pillars of American life, as important in the first half of the twentieth century as television would be in the second. However, magazines, like newspapers, also changed as a result of economic pressures, though later than the newspapers had. It was only toward the end of the nineteenth century that magazines experienced the general lowering of prices that newspapers had gone through before the Civil War, necessitating focus on other sources of revenue.

This economic factor changed the magazines dramatically, for advertising began to take a bigger and bigger slice of the page count, and even the editorial pages had to take on a brighter and bolder look so that they wouldn't be lost among the louder and louder ads. No longer could the monthlies like *Harper's* or even the *Atlantic* keep quite the elevated tone they had established. They now had to recognize their places in a competitive marketplace, making editorial decisions on that basis in order to survive. In addition, advertisers had discovered that magazines could offer a breadth to advertising that newspapers could not, thereby putting the magazines under the same pressures to increase circulation for the benefit of advertisers that newspapers had been feeling for years. Just as had happened with newspapers, a new and stronger relationship began to grow between the magazines and the advertisers. Every time one magazine took advantage of the new revenue stream and lowered prices to produce even greater circulation, other magazines felt they had to follow suit, making all of them, ultimately, much more dependent on the advertisers than they had ever been before.

The impact of the new business model was dramatic: in the quarter century before World War I, advertising expenditures more than tripled, much of that going into new and immensely popular magazines, with the *Saturday Evening Post* leading the way.[14] Hearst, of course, had long since noticed this trend. Not only did he, like Pulitzer, counter the growing popularity of magazines by making his newspapers even more visually attractive, but he also decided to move into the magazine business himself, a radical move at the time, coming just decades after the printing industry had split into its factions.

Hearst's first major general-interest magazine was *Cosmopolitan*, which he bought in 1905, much to the dismay of his advisors, both financial and journalistic. That newspapers and magazines had once been products of the same business had been pretty much forgotten. "Newspaper publishers did not publish magazines. The two media had dissimilar audiences, distant production and editorial requirements, and very different distribution practices."[15] This did not bother Hearst; he already understood the synergy that would result from bringing the two back together. He knew that the needs of advertisers would be the key to this synergy and that it was a mistake to concentrate only on differences in means of production rather than on what the two could do for each other in the marketplace.

The impact of the advertising dollar on all news media in America cannot be overestimated—and Hearst knew this certainly. Steadily, the needs of advertisers overtook those of readers, with the publications serving as simply the most efficient means of gaining access to the readers as consumers (the model that underlies media economics even today). Growth, and not quality, became the watchword, and advertisers had an increasingly powerful voice over even editorial content—especially when they felt it might have a negative impact on circulation. This new fundamental fact of the business, though many have tried to imagine it away by (among other things) positing an inviolable wall between the newsroom and the business office, kept the reader and (later) the viewer at arm's length for a century. This has proven to be the basic reason that few in the news media know how to react at all to the blogs, which don't serve either readers or advertisers.

To Hearst, the necessity of catering to two bosses, so to speak, did not present a problem. He felt he could please both readers and advertisers by playing on the tensions between the two, by balancing them out, so to speak. And it worked. By the start of World War I, his newspapers had blanketed the nation, and his growing magazine empire included *Good Housekeeping*, *Hearst's Magazine* (which he had bought when it was called *The World Today*), and *Harper's Bazaar*. He had gotten into the magazine business at exactly the right time. In terms of the sizes of previous media entities, the growth of magazine circulation was even more staggering (for all magazines, not only Hearst's) than the growth of newspaper circulation had been just decades earlier (a growth that was continuing unabated into the twentieth century).

Whereas the Civil War, for various reasons, had hurt the magazines while helping the daily newspapers, World War I, when it came, helped both, though the increase was more evident in the magazines. *Collier's*, for example, though a great success even before the war, doubled its circulation during the conflict to two million.[16] The space necessary for this phenomenal growth in magazine sales was created by decisions in the newspaper business dating back to the time of Bennett, decisions taking the newspapers away from direct participation in the public sphere, making them primarily commercial entities that concentrated on articles that could be read quickly, on topics that tended toward the salacious. The reading public, however, still wanted to participate in—or, at least, view—public debate, and the magazines gave them that in more depth than newspapers could (even though the biggest and most successful were again following the path newspapers had taken and were beginning to dumb down their offerings for a broader appeal).

It was in the magazines that the "muckrakers" found their best venue, for there was a large audience for real exploration of the problems of the day. Though newspapers did try to cater to these interests, they could not do so with the depth of the magazines, simply because of the realities of limitations of time and space. On the other hand, spectacular newspaper stories could be created out of daily events, something the magazines could not as easily do. To compete with newspaper sensationalism drawn from events, the magazines had to find a way of creating their own events. Lippmann describes the situation they faced: "When public affairs are popularized in speeches, headlines, plays, moving pictures, cartoons, novels, statues or paintings, their transformation into a human interest requires first abstraction from the original, and then animation of what has been abstracted. We cannot be much interested in, or much moved by, the things we do not see. Of public affairs each of us sees very little, and therefore, they remain dull and unappetizing, until somebody, with the makings of an artist, has translated them."[17] What resulted from recognition of this "fact" was what is sometimes referred to as "the era of the muckrakers."

The writers associated with the term, really nothing more than early investigative journalists (and with many similarities to today's investigative "citizen journalists" and bloggers), created sensational stories by digging into what had been hidden affairs, generally affairs that harmed the public in one way or another and whose exposure was guaranteed to create interest. The investigative stories were also (not unlike the blogs a century later) a response to popular dissatisfaction with government, especially in its oversight role relating to business. In fact, the parallel between bloggers and muckrakers can be taken a long way.

Like bloggers, muckrakers reflected the dissatisfaction that a part of society felt with the powers that be, and they advocated reform. In both cases, the writers have managed to get politicians to respond (though this ability is still in its infancy for the bloggers). In the case of both, their arrival created a whole new debate, catching politicians and many in the news media flat-footed. Though we don't yet know what the ultimate effect of the bloggers will be, the parallels may continue, with bloggers proving to be responsible for fundamental changes in American society, just as the muckrakers were.

What happened to this muckraking movement, however, may also serve as a cautionary tale for the blogs. Eventually, many readers began to turn away from them, finding them too shrill and not in keeping with an increasingly prosperous time. People who had once agitated for change to a responsive audience were much less able to find such audiences once World War I was over and the economic boom of the 1920s propelled American society in different directions. The upshot was that the muckrakers who survived toned down their rhetoric and were assimilated into the popular and powerful newspapers and magazines of the time. Though the economic reasons may be different, a similar process is likely to occur with the blogs, an assimilation of them into the broader commercial structure of news media. To date, no one has found a way to really cash in on the blogs, but someone will—and this "revolution" may also be co-opted into the mainstream. In the meantime, though, the blogs, like the muckrakers before them, are expanding the public sphere beyond the constrictions that had been placed on it by the commercial news media.

Though they did not last as a movement, the best of the muckrakers managed to have an impact on American society that is still being felt, and not only because there still are occasional crusading muckrakers finding their way into print and onto the airwaves. Although many were shrill and strident, producing more yelling than anything else, others were like *McClure's* Ida Tarbell, who wrote an eighteen-part, two-year expose of John D. Rockefeller's Standard Oil. Tarbell's care with writing and attention to the details in her research are reflected in the best of today's "citizen journalism" on the blogs. There was an evenhandedness to Tarbell's expose that is not generally associated with muckraking. She recognized the contribution of the oil industry, but wondered if the price paid for it had been too high: "inflated charges to the public, corporate behavior that was at best unethical and most probably illegal, the ruthless use of power to stamp out opposition, and, in the end, destruction of competition in the oil business."[18] Her arguments were reflected in the government's later moves to break up Standard Oil's near-monopoly. One day, a blogger will likely have similar impact.

One of the criticisms of the blogs has been that they offer nothing outside of criticism—a state of affairs that bloggers such as Markos Moulitsas of The Daily Kos are trying to counter (among other purposes) as they turn their blogs into political organizing tools along the lines of antebellum newspapers and their networks. Others are following Tarbell's example, trying to dig carefully and to clearly present stories that cannot be easily broken down into good guys and bad guys. Among these is the citizen journalist group ePluribus Media. These bloggers understand the limitations of criticism and know what happened to the muckrakers. They recognize that for all that the muckrakers accomplished, there was no goal beyond the uncovering of perfidy. Rarely were the muckrakers parts of political movements because when they were, they often found themselves stomped on unmercifully—as happened to Upton Sinclair when he ran for governor of California. Recognition of the tenuous place of reformers within American political structures led Moulitsas and Jerome Armstrong (the founder of the blog MyDD) to write their book *Crashing the Gates: Netroots, Grassroots, and the Rise of People-Powered Politics*, an attempt to move the liberal blogger movement toward becoming a force for political change rather than just a group of disgruntled critics.

The milieu that Hearst helped create, however, was much different from the world today, and the muckrakers came to be seen as something of an aberration—certainly not as a model, certainly not as a movement that could help effectively organize to meet political or policy ends (though the muckrakers, especially Sinclair, certainly did try).

Lippmann, writing at the height of the Hearst era, expressed the common opinion about mass movements of the time and about where real leadership came from:

> Programs do not invent themselves synchronously in a multitude of minds. That is not because a multitude of minds is necessarily inferior to that of the leaders, but because thought is the function of an organism, and a mass is not an organism.
>
> The fact is obscured because the mass is constantly exposed to suggestion. It reads not the news, but the news with an aura of suggestion about it, indicating the line of action to be taken. It hears reports, not objective as the facts are, but already stereotyped to a certain pattern of behavior. Thus the ostensible leader often finds that the real leader is a powerful newspaper proprietor.[19]

Hearst, though he was never to make a successful jump into politics (though he did serve in the House of Representatives), had shown where the power, at the time, really lay. The lesson was not lost on his successors, especially on the Rupert Murdochs at the other end of the twentieth century.

Nor is the lesson lost on the bloggers, though they disagree completely with the Murdochs and other consolidators of news-media power. Unlike the press barons, the bloggers want to bring that power away from the media centers and back to themselves and the public sphere.

Chapter 8

DOMINATION OF THE PRESS BY ELECTRONIC MEDIA

The first really revolutionary change in the news media in America since the advent of the penny press in the 1830s was the expansion into broadcast media that began in the 1920s. At first, it looked as though the amateur side of radio would be as important as the commercial, but for a number of reasons (not the least being restrictive regulation), it was the commercial that eventually dominated, delaying an electronic resurgence of the public sphere until the time of the Internet. Even so, the changes in the news business, over the two decades after World War I, were dramatic.

The United States was far from the vanguard in development of electronic news media, in part because newspapers were hesitant to get involved, a reluctance in the face of new technology that seemed to become a basic part of almost all electronic media in America for the rest of the twentieth century. Even so, as early as 1920, news was accepted as a part of what the newly popular medium of radio would be providing. An article describing a new portable radio in *Radio News* stated that a "desirable feature connected with the instrument is that it is very simple of operation and does not require an expert electrician or radio man to set it in operation. This fact alone opens up considerable future possibilities in the commercial field. . . . [The listener] can keep in touch with the news, weather reports, radiophone conversations, radiophone music, and any other information transmitted by radio."[1] The possibilities through radio for instantaneous news transmission had been known for decades, through actual usage and, of course, through the example of the telegraph. The trouble with radio, for newspapers, was that it threatened to cut them out completely—something that they knew wouldn't happen with the telegraph (it took training and practice beyond what most of the public would willingly endure to "read" a telegraph transmission). The relative permanence of a newspaper edition, however, gave the traditional press an influence and lasting power that radio would find impossible to match, not even when recordings became more commonplace. So only after the inception of other electronic media, particularly television and then the Internet, did print start to be eclipsed. Even today, the news in print tends to be taken more seriously than news presented in any other medium.

Although it did not even come close to killing the newspapers, radio (like television and the Internet) was quick to find its place in America. By 1923, 500 stations were broadcasting in the United States. By the start of World War II, that number had tripled (and many stations had increased in power), and there were more than forty million receivers in the country. There was hardly a place in the nation where listeners did not have access to radio as well as a number of choices of station.

There were concerns about the impact of radio as the number of stations and receivers exploded during the 1920s. The passive nature of radio listening worried certain commentators; a writer in *The Nation* even went so far as to ask, "Will it be possible for any man to think for himself when the speeches of the favored spokesman of those who control the 'broadcasting' stations night after night are sent out to every home?"[2] This concern was only one of many leading to government interest in the developments relating to this new technology.

The first effort to establish a coordinated network of stations was made by RCA in 1926, when it founded NBC as its broadcasting branch. NBC, in turn, soon established two networks, NBC-Red for popular entertainment and music programming and NBC-Blue (which eventually became ABC), which focused more on cultural programming. By today's standards, the networks were quite small, together totaling some two dozen stations. In 1927 the competing network that was soon to become CBS consisted of sixteen stations. These networks were perfectly positioned, two decades later, to become the prime conveyors of television as well as radio, making the transition to that medium relatively seamless.

William Paley, who is forever linked with the growth of CBS and the development of what was, for a time, one of the world's best and most influential news-gathering organizations, was a relative latecomer to radio, taking over the network and changing the name to the Columbia Broadcasting System after seeing what radio advertising had been able to do for his father's cigar-manufacturing business. But he soon became a significant force in the industry, especially as news over the radio started to grow in importance and interest and, later, as television became the centerpiece of the American living room.

It was at the time of the establishment of the networks that the U.S. government was also beginning to take real notice of commercial radio. The Radio Act of 1927 attempted to establish uniform governance, requiring, among other things, that 15 percent of broadcast time be reserved for educational use (rationalized as a cost for using the public airways). Regulation of the airways continued to be in constant flux (for example, the 1927 act was replaced by a new Communications Act in 1934, which established the Federal Communications Commission), continuing into the television era and beyond, and Paley wanted to make sure that he could influence the direction of the laws through maintaining an image before Congress as a public servant. Paley used every trick he could to make CBS look more like a higher-class network than its biggest moneymaking programs might suggest. He did so, in part, by offering high-profile educational and cultural programs along with his newscasts to draw legislative attention away from his highly profitable lowbrow offerings. He understood that public perception of the "elite" programming was more important than the actual amount of it; the percentage of public affairs programming was always much smaller than CBS public relations made it seem.

Like the novelist Graham Greene, who produced both "entertainments" and what he viewed as serious literary novels, Paley (at the time, at least) recognized the importance of both the highbrow and lowbrow in the creation of a sustainable media entity. Perhaps he was only reacting to the regulatory realities of the time, for he did retreat from this stance somewhat as government oversight loosened. Maybe he simply thought he could loosen regulation by appearing high-minded. In the meantime, though, a culture was built up at CBS News that, ironically, actually fought against him when he did try to reduce the public service programming at CBS. Unfortunately, in the years since his death, CBS—like most other networks (and in response to the loosening of regulations)—has almost completely abandoned any hint of a public service stance, looking even more toward momentary profits than at supporting programming meant for building the brand for the longer term. Paley, unlike contemporary media executives, did recognize, at least, the significance of the culture of the newsroom and supported it to some degree. He knew that there was importance in the product (at least, in keeping a range of product available) as well as in the profit.

Paley was never altruistic in his attitude toward his news division or other profile-building operations. He wanted to create an image of respectability and professionalism for CBS, but not because of any great love of the profession (after all, he never had been a newsperson himself). He saw image as a necessary part of sustainability of profit—not surprising, considering that he planned on being (and would be) involved with CBS and its finances for the long term. This is quite different from attitudes in most corporate boardrooms of the 1980s and beyond, where connection with commercial operations was no longer assumed to be long-term, when focus (as a result) turned more and more to the immediate profit possibility.

Even though he was sometimes far-sighted in terms of product (particularly in his early days with CBS), Paley could be extremely myopic when it came to technological developments. He wasn't alone. In fact, "it was the radio's pioneers, Paley chief among them, who worked hardest—by encouraging restrictive regulation—to hold back the very technologies that have helped broadcasting fulfill its potential."[3] Like the movie industry, which distrusted television and then video recordings, things that eventually brought the industry more profit than it had ever had, Paley feared that new technologies (including television) would undercut the foundation he had worked so hard to establish. This attitude among the media conglomerates continues today, as they fight to restrict innovation that they feel could undermine their current businesses and properties. They still do not understand that the changes will come and that (if history is any predictor) the innovations that worry them now will bring them more profit than they had before.

Reflecting Paley's attitude, CBS, as an organization, was nothing if not cautious. It was even more so once Frank Stanton, who had earned a doctorate in psychology and was already a pioneer in audience evaluation, came on board in the late 1930s. Stanton determined, for example, that simple programming on even complex subjects drew the most attention—and that short sentences are much more effective on the air than long ones. He also determined what pacing (words per minute) suited American audiences best. Needless to say, Stanton had a profound impact on the way broadcast news was—and is—presented. Unfortunately, his findings have often been poorly understood, media executives mistaking simplicity in presentation for simplicity in thought. The unnecessary "dumbing down" of the news of the last decades of the twentieth century was a result, in part, of Stanton's findings.

Not even Paley, in his planning to make CBS at least appear to be the "Tiffany network," recognized how important his news division would eventually become to that effort, at least not when that division was founded in the early 1930s. At the time, news copy was written (from wire service dispatches) by public relations specialists and was read by people selected for the sounds of their voices over the air, not for any journalistic ability or experience. There was little more to the news of the time than hourly bulletins and the presentation of public events. At best, CBS was producing not so much programs that were themselves real sources of the news through their own reporting, but shows that were simply news transmittal and, though not so often, opinion. In this way, the neophyte division was much more like the blogs (especially in relation to the print media of the day) than like the broad news-gathering organization that it would become, starting as World War II approached and the situation in Europe gained more attention from Americans.

"Legitimate" print reporters did not consider their radio colleagues their equals—one of the reasons that radio reporters, sensitive to their perceived second-tier status, were perhaps more sensitive to, and accepting of, the professional standards that were beginning to become more clearly established—certainly at CBS. Development of a clearly stated ethic for radio journalism was clearly part of its struggle to gain parity with print.

CBS had something of a fortunate disaster in the early days of its news and commentary broadcasting, having agreed to air the programs of Father Charles Coughlin, the Detroit based anti-Semitic demagogue who had been broadcasting locally on station WJR. Coughlin, who was looking for a broader platform for his commentaries, first sought simply to expand into the Chicago market. When he contacted the CBS station there, Paley heard about it. Wanting to bring WJR into his fold, and aware that the station owner was a Coughlin fan, Paley offered to place Coughlin nationwide—if Coughlin would pay for the airtime.

Paley, Jewish himself, must have had reservations about Coughlin, but he put them aside in favor of growth and profit—a decision that would boomerang on him the next year when the network's news chief Ed Klauber tried to rein in the increasingly inflammatory Coughlin. Klauber, after asking to review Coughlin's scripts in advance, found himself denounced as a censor. CBS was soon the recipient of hundreds of thousands of angry letters from Coughlin's supporters. Still, as the CBS executives certainly decided, it was better to get rid of Coughlin than to give in to him—so he was soon canceled.

In order to make sure that CBS could not be accused of any religious bias (Coughlin, after all, was a Catholic priest), Paley and Klauber instituted a series called "Church of the Air," which provided a rotating program of religious speakers from a number of faiths. This experience may have been the beginning of Klauber's later vocal insistence on fairness and balance as an underpinning of CBS news.

The lesson from the Coughlin affair—that it is not always best to go simply for short-term profit or the largest possible audience—was not lost on either Paley or Klauber. The experience also taught them that it was advantageous to them to keep news to the side when considering profit centers—then they wouldn't be tempted by future, well-funded Coughlins. The value of the news, anyway, Paley and Klauber (like NBC executives) were discovering, lay elsewhere. Paley, who understood this quite well, is "famously quoted as telling his correspondents, 'You worry about the news. I've got Jack Benny to bring in the profits.'"[4]

By the mid-1930s, Klauber had managed to cut back on editorializing in CBS broadcasts, limiting it to discussion panels where the variety of viewpoints kept CBS from being associated with any particular one. This strategy came about in part through recognition of the success of the "Church of the Air" formula for avoiding controversy, but also from the deep regional divides that kept the national network from presenting editorial views that, on whatever side of whatever issue, could alienate a large percentage of the population.

With this growing emphasis on objectivity and neutrality concerning national issues, it seemed prudent for the network to develop a formal code of ethics that all employees, employees of the news division in particular, could refer to and follow. It was instituted in late 1937. "In a speech to a conference on educational broadcasting, Paley declared that CBS would be 'wholly, honestly and militantly nonpartisan. . . . We must never have an editorial page. We must never seek to maintain views of our own. . . and discussion must never be one-sided as long as there can be found anyone to take the other side.' Nor would sponsors be allowed to buy time for propaganda again—except during election campaigns, when politicians could pay for time to present their views."[5] This was Paley's version of Adolph Ochs's statement upon taking over *The New York Times* forty-one years earlier. Both men wanted to clear their news entities of contentious journalistic styles, presenting a calmer, more considered approach. Both felt such a move was in the best long-term interest of their organizations.

There are problems with such an approach, however, some of them inherent in the nature of the profession and expressed well by Davis "Buzz" Merritt:

> Because journalism operates with no external proscriptions or rules for participation or other legal requirements, excesses are not only possible but inevitable. To fend against the threats to the First Amendment that such excesses spawn, the mainstream journalism community has, over time, developed certain conventions, generally agreed-on ways of operating. Although these mores are self-generated and adherence to them is

voluntary, they take on the patina of membership requirements, sometimes even of canons. Those who subscribe to them believe that good journalism is that which adheres to the generally accepted mores, and anything else is less than good journalism. . . .

One result of journalism's self-conscious defensiveness about its great latitude is that mainstream journalism is reluctant to question and slow to change those mores that, through general acceptance and long use, approach the status of canons. Yet the practices that underlie those canons constantly change.[6]

The best of journalists were justifiably proud of the Ochs approach and of the way CBS News began to position itself. Lack of reexamination and resistance to change, however, would eventually see the ethical codes that developed over the fifty years before World War II altered into almost unrecognizable parodies of themselves by the end of the century.

As the decade of the 1930s came toward its end, events in Europe became of more concern to people in the United States. After all, huge populations had family connections to both Germany and Italy, where Fascism had taken hold, so it is not surprising that radio news, with an immediacy that newspapers could not match, came into greater and greater demand. Coverage of the Lindbergh baby's kidnapping and dramatic incidents such as the broadcast of a recording of the Hindenburg disaster also gave listeners a hint of the great possibilities radio had for live coverage of important events. As news from Europe grew more and more worrying, the necessity of foreign bureaus in Europe staffed by American reporters was also becoming increasingly apparent. Klauber, quite aware that this could become a critical component of the growing CBS News division, asked Edward R. Murrow, one of the networks young, but up-and-coming, newscasters, to head its European operation.

Less than a year after Murrow took the position, Hitler annexed Austria. William Shirer, who was in Vienna at the time, headed quickly back to London (Murrow himself replacing him in Vienna), where he gave what proved to be the first field report from Europe by a CBS newsperson. NBC, however, had better facilities and staff in Europe; its reports quickly outshone those of its rival. Seeing this, Paley quickly came to William Randolph Hearst's conclusion that his staff "needed a way to 'not only get the news but dramatize it.' At that moment, as he has recounted many times, 'out of necessity and competition I invented the World News Roundup'—the model for broadcast newscasts for decades to come."[7] Whether that's exactly how it happened (it may not have been Paley's idea) is open to debate, but the result isn't. CBS had come up with a model that the other networks would have to imitate, a model that lifted it to industry dominance and that would serve it well for half a century.

It also showed CBS that it could actually compete with newspapers, though on its own terms, especially once the network discovered that advertisers were willing to underwrite the new hugely popular news programs. With its own expanding staff, CBS News could now develop its own complete newsroom instead of relying so heavily on wire services and outside sources. This gave CBS a new distinction and, through the personalities of its signature newscasters, its own sense of style.

All of this together contributed to CBS News's first real impact on the journalism profession. Klauber had been hiring good people and expanding his news division since the mid-1930s at least, but it takes years to build up an organization that can respond quickly and effectively in a world of increasingly instant news. But by the time hostilities started in earnest in 1939, CBS had in place the nucleus of a team of reporters centered around Murrow that would become perhaps the most famous group of newspeople the world has yet seen. It included Winston Burdett, Charles Collingwood, Richard Hottelet, Eric Severeid, William Shirer, and Howard K. Smith, all destined to become nationally known figures.

One of the ironies, in terms of broadcast news, of the early years of World War II (before U.S. involvement) was that many of the newscasters, though outraged by what was going on in Europe, either felt they had to appear neutral or were forced to by their networks. After all, the United States was still a neutral country. The impact of this assumed neutrality was strong on reporting, affecting the developing standards that Murrow and the CBS News teams carried with them even after hostilities had ended. One of the network's commentators, Cecil Brown, even objected to the much more patriotic stance taken by the network once the United States had entered the war in a letter to executive Paul White: "News policy as enunciated by you is not, as you suggest, intended to make CBS reporters neutral, passive spectators of the war, but to make them creatures of your own editorial opinion of what constitutes the news."[8] Even when most Americans were agreed on a common end, reporters held on to the new ethical standards that had been developing over the last decade.

Most of the new type of reporter had been hired by Klauber, who set the tone for the CBS news division with a vision that brooked little challenge. "'Ed Klauber was an intolerant man,' said Edward R. Murrow many years later, 'intolerant of deceit, deception, distortion, and double talk. . . . If there be standards of integrity, responsibility and restraint in American radio news,

Ed Klauber, more than any other man, is responsible for them.'"[9] Klauber emphasized fairness and balance in a way that is only parodied by Fox News with its "fair and balanced" slogan. The Klauber concept of "fairness" became part of the FCC's "Fairness Doctrine" in 1949, instituting the concept that broadcasters had a responsibility not only for covering controversial issues, but also for making sure that all significant sides were reasonably represented. Eventually, this would devolve into a "he said/she said" presentation instead of exploration and evaluation of competing views—and would be used as part of arguments insisting that anything from creationism to Holocaust denial be given "equal time." In the 1950s, however, the policy was still seen as a means for ensuring responsible debate.

By the start of the war, Klauber and Murrow had developed an extremely precise and careful sense of what journalism should be, and by war's end, they had spread their views throughout the entire division (perhaps even the whole profession). An idealist, Murrow saw journalism as a profession separate from the public sphere but playing a role in sustaining it. He "believed that broadcast news should inform the citizenry not only about the accomplishments of government but about its problems and conflicts as well."[10] As a fundamental part of a functioning democracy, the news media, in his view, has a responsibility for providing sufficient data for the populace to be able to hold a real debate within that public sphere (though he would not have been aware of that term). The professionalism of the news media was extremely important to Murrow, who saw it as the bulwark against the biased ravings of a Coughlin or even a Hitler, as the very thing that made his reporting a viable basis for the popular decision making necessary to a democracy. More than any other single person, Murrow fostered a culture of honesty and honor, especially in the broadcast news media, a culture that carried through the 1970s and that was responsible for the forthright reporting on the Vietnam War and even for how the news media approached the Watergate scandal. To him, a motto like that other one of Fox News, "We report, you decide," meant that the reporter had a responsibility for broadening and deepening the information presented to the news consumer, even if that information was distasteful to the consumer—the complete opposite of the way Fox, which tries to narrow debate to simple dichotomy, tries to present the news.

One problem with Murrow's attitude was that it conflated news and truth. These, as Walter Lippmann pointed out more than a decade earlier, "must be clearly distinguished. The function of news is to signalize an event, the function of truth is to bring to light the hidden facts, to set them into relation with each other, and make a picture of reality on which men can act.

Only at those points, where social conditions take recognizable and measurable shape, do the body of truth and the body of news coincide."[11] Like Klauber, Murrow believed that truth could lie in the news, if the reporter had a strong enough commitment to truth. This idealistic focus ignored many of the realities and needs of the public sphere. As Lippmann writes, "the environment with which our public opinions deal is refracted in many ways, by censorship and privacy at the source, by physical and social barriers at the other end, by scanty attention, by the poverty of language, by distraction, by unconscious constellations of feeling, by wear and tear, violence, monotony. These limitations upon our access to that environment combine with the obscurity and complexity of the facts themselves to thwart clearness and justice of perception, to substitute misleading fictions for workable ideas, and to deprive us of adequate checks upon those who consciously strive to mislead."[12]

This was the danger in the Klauber–Murrow ethics: because it did not recognize anything outside of a very narrow prescription, it opened itself for abuse and almost parody—as Fox News began doing with their precepts fifty years later.

Though he disliked what he saw happening to television in the 1950s, Murrow believed television could contribute greatly to democracy (a view he would probably extend to the Internet and the blogs were he alive today). In a speech before the Radio and Television News Directors Association in 1958, "Murrow urged the networks to make a 'tiny tithe' to increase news and public affairs programs. 'This instrument can teach, it can illuminate,' he said. 'Yes, and it can even inspire. But it can do so only to the extent that humans are determined to use it to those ends. Otherwise it is merely wires and lights in a box.'"[13] The power of the medium, in his view, required a responsible use of it and not simply a profit-making one. Because there was only limited access to television broadcast possibilities, those with that access owed a debt of public service to the public whose airwaves they borrowed.

The greatest weakness in the Murrow philosophy was that it posited the importance of that fourth estate as an entity removed from the people—for them, not of them. This could, and did, lead to a sense of difference and entitlement on the parts of some individuals within the profession, something the public could not help but notice—and react to negatively. Though intentions were good, the result was "replacement of a reading public that debated critically about matters of culture by the mass public of culture consumers."[14] When something is done *for* the public, assumption is of a passive public of consumers, not actors, just as that writer for *The Nation* had worried decades earlier.

One of the weaknesses of CBS News to which Murrow objected most strongly was the fact that news shows often had single sponsors, giving those advertisers a de facto veto over what might be covered. It wasn't until the 1960s that spot advertising became the rule for news programs, lessening the influence of any one advertiser. Prior to that, an irate advertiser could cause a show to lose its only sponsor, making the newscasters too aware of that situation at the expense of responsibilities to the public. Though this changed, the attitudes of network executives did also, moving their focus more toward pleasing advertisers in general and promoting viewership numbers—and away from providing the best newscasts possible.

Paley, whatever his weaknesses (and they were many), did recognize that it was ultimately better for his CBS to have a vibrant and aggressive news division, even though it angered him at times and cost him a lot of money, than to increase current-year profits. Fortunately for him, he could also afford this, for profits in the broadcast industry grew substantially from the 1920s through the 1970s. Partly as a result of financial difficulties starting in the 1980s, Paley's generation of executives, people who were generally committed to just one company (and who rarely had worked for many more), was the last to be able to act on the idea of long-term viability without feeling they were pinching short-term profitability too tightly—and the country has been paying the price ever since.

Chapter 9

ALTERNATIVE JOURNALISM

One of the greatest problems faced by the small "alternative" publications of the twentieth century was continuity of conversation—the same problem that had limited the effect of coffeehouse discussion in the seventeenth century, until the journals that sprang from them started to appear, giving the arguments more substance. Only a few of the alternative publications have ever had enough of a subscription base, or continuous readership, to be able to build up what amounts to continuing argument. Of the proprietors of such publications, I. F. (Izzy) Stone was perhaps the most successful at building up an audience and a sense of continuity without eventually being co-opted into the commercial news media. Certainly, he was the best known. His *Weekly* lasted several decades and made him at least comfortable, even if not rich. Most other alternative publications lasted only a few issues, the articles in them quickly disappearing completely. As a result, their impact, for the most part, was minimal.

Conversely, on the Internet, nothing disappears (this has now become something of a "truism"). Something someone writes one year can be found again the next, even if the site it appeared on has been thoroughly "scrubbed." This gives amateur and alternative journalism greater impetus than it has had for a long time, for the "I told you so" can now be proven—and the writers can feel that they are partaking of a larger, ongoing debate. No other single factor relating to the blogs, outside of their low cost of production, will be liable to have greater impact on the likelihood of a continued or growing blog presence in American society. Though it did have its moments of glory, the older alternative press has had relatively little impact—chiefly because of this ephemeral aspect of its nature.

As inheritors of the mantle of the alternative press, the blogs also have to be careful somehow that they won't be enfolded into the "mainstream media" (which many bloggers call "MSM"), something that has happened to many of the more successful examples of alternative media. *The Village Voice*, for example, was eventually owned by Rupert Murdoch, and like many of the papers that originally were small, independent, local alternative newspapers, it is now part of a chain. Its current owner, renamed Village Voice Media, controls more than a dozen papers that once would have been called "alternative."

As of yet, no one has found an effective way of turning blogs into the money machines that first newspapers and then sequentially magazines, radio, television, and the Internet itself have become. This allows them to remain relatively independent of the pressures of commercialization, allowing the bloggers to follow their passions, rather than looking to what might entice the largest audience (though the desire for a wide readership is certainly part of the blogs).

If Benjamin Franklin is the one person who should be nominated as the patron saint of the blogs, it's only because Izzy Stone never achieved the breadth of accomplishment relating to both the press and technology that Franklin did. The political bloggers wear their passions and ideologies on their sleeves and are as unapologetic for their attitudes as Stone was. And the best of them are as devoted to research as he was.

Though he had established the power of his research long before, it was during the Vietnam War that Stone showed just how effective the type of research he conducted could be. It even seemed, for a while, that he had set a new standard for the entire field, that real in-depth research would become a standard tool in the journalist's box. By the 1990s, however, when CNN was dominating the airwaves and *USA Today* had become a big print player, research of the type associated with Stone had almost completely disappeared—though it has since returned with the rise of the blogs and citizen journalism. In fact, after almost completely disappearing, Stone's place as a model is no longer of questionable significance, his once unique stance having become a model for the blogosphere, no longer just the anomaly it increasingly seemed before the arrival of the Internet, the new and associated research avenues, and the cadre of committed amateur journalists now able to follow in Stone's footsteps.

As a high school student in 1969, and as one influenced by I. F. Stone (among others), I "published" two issues of a mimeographed underground newspaper. It was as amateur as the weakest of the blogs today, but unlike a blog, it had the further disadvantage of disappearing completely within a year, irretrievably. Today, if anyone wished to look at it, they would have quite a difficult time: I doubt a single copy exists anywhere. Even at the time, I knew that the effort was hardly worth the result, which is one reason *Bullitt* lasted only two issues.

As late as the 1980s, for all the technological advances through the 1970s, a publication could disappear without a trace—and most did. For almost half of the decade, I edited *Free Environment Monthly* (later called *Chinook Winds*), a monthly tabloid dedicated to environmental issues. A copy of each issue was sent to the Library of Congress in Washington, but I suspect it would be quite difficult even there to locate a copy of any of the forty or so issues I edited. Compare that with the Internet, where anything I have posted in the decade and a half since the establishment of the World Wide Web can be found, and without too much effort. Clearly, though the alternative press contained the seeds for the blogs, it had few of the abilities of the blogs for producing a lasting impact—or for lasting at all. That it accomplished as much as it did is a testimonial to the passion and dedication of its participants, not to technology.

By the time I was editing *Chinook Winds*, I had my sights set on career goals aside from journalism. The small tabloid helped support me during my first years in graduate school, though not through advertising or subscription (we were subsidized by University of Iowa student fees). Mostly, though, I worked the job because of my commitment to the environmental movement and not for the money (which was never very much). And that's another reason publications of this nature had short success (if any at all) and tenure: they were rarely the work of committed professionals who had the wherewithal to ensure at least a certain measure of longevity. Amateurs, no matter how talented, have other priorities, often even having to leave the area their publications serve in order to follow their careers. Today, of course, with the Internet, location hardly matters. One can keep up a blog from anywhere in the world.

The surest way to make an alternative publication work—before the Internet—was to come to it with something of a reputation in mainstream journalism. On the other hand, the alternative press was often seen as one possible stepping-stone to a journalism career, but what was good for the individual was rarely good for the publication. Today, the blogs can also provide a way into a journalism career, but the blogs themselves don't have to suffer the resulting loss of talent. In fact, the blogs, extremely flexible, can easily be incorporated into future careers—and are even now being incorporated (with varying degrees of success) into commercial news media entities.

If he had been born seventy years later than he was (in 1907), Stone would certainly have been a blogger. Lacking the Internet, he did what he could to find an outlet for the opinions that were crowding his head. His first publication, the ancestor of his eventual *I. F. Stone's Weekly*, was called *The Progress* and even then showed Stone's leftist leaning. It championed "the League of Nations, while condemning William Randolph Hearst's yellow peril campaign and the fundamentalist stance of William Jennings Bryan."[1] Even in the 1920s, Stone knew that he had something to say. Not just a leftist, but a loudmouth, too, he also knew that his political leanings meant that he was going to have to take responsibility for his own career, that working his way up through the commercial press was going to be somewhat more difficult for him. From the first, he gravitated toward editorial writing, though as one who based his words on very careful research (later the hallmark of his *Weekly*). Although he was a fine and careful reporter, it was only through production of editorials that he could write without stifling his activist instincts.

Izzy, as Stone was known nationwide even at the height of his fame in the 1960s, blustered his way into a position as an editorial writer on the Philadelphia *Record* when he was still quite young, more on the strength of his writing than on his opinions or track record. The newspaper's publisher, J. David Stern, was quite liberal, however, and liked the work Stone produced—until the election of Franklin Roosevelt in 1932. Though he supported much of what Roosevelt did, Stone found the new administration neither active enough nor leftist enough. Stern, however, was close to Roosevelt and did not care to see his administration attacked too often, especially not in one of his own papers. "Although not uncritical of the new administration . . . Stern was not about to lend his newspaper as a forum for the kinds of analyses employed in 'Roosevelt Moves Toward Fascism.'"[2] Not for the last time in his life, Stone found himself somewhat muzzled. Though he wrote for left-wing periodicals on the side, it would take more than twenty years for him to establish a platform from which he could really speak freely. As a blogger, he could have done so from the beginning.

One of the reasons Stone preferred working as an editorial writer and not a reporter was that he could not abide by the growing "rule" of impartiality that had been developing in the journalism profession since the height of yellow journalism, the rule of staying outside of the story. He considered objectivity a dodge, a means of not having to commit to any sort of truth. At the same time, he did not accept that it was possible to avoid politics; there was always a political stance underlying any coverage of government. Here again, Stone was much more in line with the attitude of the twenty-first century blogger than with his fellow twentieth-century journalists. After all, he was an idealist who had grown to intellectual maturity in an era of political activism. He felt that it was morally incumbent upon him, as an activist and an intellectual, to take clear and forceful stands on the issues of the day rather than pretending he could look in upon them as a disinterested observer.

Certainly, in Stone's view, a reporter, by the constraints of objectivity, could never be an intellectual. Stone much preferred staying on the side of the intellectuals. For one thing, intellectuals respected research to a higher degree than did most reporters (who admittedly had little time for it) of his time—or of the later time. Though they always claimed to respect research, few reporters, as Stone discovered in his own career, acted as more than stenographers, taking what they were told without question and transmitting it through their publications. That never could have satisfied Stone. Stone, like the muckrakers before him, lived by his research and not by the breaking story—nor by rubbing shoulders with the rich and famous.

In his early years, Stone was an employee of an organization and not an independent entity, so when asked to go to Washington and report from there, he did so. He had to, or he would have lost his job. But he knew, even before he got to the capital, that he would not be happy with the standard press operations he would find. Washington, then as now, was known as a "place where insider information prevailed, where correspondents had come to rely on press conferences, official handouts, press releases, and a near-incestuous relationship between themselves and politicians."[3] That was not something Stone ever envisioned for himself. His feelings about his fellow reporters, in fact, were not that different from the feelings bloggers today have for members of the established press. Neither found much to respect in the commercial and professional news media.

It wasn't that Stone turned completely away from the routines the press had fallen into—at least, not right away. But he realized quite quickly that the Washington events for the press that he attended didn't tell him much, not even when they made for good stories. Dissatisfied, he began to look behind the public statements, at the documents that were (and still are) available to the public there in Washington. He quickly found that if he con-ducted a little work, plenty of information was available to him, information that often told stories different from the official versions that other reporters were taking as gospel.

Working from the center of the American governmental bureaucracy, Stone quickly gave evidence to the truism that bureaucrats can never bear to part with anything—even if it is something that makes them look bad. At best, they would file it away in an obscure location that an investigator less diligent than Stone would likely miss. Like the cadres of Internet blogging researchers who unearth things such as the past of supposed reporter Jeff Gannon (who had attained access to the White House press room by unusual means), the more serious bloggers are, for the most part, uninterested in breaking news. Like Stone, they haven't the resources to chase stories the way reporters do, so they concentrate on looking into the backgrounds, generally through publicly available documents—just as Stone did half a century and more earlier. It's not really surprising, then, that the "myth" of I. F. Stone has been revitalized and continues to build now that the blogs have appeared.

Throughout the early years of his career, in addition to his newspaper duties, Stone wrote for a variety of left-wing publications, chief among them *The Nation* (continuing, even there, his penchant for stepping outside of the publication's "conventional wisdom"). This led to a high-profile position on the left during the 1930s, one that he was eventually able to utilize when he began his *Weekly*. According to Robert Cottrell, Stone's reputation before World War II probably pleased him, for he "was a proponent of the two leading left-of-center movements of the decade—Franklin Delano Roosevelt's New Deal and the Soviet-backed Popular Front—both of which seemed to support broadly based reform efforts to head off the threat posed by economic and political collapse. . . . And that very level of commitment eventually led him on a reportorial path that involved more investigative journalism and a position on the editorial board of *The Nation*."[4] It was, however, commitment coupled with a fierce belief in careful research and intellectual honesty. Stone's type of investigative journalism never sought sensationalism, never took part in the muckraking at its worst during the decades before World War I. His journalism was always tempered by his ideological stance, something he never hid, though this could cause him problems not only with the people he interviewed and wrote about but also with his editors, who often wanted a more distanced approach.

Like many of today's bloggers, Stone often seemed (especially to his detractors) as though he were looking for a fight through his research. He sometimes seemed to be fishing for contention, hoping to draw others into debate where he would, much more often than not demolish them.

By the 1950s, in the repressive climate of the McCarthy witch hunts, Stone had started to find it harder and harder to work within the claustrophobic boundaries of the commercial press or even for *The Nation*, which had its own political and editorial ideas, sometimes at odds with Stone's. Perhaps it was upon looking back to his teen years and his little paper *The Progress* that Stone decided to go it on his own, capitalizing on his reputation to produce *I. F. Stone's Weekly*. At the time, however, the early 1950s, he was certainly bucking the current trends in journalism. Looking back, it seems unlikely that anyone as far left as Stone could have made a success of a journalistic enterprise in the repressive atmosphere of McCarthyism—but Stone managed it. In part, he succeeded because the cold warriors of the day didn't know what to make of him. Instead of seeing the international situation in black-and-white, "us against them" terms, Stone was more than willing to criticize both sides. The Soviet Union got no more of a free ride from him than did the United States. Though he found himself denied access to most political figures (the greatest fear of many of today's professional journalists), Stone never let that stop him. In fact, he turned it to his advantage, letting other journalists concentrate on the people while he unearthed the background story.

Stone was certainly proud of the notoriety that kept him from "access." To him, it meant that he was doing something right. He knew what *Wichita Eagle* editor Davis Merritt discovered decades later: that making where he stood clear increased, rather than harmed, his credibility. Merritt writes that "true credibility with others cannot arise from a person, profession, or institution openly professing not to care, not sharing at least some broad common cause with others. People do not value that which they do not trust, and they do not trust (i.e., place credibility in) that which they feel is not useful to them in accomplishing that broad goal of improving their lot in life."[5]

One advantage of Stone's unwillingness to hide or put aside his views was that he could not be accused of having a hidden agenda or of being a propagandist mouthpiece for others. His views were always clearly his own and were based on careful research painstakingly presented. Even those who disagreed with him had to respect him, finally—for he was proven correct, over and over again.

What Stone was attempting was not without precedent. Though there was nothing comparable at the time he began publication, there "was a model for such a journalistic enterprise, *In Fact*, published between 1940 and 1950 by George Seldes, Izzy's good friend and a fellow veteran of the Old Left. *In Fact*, thanks in part to Seldes's ties to left-wing labor unions and political organizations, had boasted a subscription total of 176,000 at one point. The changed political climate of the postwar period, however, which resulted in FBI harassment on the one hand and attacks from the sectarian left on the other, caused that newsletter to close shop."[6] With a small operation keeping costs low, Stone felt he could succeed where Seldes had failed.

Immediately after deciding to take the plunge, Stone started doing just the sort of research he loved, working through amazing amounts of data with precision, sorting and filing information for future use. He never worked on one story only, but kept track of numerous lines of pursuit, filing information away for later use. Readers of the *Weekly* were often astonished by the variety of sources that Stone had used for any one story, not being aware that some of the information may have been in Stone's possession for months, if not years, before he found a place for using it. Though he died on the eve of the Internet (in 1989), with his passion both for research and for squirreling away the nugget of information, Stone really was the proto-type for that most significant type of blogger, the citizen journalist. Citizen journalists are ultimately much more important and influential than the popular typists in pajamas that fast became the disparaging stereotype of the blogger, promoted especially in the news media that was quick to see a threat from bloggers as a whole.

One of Stone's more notable (though typical) research successes con-cerned claims by the Atomic Energy Commission in 1957 (during test-ban negotiations with the Soviet Union) that seismic waves from underground tests could be recorded no more than 200 miles from the test site. Curious to see if this was true, Stone began collecting stories claiming detection of seismic incidents that could be related to atomic tests and discovered that 200 miles was a ridiculously small estimate—tests could be recorded from thousands of miles away. Once he had clearly established his point, Stone presented his findings to the AEC, which immediately changed its claims. This story remains an example of what one person can accomplish with enough dedication and know-how. As Cottrell writes, it "was also the type of journalism that few others were then producing, since they were deter-mined to display a veneer of objectivity."[7] Few others, outside of the blogs, produce it today.

Later, in the 1960s and 1970s, Stone did begin to have an influence on other journalists, and the sort of investigative reporting at which he excelled developed a new vogue (more in response to the Vietnam War, Watergate, and social changes than to Stone, it must be admitted). Few of the inves-tigative reporters, however, had the freedom Stone did from the business pressures of commercial journalism. As sole proprietor and surviving on subscriptions alone, Stone had no obligation to advertisers, who subsidize most periodicals in exchange for access to the customer base and, to some degree or another, for influence over editorial content.

By the time the Vietnam War heated up, Stone was in his late fifties and had poor hearing to boot, so he was not really in a position to report directly from Vietnam. However, it was Stone in Washington, not the reporters in the field, who uncovered much of the truth of what was going on in Vietnam, from the Tonkin Gulf resolution on. As Cottrell writes, Stone made discoveries by studying Pentagon documents: he "noted that the guerillas were acquiring the vast bulk of their weapons not from Communist nations, but from the United States. The State Department document also failed to acknowledge the roots of the insurgency, including American-South Vietnamese violations of the Geneva accords, the repression that had been commonplace under Diem, and the absence of authentic land reform of any sort."[8]

If it was the Iraq War that gave voice to the blogs (especially the liberal blogs, though the conservative ones have been nearly as vocal in their support of the conflict that the liberal ones, for the most part, disdain), it was Vietnam that made Stone into a national figure, known well beyond his traditional base among the Old Left. In both cases, the refusal to accept the statements of the politicians who led the United States into war was what spurred the specific research and attention to the details that disproved what the country's leaders were saying. Whether inflated body counts from Vietnam or weapons of mass destruction in Iraq, Stone and his blogger descendents were quickly able to put the lie to military and government pronouncements. People, for the most part, have a willingness to trust their leaders and governments. Stone, like most bloggers (both of the right and of the left), was much more skeptical of what he was told. Unlike Ronald Reagan and his "trust, but verify" saying, Stone's mantra was simply "verify."

Stone set a standard that looked, for a while, to become that of the profession of journalism as a whole. Unfortunately, commercial powers proved stronger than professional ones, and journalism regressed to "gaggle" status in the 1980s and stayed there—until, that is, the impact of the blogs started to be felt more than a decade after Stone's death.

The similarity between Stone's research method and that of Internet researchers is certainly striking. Today, many journalists look upon the bloggers with disdain, seeing them as doing no reporting. What they mean is that the bloggers aren't on the spot, watching a war unfold or asking a president direct questions. But what Stone discovered and what bloggers are rediscovering is that effective reporting entails a great deal more than direct observation. In fact, in this view, what has come to mean "reporting" over the past years isn't real reporting at all, but merely the recording of events.

Of course, not every blog researcher works with the care and skill of an I. F. Stone. The same was true of most of the rest of the alternative press, where conspiracy theories could be as rife as they are on the Internet today. It takes a special sort of mind to be both a committed activist and a skeptical researcher, and few today (if ever) develop the required rigor. As a result, much that came from the alternative press (as from the blogs today) was laughably naïve and generally quite sloppy in its preparation. Izzy Stone, though perhaps the most famous and respected writer for the alternative press, worked on a level far above that of most anyone who might have dared to call themselves his peer.

Still, though he ultimately had very little impact on the journalism profession or even on the alternative press, Stone has shown the way for thousands of diligent, committed researchers of an era that began after his death. He showed the way to a type of journalism, whether professional or amateur, that needn't divorce itself from ideology to be recognized as significant and diligent. He demonstrated "how the journalist could use investigative skills; the intellectual, political activism; and the lone actor, his own maverick qualities, to challenge the supposed certainties of both governmental policies and the movement to which he belonged."[9] Almost any political blogger, either on the left or on the right, would be proud to be so described. In fact, that description could be said to set the bar to which the best of the political bloggers aspire today.

Chapter 10

THE FAILURE OF THE AMERICAN NEWS MEDIA

In the days before the proliferation of electronic media, Americans participated directly in public debates. They might also listen passively as speakers argued, but they listened as groups, not individually. After the speeches, they turned to each other for discussion. Of course, even then, there was a commercial aspect to much of what went on in the public sphere, but it had not yet become the controlling factor, nor did it seem to threaten to manage the entire debate. Certainly, there was always an aspect of commerce to art and information. Even with libraries and free museums, people paid for their books, for theater, and for newspapers. But, as Jürgen Habermas writes, "not for the conversation about what you had read, heard, and seen and what you might completely absorb only through this conversation."[1] That, as they say, was then—and it was free and open for active participation by anyone who cared to join in.

Habermas goes on to claim that by the second half of the twentieth century, even conversation had become a product in the marketplace. Professional speakers aren't the entertainers of Samuel Clemens's day, but provide the type of discussion that was once overheard in the local saloon or café. The fact that bars today are dominated by television screens showing either sports or cable news networks demonstrates just how far we have come from a time when discussion belonged to the public and not to a "punditocracy," when discussion did not have a commercial value. Though he was describing this type of transformation in the 1960s, the changes Habermas noted were even more clearly delineated in the 1990s than they had been thirty years earlier. Discussions of all types seemed to have been ceded to the commentators by an increasingly isolated audience, particularly to those who styled themselves as "journalists."

This process admittedly began long before the 1990s. Even by the 1920s, the public sphere had all but disappeared, a result of the usurping of the individual's role in public debate by the press, reducing the role of the public to that of picking between alternatives. As Walter Lippmann (who did not seem to believe that real publicly defined discourse was possible) wrote, "out of the private notions of any group no common idea emerges by itself. For the number of ways is limited in which a multitude of people can act directly upon a situation beyond their reach. . . . But by mass action nothing can be constructed, devised, negotiated, or administered. . . . The limit of direct action is for all practical purposes the power to say Yes or No on an issue presented to the mass."[2] Seeing no discourse arising from the public sphere, Lippmann assumed that it could not (or, at least, did not) exist.

Though many journalists today like to think of theirs as a profession, it really is not—certainly not in the terms that define the "traditional" professions such as medicine, law, and the clergy—for it has no system of certification or enforceable code of professional conduct and, thus, no means for stopping itself as it moves from its original function into new areas, making discussion part of its business, for example.

Anyone can set himself or herself up as a journalist; success in the field depends solely on readership (listenership or viewership) and influence. It is never defined by results or predicated by any series of formal steps. Many, like media critic James Fallows, see this as having had a generally positive impact, providing flexibility that has allowed the field to change, to grow in positive ways. He mentions such journalism luminaries as John Gunther, Ernie Pyle, and Theodore White and, more recently, writers as varied as Hunter S. Thompson, Tom Wolfe, and Norman Mailer (among others) as writers who have contributed new and more effective (for their times, at least) means of telling news stories.[3] After the direct influence of Woodward and Bernstein began to wane, the remaking that became evident in the 1980s and reached its zenith in the 1990s was not nearly so positive.

Perhaps because it lacks strict guidelines, journalism certainly can adapt itself quickly to new situations, technological or otherwise. Unfortunately, this also means journalism can *fail* to adapt, in part through a lack of any real process of self-evaluation. The field has never had strict standards by which to judge itself, so, not surprisingly, it sometimes does not evaluate itself well (to see what wrong turns it might have made). Thus, it has allowed itself to become a tool for the debasement of the public sphere.

This inability to evaluate itself by any rigid standard is one of the reasons (but only one) that American journalism had come adrift by the end of the twentieth century and had discovered itself shaken by the wake of the cultural commentators who had even stolen journalism's name.

One of the oddest aspects of the news media in the 1990s was the inability to understand just how they were viewed by the public and their unwillingness to accept responsibility for their cynical reputation. Good observers even then, they knew that the public saw them as callow—but they continued to deflect blame from themselves. "They are simply reflecting the world they see. They say that their cynical tone is justified—even required—by the relentless 'spin' of the politicians they write about,"[4] says Fallows. The problem was that the reporters had not bothered to consider the situation from the viewer perspective and then adjust their presentation in light of the needs of their audiences—once a key part of any journalistic endeavor. Another part of the problem was that there was only limited venue for expression of that perspective.

As a result, the profession watched helplessly as its audiences dwindled and respect from the general public disappeared. Instead of looking within, the press scampered shamelessly in pursuit of what remained of its readership, viewership, and listenership. As a former Knight Ridder editor Davis Merritt writes, rather "than accurately diagnosing the problem and devising a useful remedy, . . . journalists set out in frantic pursuit of the departing audiences. Concerned about our weakening commercial franchise, we ignored our true and far more valuable franchise: the essential nexus between democracy and journalism, the viral connection with community and our role in promoting useful discourse rather than merely echoing discontent."[5] Concentration from within the profession remained on the profession, rarely seeking the roots of its problems within its relation to its audience and the public debate underlying the very place of the press within a democracy.

To be fair, the 1990s were a problem time for journalism for reasons far beyond what the profession could do anything about. The news media had come to be dominated by the three major television networks, ABC, CBS, and NBC, but these no longer were in the comfortable financial position they had once claimed—and competition was finally eating into their hegemony. Money, in fact, started to drain away from them:

What explains the sudden collapse of network revenues? The causes are many: The recession [of the early 1990s] obviously gutted advertising budgets; as network audiences shrank, advertisers sought other outlets; the decision of the networks to try and make up for lost revenues by running from 4 (ABC) to 8 (NBC and CBS) more ads altered the psychology of the marketplace, shifting leverage to advertisers who had no reason to panic since they now knew network time wasn't scarce. The war with Iraq took a toll as well. In its first days, the war cost each network up to $6 million a day in lost advertising; NBC calculated that the Gulf War cost it $50 million between August 2, 1990, when Iraq invaded Kuwait, and February 1991, when a ceasefire was achieved.

In a less quantifiable way, the war in the Gulf may have cost even more. Instantly, the public glimpsed the cataclysmic changes in the television industry. Viewers realized that CNN, not the three networks, was the channel of convenience for live, up-to-the-minute news. With relatively few overseas bureaus—by mid-1991 each network had shrunk to between four and nine bureaus, not including a handful of offices scattered elsewhere—the networks no longer qualified as a worldwide news service, if they ever did. Even though the war boosted interest in news, by early 1991 the three network newscasts together attracted only 54 percent of those watching television, a loss of nearly one out of three viewers in less than a decade. All at once, everyone seemed to be talking about whether network news had a future—indeed, whether the networks had a future.[6]

The fault, certainly, for the malaise of the commercial and professional news media did not lie solely within the profession. Overreliance on television news, with its pictures, made the appearance of good spot-news coverage more important than the reality—which had always been sketchy, anyhow. Overreliance on profits from other divisions within corporate structures left news divisions vulnerable to cuts when growth was not as great as expected. Overconfidence in a status quo that was already being eroded by new entities such as CNN undermined the base for all older news media.

In trying to explain what had happened to their profession, Leonard Downie and Robert Kaiser, editors of *The Washington Post*, provide a good nutshell description of how the journalism profession viewed what was happening: "The 1990s were not a happy decade for American journalism. A few fine news organizations continued to thrive, but many more suffered. The pressures from owners to make more profit undermined good journalism; frivolous subjects often displaced more important topics; celebrities became more important newsmakers than presidents and potentates. Many in the news business thought traditional news values were in grave jeopardy."[7]

But it was worse than that. In addition, what Downie and Kaiser were not able to see was that what had come to be viewed as "traditional news values" were themselves part of the problem. Instead of promoting the good of the profession, these had turned into a means of shielding journalism from its very necessary participation in the greater life (and discussions) of the community, actually making it *easier* for packaged commentary to replace journalism. The concept of "objectivity," for one, had become a way of distancing journalists from both the stories they covered and the communities they supposedly served, making them consider themselves outsiders in terms of the greater society, looking in as observers, not participants. Paradoxically, because they refused to accept a stake in the debate, they were more willing to comment, believing, perhaps, that they would offend no one.

In describing the points of a speech given by former *New York Daily News* editor Michael J. O'Neill, journalism scholar Jay Rosen says that, by "continuing to see themselves as outsiders, journalists fell victim to some dangerous illusions: that they had no investment in the health of the political system, that they could continue to watch the craziness—and feed it—without substantial cost, that their intention to be in no one's pocket meant that they were free of politics, when the reality was they were implicated in everything politics had become."[8]

There was also a great deal of smugness in that "outsider" attitude, something that the general public certainly did not fail to notice. So the reputation of the press, still so high in its own estimation, was able to fall lower and lower in the eyes of the public without members of the press ever taking serious notice. The public, they might have said, just didn't understand, and so wasn't worth listening to.

The outsider stance, coming from that assumption of "objectivity," lies behind a great deal of the journalistic self-satisfaction that grew large in the 1960s and 1970s. But it is an objectivity that has always been more myth than fact, especially in the eyes of newspaper readers, even while allowing practitioners to pretend to distance themselves from the activities around them. Journalists are constantly making decisions about the news. Never are they simply objective reporters, and readers know this even if journalists refuse to acknowledge it.

And that knowledge is not new: the interactions between reporters, editors, and readers have always been complex and dynamic, the assumption of an objective viewpoint on any part rarely entering into consideration. Writing in the 1920s, Walter Lippmann described what the news process was then (much as it is now):

> Every newspaper when it reaches the reader is the result of a whole series of selections as to what items shall be printed, in what position they shall be printed, how much space each shall occupy, what emphasis each shall have. There are no objective standards here. There are conventions. Take

two newspapers published in the same city on the same morning. The head-line of one reads: "Britain pledges aid to Berlin against French aggression; France openly backs Poles." The headline of the second is "Mrs. Stillman's Other Love." Which you prefer is a matter of taste, but not entirely a matter of the editor's taste. It is a matter of his judgment as to what will absorb the half hour's attention a certain set of readers will give to his newspaper. Now the problem of securing attention is by no means equivalent to displaying the news in the perspective laid down by religious teaching or by some form of ethical culture. It is a problem of provoking feeling in the reader, of inducing him to feel a sense of personal identification with the stories he is reading. News which does not offer this opportunity to introduce oneself into the struggle which it depicts cannot appeal to a wide audience. The audience must participate in the news, much as it participates in the drama, by personal identification.[9]

If nothing else does it, this last fact obviates even the possibility of a *real* objective posture anywhere in the process.

There's another aspect of the business that Lippmann left out of his description, and that is the influence of advertisers. Even when there was a wall between the newsroom and the commercial aspects of journalism, that wall was frequently breached. Today, in many parts of the news media, it is hardly there at all. Tom Fenton, formerly a correspondent for CBS News, writes that, today, news organizations "are in the business of creating product both for viewers and for advertisers. Every day, their product needs to be selected, edited, sequenced, and bundled into neat and tidy productions. The executive producer has to decide what down-beat story to place next to which commercial, followed by a more uplift-ing segment, and piece it all together into a coherent reassuring whole. There's nothing new in that. But that doesn't make it right. The world is not neat and tidy, and the packaging of shows skews the news."[10] The influence of the advertisers, always greater than most journalists were will-ing to admit, had come by the 1990s to be an accepted part of almost every news operation, but especially those beyond traditional print journalism. With that has come a new view on just what ought to be presented as "news," with the gathering of stories themselves and direct experience with the events commented on fading in importance. Haber-mas writes that editorial "opinions recede behind information from press agencies and reports from correspondents; critical debate disappears behind the veil of internal decisions concerning the selection and presen-tation of material."[11]

At the same time, Habermas goes on to say, the important issues making up a portion of the news start to be pushed aside for the fluff, the "immediate gratification" pieces about missing children, auto accidents, fires—and even the purely entertaining, the comic strips and advice comments and such. Why? Because these are what the readers turn to first. To compete, the news stories have to be formed into entertainment as well, with "story" becoming more important than content. This, in turn, leads to a blurring of the line between actual events and the stories that can be generated from them, between the facts of the case and what can easily become the fiction of the telling. But readers (and listeners and viewers) aren't stupid. Having put up with this for decades, even before Habermas was writing about it in the 1960s, they have become increasingly frustrated. They know when they are being pandered to, and they know that a great deal of what goes on in journalism is, frankly, pandering to increase circulation.

Consumer frustration came to a head in the last decade of the twentieth century, a result of the pandering getting quickly much worse and more obvious. By then, an increased concentration on profits was determining almost everything about the news—at the expense of the obligation to inform that had once been part of the news-making ethos, but that had been pushed aside under the smokescreen of objectivity and balance. The news itself had taken a seat well behind gain and the profession's need to see itself as separate, as special. For, as Fenton says, "it's all based on a contempt for the audience's intelligence. Sound-bite snippets, emotional 'moments,' pandering to the star system—such methods assume that the dumbed-down audience will only respond to showbiz techniques."[12]

Even as early as the 1980s, however, it was actually possible to be proud of such pandering. About USA Today's start in 1982, Peter Prichard writes that its "front page would boldly pick homegrown princesses over foreign presidents, its headlines could single out survivors as well as victims. USA Today would be edited, its creators maintained, not for the nation's editors, but for the nation's readers. . . . 'Its aim,' [Al] Neuharth wrote in his page one letter in the first edition, using the frequent alliteration that was his trademark, was to be 'enlightening and enjoyable to the nation's leaders; challenging and competitive to the nation's journalists; refreshing and rewarding to the nation's advertisers.' And then he added, in a new twist on what was an old theme for him: 'USA Today hopes to serves as a forum for better understanding and unity to make the USA truly one nation.'"[13]

That first day's coverage led with the death of Princess Grace of Monaco over coverage of assassination of Bashir Gemayel, Lebanon's president-elect. On no level of newsworthiness can the former be considered more important than the latter, yet the paper justified its choice by claiming this is what the readers wanted. The point was to sell more papers, pure and simple, based on the fact that Grace Kelly had been better known to more Americans longer than Gemayel. No obligation to inform or to bring the public information entered into the consideration. The headline about an air crash on that same first front page pointed out the number of survivors, not simply the number killed—an attempt to pander to those who complain that the news media only focus on the bad news, not the good. All claims to the contrary, this is not news "for the reader" at all, for it provides the reader nothing useful, nothing for participation in the substantive discussions of the day. It plays only to the same voyeuristic impulse that also makes us slow down and look at auto wrecks. We may claim we're happy to see survivors, but it's the bloody wreck that fascinates us. The editors of *USA Today* know this—and their readers know they know it.

Claiming they were designing this new paper "for the nation's readers" is not only a bit of self-deceit but is also just another example of the paucity of vision that led to what has amounted to a national disgust with the news media. By the 1990s, readers knew, even if they were not able to verbalize it, that the news was now nothing more than a vehicle for advertising. As Habermas writes, "The selection of material became more important than the lead article; the processing and evaluation of news and its screening and organization more urgent."[14] The "what" had been finally and almost completely replaced by the "how." And, finally, as Habermas also says, "Critical publicity is supplanted by manipulative publicity,"[15] meaning that the news business has been debased through this process, leaving, as Merritt writes, "a thin shell of public relations gimmicks that pretend to be public service and entertainment that pretends to be news."[16] The debasement was so extensive that "in-depth" had become "in-a-second." Fenton recalls that one "promising young CBS News correspondent told me about being asked at three o'clock in the afternoon to do an 'in-depth' investigative report for the 6:30 news that evening. The public never knew that the reporting behind the story was paper thin, but the correspondent did."[17] I suspect that Fenton is wrong, that the public did know that something was wrong. Even if people weren't able to put their fingers on what it was, they knew something was amiss—and resented it. And they resent even attitudes like Fenton's, which assume that the viewers can't even see through a light fog.

Specifically, two related forces have come to symbolize the decline in American news media from the 1970s through the 1990s: first, the rise of big-money television news shows—*60 Minutes* being the early exemplar—and second, the growing importance of numbers in relation to all news media, *USA Today* being the early exemplar. *60 Minutes* changed the profession of journalism simply by showing that news could become a television profit center. Soon, all the networks were demanding economic performance from their news divisions, and they found themselves paying top dollar for the news faces that, they felt, could attract even larger audiences and greater advertising revenues—bigger numbers. Journalism suddenly became a field where one could aim for a financial top never before imagined. As Fallows points out,[18] prior to the 1970s, news operations were seen by the television networks as "loss leaders" and creators of prestige through the names of newsmen (and they were men, almost exclusively, at that time) associated with each of them. The power that Edward R. Murrow and Walter Cronkite could wield within the CBS network had more to do with status than with contribution to the bottom line. Freed from economic contribution, the news divisions were able to concentrate on their primary task—until, that is, *60 Minutes* showed that even news could become a profit center.

The success of *60 Minutes* woke up the network executives. They soon came to view the news divisions differently and to pay more attention to them, expecting something from them other than public service, which had been intended, in large part, to generate a better public image. News divisions were now expected to act like every other division of the corporations, as profit centers. News was no longer treated as a profession, but simply as a business. Of course, as demand for profit grew, pieces of the news divisions started to be chipped off as dead weight. The most glaring example, and the one that still rankles long-standing members of the journalism profession, was the folding of foreign bureaus in the wake of the collapse of the Soviet Union. These no longer seemed to have significance—at least, not insofar as pulling in viewers.

With profit growth comes demand for continued growth (especially when more and more news media are owned by publicly traded companies)—and that means finding ways of increasing audience even further, and doing so quickly. For journalism, this meant that the complicated stories, ones that could not be explained quickly, were less and less attractive to those making editorial decisions. They looked instead for stories based on what people already knew. One of *USA Today*'s 1980s "innovations" was to de-emphasize "foreign news in favor of domestic news culled from every corner of the country, which was reported in state-by-state round-ups on its 'Across the USA' pages."[19] Ease and familiarity along with sensationalism—these, as James Gordon Bennett had proven a century and a half earlier, could lead to quick increase in numbers. And, for the media executives, that was now all that mattered.

But, as journalists have always found, these numbers could not be sustained by simply maintaining the past level of sensationalism. By 2000, it was taking far more outré stories to engage audiences at all than at any time in the past. The "ease and familiarity" remained, but it was the strange things going on in a neighbor's basement that now brought people to the news. The success of Jerry Springer's television show was based on much the same premise that now dominated the news: find the weird in the familiar, and viewers will come. The problem is that next time, the story has to be stranger still.

However, it wasn't just the increasingly banal (though bizarre) nature of much of the news that brought the news media to their crisis in the 1990s. Again, part of the problem stemmed from that growth of profitability in almost every aspect of the news media from the 1960s through the 1980s. This led to new demands for more growth and also led people in the media into an almost smug and most definitely complacent attitude toward journalism itself. If the money was rolling in, the journalists told themselves, they were certainly doing a good job. Few were willing to look beyond that far enough to recognize the dangers that lay in wait. After all, it was comfortable to be around all that money.

The self-satisfaction of the media led not only to the ossification of many media attitudes but also to an increased sense of importance and separation on the part of many actively involved in journalism. At the beginning of his 1996 book *Breaking the News: How the Media Undermine American Democracy*, Fallows relates an exchange between Mike Wallace and Peter Jennings during a panel conversation at New Jersey's Montclair State College in 1987. The following question was asked (though I paraphrase): Would you warn American troops if you happened to be following a story with enemy troops who, you discovered, were about to ambush the Americans? Jennings said he would.

> "I am astonished, really," at Jennings' answer, Wallace said a moment later. He turned toward Jennings and began to lecture him:
> "You're a *reporter*. Granted you're an American"—at least for purposes of the fictional example; Jennings has actually retained Canadian citizenship. "I'm a bit at a loss to understand why, because you're an American, you would not have covered that story."[20]

Jennings quickly reversed course, agreeing with Wallace—while the rest of the panel, which included a number of military men, stared at the two, dumbfounded.

This exchange shows, as well as almost any example can, the attitude of American journalism toward itself at the end of the twentieth century. It also shows how diametrically opposite the newer journalism was from that prevalent two centuries earlier, when almost all journalism was determinedly partisan, when a state of "neutrality" would have been seen even by many within the new profession as tantamount to treason.

Significantly, the others on the panel reacted much as early American journalists might have. One was "George M. Connell, a Marine colonel in full uniform. Jaw muscles flexing in anger, with stress on each word, Connell looked at the TV stars and said, 'I feel utter. . . *contempt.*'"[21] Connell's reaction is indicative of the divide that had grown between the press, with an implicit code of ethics that it had been fine-tuning for a generation (not to mention that growing vision of itself as somehow distinct from the broader culture), and the population at large. In addition, journalists, once generally of working-class (non-college, at least) families and of income comparable with much of the middle class, now tended to come from much more elite backgrounds (at least in terms of education)—and, if they are successful, they now stand to make much more money and attract much more attention than people in all but a few professions. This sets them apart from the mass of Americans in ways that the press of the past never experienced.

Further separating the press from the population it "served" was a sense of pride that reached its height at the time of the Watergate scandal but that began to really build during World War II, with what were seen as the "heroic" broadcasts of the likes of Edward R. Murrow and William Shirer from Europe. Even today, with the press under constant attack, that view of journalists as knights on white horses continues in some quarters: in 2005, George Clooney, himself the son of a newscaster, released *Good Night, and Good Luck*, a film he cowrote, directed, and even appears in, a laudatory presentation of the role of Murrow and CBS in the downfall of Senator Joseph McCarthy in the 1950s. The movie leaves the impression that Murrow and CBS were the real cause of McCarthy's downfall, more so than the growing public revulsion and McCarthy's own self-destructive tendencies.

That there was a disconnect between the concept of the crusading journalist and that of the objective journalist didn't seem to bother many people in the media. Nor did the fact that both concepts are, essentially, mythological. The self-satisfied self-image led only to complacency and error in the face of an eroding public image—not to mention a declining news-gathering (not to mention analytic) capacity. And it was the fault of the industry, not of unforeseen outside forces. Many journalists, including Fenton, saw what was happening and seethed: "the behavior of the news media in the 1990s amounts to more than a few stray mistakes; it represents a pattern of fundamental misjudgment that played out over a long period of time. The industry might have a better alibi if it had spent those years increasing the resources available to its hard news organizations, or if it displayed any real concern over threats to the homeland—in short, if its sense of public duty had visibly come before corporate calculations. As the evidence shows, the reverse is true."[22] To more and more people, the news media seemed out of touch with themselves, with the public at large, and with their own purported mission. They had become timid, reverting to what they assumed had been decided the "conventional wisdom." Mary Mapes, the former CBS producer who was at the center of what came to be called Rathergate, recalls having lunch with a former compatriot in the industry, writing that it "was as though I was having lunch with the personification of 'conventional wisdom,' the group-think that has taken over press coverage in Washington. Conventional wisdom—or the CW, as *Newsweek* magazine's self-aware column calls it—doesn't consider anything outside of what 'everybody knows' or 'believes.' It doesn't question authority too aggressively or step out of line. CW is complacent and self-satisfied."[23] Obsessed with conventional wisdom, with remaining safely in the mainstream, few within the news media could see what millions outside were now trying to point out.

Just a few years earlier, certainly by the mid-1970s, building in part on the reputations of Murrow and Walter Cronkite, the news media had attained as exalted a status in America as it had ever had. The CBS that William Paley had built seemed to actually be living up to its "Tiffany network" brag, and its crown jewel, the news division, was in good part responsible for this. It's true that the Cold War conflicts kept American attention on the world, but—for all the claims that the Cold War's end led to a turning inward— American journalism wasn't ever known for looking too far from home for its stories. Because of the prestige that news divisions brought, they were lavished with money for foreign bureaus and correspondents—but not because this was felt to be important in its own right. These were considered frills, not underpinnings, and so when it proved more desirable or necessary to look to profits rather than to prestige, the foreign bureaus were sacrificed.

The five decades before the 1990s had seen vast changes in news media, with tremendous growth in almost all areas—much of it greater than needed for simply good reporting and comprehensive coverage. Newspapers and magazines had had to learn to exist in a new environment, one including television in addition to the radio news that had come into its own at the beginning of World War II. The Kennedy assassination not only had shown what television could do, but also had convinced newspapers that they could not compete in the breaking-news arena—so they had begun to concentrate on analysis and opinion, the "after the fact" of the news. It's no surprise that the op-ed page first appeared in *The New York Times* a mere seven years after Kennedy's death. CNN, the first of the cable news networks, got its first real boost by bringing the first Gulf War instantly into American homes.

But, as the success of *60 Minutes* would show, television did more than merely shift the various media into new niches. It began to blur boundaries that were once sacrosanct, especially between news and entertainment. It all became simply spectacle with the sole purpose of increasing profits. Journalists, of course, were aware of this, and it influenced how they planned their careers, de-emphasizing the work of reporting in favor of the show, the presentation. Emphasis, then, began to turn from the story itself to the person reporting it. The unglamorous parts of the profession, the research, the time spent exploring but coming up with nothing, began to disappear at the same time that pride in the profession was growing unbounded—and unwarranted. "There's no story in this" became a cover for "it won't do anything for my career." By 1990, too few working journalists had entered the field for the work of discovery, of unearthing a story. Instead, a large percentage were now looking simply for fame.

To cut costs and increase profits after the end of the Cold War, the television networks cut back extensively on their foreign bureaus and foreign coverage in general, relying instead on stringers and on their ability to get a team almost anywhere in the world quickly. Unconvinced that these were cornerstones of the business (and aware of the flagrant overspending that had grown pervasive before the 1980s), they saw no importance to the foreign bureaus in themselves.

By adopting this attitude and the stringer strategy, they also ignored a problem that A. J. Liebling had pointed out decades earlier, at the time when foreign television news bureaus had not yet begun to grow to the extent they would in the wake of the Vietnam War: that reliance on foreign stringers carries with it quite a number of potential problems, "since their necks are in imminent danger if they deviate from the Government line in many countries, and their livelihoods are in peril if they do so in others, it is the Government line that they stick to."[24] When the American correspondents are given only limited time in a particular locality, they have to rely on the people who are there permanently, no matter how great their own expertise in the region or the matter at hand. To make matters worse, they haven't the time to carefully check behind their stories before jumping on a plane and flying off to the next assignment. No matter how skillful or knowledgeable they may be, they become severely limited as reporters.

Liebling is careful to point out that stringers can be most useful, providing leads and insights, but they should be viewed as contaminated sources under the best of circumstances, especially in places where the regimes have little respect for the freedom of the press. The stringers have to look to their own skins first and to their lives in places where most American correspondents visit only briefly. As a result of the renewed reliance on stringers (such reliance decreased during the heyday of American television news, roughly from the 1960s through the 1980s), most foreign news departments have once more become simplistic and focused on the sensational (the easy) story or on the conventional and safe.

Fenton describes the more contemporary practice (but similar to the one Liebling discussed), explaining how the networks now find it sufficient to fly a team into a crisis spot and film a story almost as soon as the team has landed. The assumption, he claims, is that the viewers won't know the difference anyway; the reporter is on the spot, so the news must be factual. But, he continues, a "news organization that closes down a bureau loses its eyes and ears on the ground. The best it can do is to react to events in that country"[25] instead of providing analysis. Though the reporters themselves were aware of the dangers, the network news divisions (and much of the rest of the news media) had been reduced to packaging already-bought footage (or other information) for their reports. This further degraded news coverage (here again are shades of Liebling's concerns), for the correspondent or announcer is now even one step further from the actual gathering of material. Instead of shaping and reading the work of someone whose inclinations and training are known, the story is now based on video, audio, and other information prepared by an unknown party. This preparer could be someone in thrall to the subject of the story, could be an agent of some government—could be anyone. The base information, in other words, is not trustworthy.

Also by 1990, another factor had started to influence journalism, the growing centrality and power of the famous television pundits, the highly paid, well-connected commentators who, during the 1990s, came to dominate cable television news channels, talk radio, and the television panel news shows. These became a part of what Habermas describes as a "group of well paid cultural functionaries [that] has risen from lumpenproletarian bohemia to the respectability of the managerial and bureaucratic elite."[26] Increasingly, the entire profession has been judged by them; their clear failure to provide anything but entertainment has alienated many viewers from the profession of journalism as a whole. The fact that it is controversy that fuels their careers makes their influence even more pernicious. They have no interest is resolution or reconciliation, but do everything they can to fuel discord, knowing that will best bring viewers. As Fallows says, their work actually "undermines the entire process of journalism, by suggesting that it should be viewed as a sideshow, most successful when it draws gawkers into the tent."[27] Their work, in other words, makes the real task of reporting often seem irrelevant—and decreases the likelihood of anyone entering the field to do it.

Furthermore, much of what these commentators are engaged in is promotion, either of themselves or of a particular political agenda, giving them more of an advertising edge and reducing any relationship they might have to "real" journalism. Habermas calls what they are doing "opinion management" as opposed to advertising for the simple reason that its end is not sales, but ownership of the public sphere. In addition, there is a subterfuge involved that, in his view, is not so often an element of advertising: "The sender of the message hides his business intentions in the role of someone interested in the public welfare."[28] Be that as it may (and I find it debatable, seeing much the same thing in a great deal of commercial advertising), it pulls the commercial realm more fully into the editorial. Because of the wall that once existed between the news and business sides of the journalism business, advertising's encroachment on public discourse once could be kept to a minimum, but no longer.

In addition, traditional advertisers, seeing how "opinion management" can work, begin to use it themselves, turning what might once have been simply pitches for products into promotions of lifestyles and ways of looking at the world and (by unspoken extension) even promotion of political issues. Here, again, the public has sensed that something is wrong, but has not been able to find a way of expressing its frustration with the substitution of "opinion management" talking heads for real news coverage.

One argument against paying too much attention to the television panel shows and the radio talk shows is that everyone knows that they are entertainment, first and last, albeit entertainment that uses the news as a basis. According to this argument, such so-called news shows are no more significant than Comedy Central's fake news shows *The Daily Show* and *The Colbert Report*. In fact, this is generally the case. But unfortunately, as Fallows notes, "the fact that. . . no one takes the [panel news] shows seriously—is precisely what's wrong with them."[29] They can't be taken seriously, yet they still pose themselves as journalistic endeavors and reflect on the profession as a whole. The image of a journalist, because of the high profiles of these shows, has increasingly become that of people obsessed with each other and with the picayune details of politics. Instead of trying to educate people, they seem to be interested only in making their points to the detriment of the points of others. The fact that many of these "bloviators" (as they are often publicly perceived) are frequently seen arm-in-arm with the real movers and shakers of the country gives them additional credibility in some eyes yet further debases the image of journalism as a whole in the estimation of many others.

What has been lost? Are the pundits *not* presenting anything that the news consumers want? This is the question that most of those managing the news today answer, "No." However, it has led to a milieu of commentary at a remove from actual experience with the situation under discussion. After all, the pundits are more concerned with what they will say on a topic than with finding new information about it. This doesn't mean that they won't study, but means simply that their focus is on what is useful to them rather than on the topic itself. They have abandoned the older approach of immersing oneself in a topic with an open mind, letting the information itself begin to form an approach to the topic and even a point of view. Instead, they bring their points of view to the topics—and necessarily, for they are expected to provide a consistent stance in their public presentations.

A further problem is that such "journalists" are at such remove from their topics that they are unable to formulate follow-up questions when conducting interviews. Generally speaking, even the original questions have been developed by producers or by someone other than the on-air personality.

This leads to interviews that often frustrate viewers, who do not see the questions they want answered addressed. The viewers, not stupid, quickly come to understand that the news show stars have become ex-journalists, people no longer directly involved with the detailed background work that goes into preparing an interview. But the audience (and this is the other side of the coin) is deemed less and less important than the political machinations being covered.

In addition to the new stars of the news programs, the pundits on the ubiquitous panel news shows further warp popular perception of journalism. Though the panelists are often presented as journalists or experts of some sort, their function is simply one of entertainment, each with a specific role in contrast to another, each fulfilling expectations indicated at the start of the show or in previous shows. To maintain interest, each new show has to overreach the last, leading to hyperbole and overstatement, what Fallows calls "an ethic of polarization and overstatement."[30] It also makes the journalists into performers, more concerned with the perception of their act than with the content of their comments.

One of the spin-offs of the panel show phenomenon has been increased demand for recognizable journalists on the lecture trail. This, too, has harmed the news media's reputation. Not only does it make the journalists more clearly entertainers, but it also can lead to obvious conflicts of interest when they address (for large amounts of money) the very groups that they may write about. When even minor journalistic celebrities can earn more by lecturing than their base salary, a problem of integrity certainly arises. As participants in a cycle of radio and television appearances and speaking engagements, people start to recognize each other from meetings in green rooms and other places on the circuit, developing a clubbiness and comfort with each other, as reflected in the contents of producers' Rolodexes in their own particular areas of "expertise." This is a system that builds on itself, rarely on anything or anyone from outside. As Fallows declares, "There are people who will *kill* for two minutes on *Good Morning America*, because it brings in another raft of lecture dates.'"[31]

The glamour and money of celebrity journalism have moved many once-competent reporters so far away from their craft that they may never be able to find a way back to it. Instead, they have become immersed in the Washington political game, wanting to be players as much as the politicians. Their corporate bosses have even encouraged this, for it raises the reporter's profile, making him or her even more marketable. After all, the "faces" of the news long ago became profit centers in themselves. The salary paid to Barbara Walters in the 1970s set the ground for a steep increase in salaries of all the top news readers, interviewers, and reporters. This further separated what was becoming two classes of journalists, the grunt reporters (the "producers" of television and radio) and the stars.

This development, along with the devaluation of reporting skills and the knowledge such skills produce, has led to the unfortunate situation where the main expertise of many commentators is the political process itself. They are often based in Washington and rarely go beyond the political circuit. Yet they are asked to talk about almost any topic in the news from anywhere. Daniel Shorr, for example, one of the great correspondents of his generation, is still able to talk with authority on a wealth of issues with which he has little direct experience—after all, he is in his nineties and can't possibly do the traveling or research that he once could. So even Shorr often finds himself reducing the stories to the arena he knows best—American politics.

By the 1990s, it was the "inside baseball" aspect of political leadership that the top news people naturally turned to in just about all instances—for it was all they knew any longer. Viewers, however, not nearly so stupid as media executives assumed, hated what they saw of this world so cut off from their own, but that world still may have seemed fascinating to those so close to the people directly involved. What the people in the media did not understand—and, for the most part, still do not understand—is that they have created a further divide between the public and its need for news and the media's own fixation on themselves and the inside-the-beltway struggles that fascinate them so. They made the problems that should be the center of the stories secondary to the maneuvers of the politicians who are using the problems for their own gain.

It should be no wonder, then, that the frustrated viewing, reading, and listening public proved open to a new avenue of both news presentation and discussion when it appeared at the beginning of the next decade. It should have been no wonder that the blogs would become so popular so quickly— and would do so even while they were being dismissed by the "legitimate" news media as an army of the uninformed in pajamas.

With the traditional news media far removed from the public sphere and becoming, in fact, an impediment to it, it's not surprising that many in America have begun to side-step it completely, finding other sources for the information they need—both for good and for bad.

Chapter 11

THE MOVEMENT TOWARD PUBLIC JOURNALISM

Certainly, the political blogs have been a spontaneous response by the public to the failures of professional, commercial journalism—but that doesn't mean they have been the *only* response, or even that they address all of the needs of the public sphere abandoned by the professional and commercial news media. There were those within the journalism profession at the beginning of the 1990s whose growing discomfort with what they saw around them led to a movement known as "public journalism," spearheaded by a group within the Knight Ridder chain and centered on then-editor of the *Wichita Eagle* Davis "Buzz" Merritt, working from ideas generated by journalism scholar Jay Rosen.

They did try to address public needs in the discursive sphere, but unfortunately, the movement wasn't received well by most others within the journalism profession. Some saw it as a means to break down the wall between the newsroom and the business office. Others disliked that, in general, attempts to institute it (especially within the Knight Ridder organization) were generally top-down, something that seemed to contradict the very nature of the experiment. Yet, as Philip Meyer argues, "it was really a good idea. . . . Civic journalism was a way to use a newspaper's influence to build a stronger polity, and it benefited both the community and the paper."[1] The real problem was that "public journalism" (or "civic journalism," as both Meyer and Rosen call it) challenged the easy assumptions of a profession that wasn't, at the time, really interested in self-examination. Certainly, its precepts, as Rosen presents them, seem benign enough to hardly arouse comment: "Politics and public life, journalism and its professional identity, could be renewed along civic lines, meaning the ties that held Americans together as a community of the whole—a public. If citizens joined in the action where possible, kept an ear tuned to current debate, found a place for themselves in the drama of politics, got to exercise their skills and voice their concerns, then maybe democracy didn't have to be the desultory affair it seemed to have become. And maybe journalism, by doing something to help, could improve itself and regain some of its lost authority."[2]

Rosen gives public journalism five basic forms: (1) an "argument," a story of journalistic involvement within the community as well as a story about the community; (2) an "experiment" in new ways of contributing within the public sphere; (3) a "movement" of like-minded professionals in journalism and academia toward reform; (4) a "debate" over the role of the news media; and (5) an "adventure," a quest for a new ethical standard for the journalism profession.[3]

Involvement in such a process, however, would have meant accepting the fact that journalism itself was partly to blame for the decline in civic participation in America, something few journalists were or are willing to do. After all, "They were accustomed to covering the news, not rebuilding the logic on which the news was based."[4] Conditioned to stay away from advocacy, they were concerned that activism of any sort outside of the narrow confines of news gathering, sorting, and analysis would bring charges of partisanship down upon them. In summarizing the other criticisms of public journalism by the profession, Rosen reports that many saw it as nothing new, as simply a "gimmick that draws attention away from cutbacks that have led to poor coverage and a dissatisfied public. A marketing ploy by an industry desperate to retain market share. A misplaced longing among editors who want to be loved. An invitation to go soft. An assault on the profession's prerogative to judge what's important. A call for advocacy journalism, which would usurp the political process and further erode public trust. A distraction from the basic task of covering the news, difficult enough without adding the duty to repair society. An arrogant and preachy movement that pretends to have all the answers. A recipe for dumbing down the newspaper and backing away from courageous stands that defy popular opinion."[5]

As a result of reactions like these, the movement toward public journalism never gained much traction within the professional commercial journalism community, forcing would-be reformers to search outside of the profession for impetus toward change. Instead of looking to its problems and finding solutions, the profession has become more entrenched in its attitudes, hunkered down, waiting for the storms against it—now blamed on the blogs (for the moment)—to subside so that it can get back to business without pesky interference from citizens.

Sensing change as attack and trying to graft the old ways onto new paradigms and technologies, the news media have remained inert at their core.

Even though many news media entities now sponsor their own blogs, for example, they often view them more in a "letters to the editor" context than as a new way for the professional journalist to relate to the public, possibly leading to an entirely new type of journalism. Instead of sensing that the blogs may provide a new intersection between citizens and journalists, many within the profession are unwilling to see them as more than unwarranted intrusion by amateurs.

Though the profession has shown few signs of renewal since the 1990s, sinking even lower in popular esteem in the meantime, only pressure from outside the profession has led to any wider recognition at all within the profession that it has problems that could render it irrelevant if not addressed. Rather than reaching out to public journalism or making other attempts to discover new alternatives to an increasingly discredited profession, however, the upshot has been predominantly hand-wringing. Professional journalists feel that they are under attack both by the government and by the citizens they are supposed to serve—but their myopic clinging to a single and increasingly irrelevant model of journalism keeps them from understanding why. Until they overcome this, they will continue to be confused and aggrieved by the increasingly contentious popular views—and by the politicians who seize on the low regard for the press in attempts to muzzle it.

As part of a study he was conducting concerning public journalism and electoral politics, Meyer, himself a former newspaperman and now a professor of journalism, used the following list to define whether or not a particular newspaper was attempting "civic journalism" in the 1996 election campaign:

1. Sponsor one or more public forums on issues.
2. Use polls to establish the issues your coverage will focus on.
3. Conduct focus groups with voters to establish their concerns.
4. Form citizen panels to consult at different stages of the campaign.
5. Seek questions from readers and viewers for use when interviewing candidates.
6. Base reporting largely on issues developed through citizen contact.
7. Provide information to help citizens become involved in the political process in ways other than voting.[6]

Each one of these tasks requires an interaction with the public on a basis different from what most traditional journalists have ever admitted to having done. Instead of presenting *to* the public, they were being asked to present *with* the public. Though he found elements of public journalism in quite a number of papers and found a spectrum rather than a divide, what Meyer found was that many of the tools for public journalism were already in place—only the mindset necessary for placing it front and center, perhaps, was missing.

One of the reasons for lack of interest in public journalism within the profession must be seen as ironic: the surface cynicism of the news media often masks a real idealism—one that led many of America's best young people into the profession in the 1970s, in the wake of what was seen as heroic coverage of civil rights, the Vietnam War, and Watergate. To these people, journalism is not just an important part, but an integral part, of any successful democratic system. They started out in a relatively low-paying trade because they believed in journalism's mission. But they had to hide such feelings and hid them so well that many were unable to ever find them again.

To their surprise, members of this generation of journalists had often found themselves in situations where their idealism had to be masked, a result of the prevailing newsroom ethic of dispassionate observation that had devolved into a policy of "don't let your feelings show." Everything had to be compartmentalized—a particularly hard mindset to break once it has set. As Merritt writes, the "operational ethics require that editorial functions are separate from advertising functions; news from opinion; facts from values; reality from rhetoric. The newspaper is separated from other institutions by its duty to report on them, journalists are expected to separate their professional identity, and truth telling is separated from its consequences so that we can tell it like it is. How the journalist feels about something must be separated from how the journalist reports on it."[7] This had once seemed a fine ethical standard, and it did work for some time, but it is based, unfortunately, on a certain type of dishonesty and deception (even though it is a kind of dishonesty that many have tried to justify), one blanketing true relationships and feelings— and one that can't continue forever without others recognizing the hypocrisy behind it and manipulating it to their own ends while others still, also recognizing it, turn away in disgust from the profession as a whole.

If everyone in the profession is wearing masks, not only is it impossible to segregate the deceivers from those who have the masks on only out of necessity, but it also makes observers feel that they have no basis for judging anyone at all. How is the receiver of news to tell the difference between a dedicated newsperson and a propagandist who masks himself or herself in the trappings of the news media when neither "newsperson" is presenting an honest visage? Talon News, with its "White House correspondent" Jeff Gannon, looked legitimate, if one viewed its Web page in 2004. Only real journalists, for a time, recognized the imposter—but few called him out on it, and he continued to attend White House press briefings for a year—on day passes. It wasn't until his questions outraged enough people in the general population that he was exposed. A huge number of other propagandists are successfully hiding as journalists—for most people have neither the time nor the expertise for the task of unmasking them. Instead, sensing something wrong, but unable to separate the good from the bad, people simply turn away from *all* journalists, real or otherwise.

Why hasn't the profession seen what is happening to it and responded either by publicly shunning the imposters or with an appropriate reform program such as public journalism—or both? According to Meyer, there's been an internal struggle within the profession, "a battle between the new professionals and the old craft persons. The old ones tend to be nonconsequentialists. They see their job as to get the truth and print it, period. Let the chips fall where they may. The craftsman needs neither to know nor care where the chips fall."[8] The chips, though, have been flying into the faces of even the craftspeople and are blinding them. Focusing on the job solely may have seemed noble in the days of World War II or the civil rights movement—or even Watergate—but it was the definition of shortsightedness even then. It's much the same as overgrazing land for immediate profit—or even the same as demanding huge returns from newspaper stock, even if it means harming the paper's profitability down the road.

Behind this movement to counter the failures of the news media is recognition that the journalism profession desperately needs new goals for professional activity and revised standards of ethics if it is going to retrieve its role as a facilitator of democracy. The press that journalists were now involved in had changed in the decades since the likes of Ed Klauber and Edward Murrow had last taken a careful (and high-profile) look at the profession, establishing new guidelines of objectivity for it (based on the stand *The New York Times* had taken since the 1890s). By the 1990s, John Dewey's debate with Walter Lippmann (in the 1920s) over the role of the press and the possibility of popular involvement in sophisticated public debate was long forgotten—to all but a few, though a few that included those pushing public journalism.

No longer did journalists consider their role in terms of the public debate or its impact on the public sphere. Journalism had come to see itself as a unique profession legally set apart from both the people and the government, with rights of its own. Journalists no longer recognized that the First Amendment's view of the press was one of extension of the popular right to free speech, that "it was originally written to empower people rather than any institution."[9] Instead, freedom of the press had come to be considered (from within the journalism profession) as a protection for a distinct institution because of its peculiar role as neither part of the public nor part of the government. It also gave journalists an almost unconscious sense of entitlement, a belief that they were set apart from both the people and the government.

Most of the journalists of the later part of the twentieth century did not consciously see themselves as part of an elite, but they had become one. Unwittingly, they had accepted for themselves a role, perhaps first outlined by Lippmann, as the shapers of debate for the public—but without ever seeing themselves as part of the debate or of the public. Through this, they narrowed their universe, putting on blinders of a sort and degrading any possible public discussion resulting from their work.

The complaints about journalism aren't so much that the profession's actual practices are wrong, but that they don't encompass either the realities of life or the needs of their audiences. Going out and finding the stories, sorting the information gathered, and even providing something of an analysis of it have become the mainstays of the profession. But, according to Merritt, they aren't enough. The profession needs to offer more if it is going to remain relevant in the United States because by "remaining on the present insufficient and restricted course, journalism will make itself wholly irrelevant. A society that considers journalism to be only an irritating appurtenance or a negative burden rather than an interested stakeholder will look elsewhere for ways of getting the information necessary for that society to function."[10]

To use one of Merritt's metaphors, the news media need to get out of the stands and down onto the ball field—perhaps not as members of either team, but as active participants in the game. If democracy is the game, the press cannot play a role in it simply from the bleachers—certainly not if it continues to pretend to favor neither side. According to public journalism, it is even necessary for each member of the profession to recognize that, even if they are not part of a particular team, they have to support, at least, the league. Meyer uses another metaphor, but to the same end, saying that a newspaperperson, like any other professional, has clients. He asks, "Who is the journalist's client? It is not the news source, although many sources think so. It is not the advertiser nor the publisher nor the shareholders. Traditional journalists consider the reader as their client. The desire of the civic journalists to emphasize the collective nature of the client makes perfect sense. Readers' interests cannot be taken into account at the level of every single individual, and so journalism's client is the community. A news medium can treat its community of users with the same care and concern that a teacher shows for a student or a physician for a patient."[11] Meyer echoes the Dewey side of that Dewey–Lippmann debate of an earlier generation, for Dewey, after all, was primarily concerned with education as a means for strengthening democracy and saw education as extending far beyond the classroom and even into professions such as journalism.

Dewey's beliefs are behind public journalism in more ways than one, not the least being his belief in continual learning and change—something the journalism profession seemed to have rejected, for itself and for its audience. One of Dewey's depictions of the public becomes almost a direct, positive challenge to proponents of public journalism: "It is not that there is no public, no large body of persons having a common interest in the consequences of social transactions. There is too much public, a public too diffused and scattered and too intricate in composition. And there are too many publics, for conjoint actions which have indirect, serious and enduring consequences are multitudinous beyond comparison, and each one of them crosses the others and generates its own group of persons especially affected with little to hold these different publics together as an integrated whole."[12] The challenge, then, is to find a way to bring these "different publics" together in a way that can allow them to develop as an "integrated whole." Merritt and Rosen believe that journalism can do that—and without sacrificing integrity.

Lippmann, on the other hand, took a less nuanced view of the public and its capabilities. He didn't believe that the general public has the ability to do more than choose between two options. The press, for the most part, has accepted that concept in practice, presenting almost everything as simple dichotomy. Because it is privy to some of the debates among politicians and other leaders, has the ability to do research, and has the flexibility to be on the spot when events of significance occur, the press has long felt that its job is to frame debates in ways the public can comprehend. Unfortunately, however, journalists have settled on a consistent either–or paradigm that does little to assist a solution. They also appropriated for themselves a self-image drawn from Lippmann, that of disinterested examiners and presenters of information *for* the people.

So public journalism has had a hard time gaining any traction within the professional journalism community. Meyer might be right that part of the problem is that the idea did not originate with journalists themselves, but with editors and scholars—and was instituted by people such as Merritt and others, within the Knight Ridder chain, in particular, as an edict from the top. But there is also the fact that journalists cherish what they see as their special status and love that detachment that keeps them from responsibility relating to the stories they cover. In many ways, this has led to an easy and, in the last quarter of a century, increasingly lucrative life that allows successful journalists to rub shoulders with the true elite. Unfortunately, though, their detachment has contributed to an integration of the journalists into the elite. Professionally nonjudgmental (in their own eyes), they have learned to believe that they have no reason not to mingle with the people on whom they report. Nor do they see themselves as having joined the elite. They assume that the distancing they try to practice professionally applies also to their personal lives, feeling that this keeps them from being part of the elite.

Yet, in the eyes of most Americans, the journalists have indeed become part of the elite, a disgrace in a country where theirs is the one profession that has been given a special status based on the idea that it is not part of the elite. On the other hand, there are many who would argue that this is a good, not a bad, thing. For this is very much the elitism that Lippmann argued is a necessary part of a working democracy of any size and world responsibility—but it is nothing like what Jefferson conceived of or what Habermas argues is a necessary component of an effective public sphere. It is self-serving, at best, and it demeans the population as a whole.

When the amount of information available both to the journalists and to the public exploded in the 1990s, one would have expected the news media to be at the forefront of finding new ways of framing that information for the purposes of debate and resolution within the public sphere. What the profession did, however, was focus only on the first half, the debate, forgetting that more than debate is needed for a resolution that can be accepted by a real majority of the populace. In fact, it soon began to seem as though the news media preferred contention to solution and so found ways of packaging this overwhelming volume of information in simple binary form with no middle ground. As a result of this, debate is presented to the public in the form of resignation to the idea that "never the twain shall meet" rather than as an exploration that could, at least, discover common ground. The journalists, with the attitude (devolving from Lippmann) that the real debate is beyond the capacity of the public anyhow, began to see what they are doing as a mere sideshow, as entertainment, instead of as a crucial part of any possible evolving compromise or even consensus.

By developing the attitude that they have no stake in the outcome of public debates—this putative "objectivity" of the news media—journalists then, even if unconsciously, end up struggling to continue the conflict instead of working for resolution, for the conflict itself becomes their métier. In this sense, the journalists step aside from even Lippmann's elite, who are meant to understand the issues and to present them simply for the population who can then make a choice between two prepared alternatives.

The perpetual debate fostered by the news media ultimately hurts even the journalists, for it has no public purpose. Without purpose in the public arena, even the journalists themselves start to lose significance, and the public turns away. When the national debates are presented as insoluble, there is no point in continuing to pay attention to them. There's nothing to do but make up one's mind and leave it at that. Seeing this, the public begins to turn away from public debate, looking to their immediate concerns, where they at least have a modicum of control. In this manner, the distance that many journalists have long believed they must maintain between themselves and the issues they cover eventually becomes so great that the press can eventually find itself an irrelevancy in any debate that does arise. This is what public journalism is meant to counter.

The idea that public journalism rejects most strongly of all the stances of traditional journalism is "balance." In some respects, in debates in the public sphere, journalists have come to see themselves as simply stenographers, taking note of events and presenting them to those not able to be present. As such, they have also decided that they have to present both sides of any issue if they are reporting dispassionately, no matter how absurd one side may be. This also keeps the reporter from risking offense to proponents of any view—seeing lack of such offense as proof of their impartiality. Not surprisingly, this is a direct descendant of Lippmann's either–or idea, the suggestion that the public can only digest two viewpoints, at most. But this stance has devolved into an idea that there are always two sides, both equally valid and both worth presenting.

This notion has even moved into our schools and universities, where people now argue that "balance" requires that "intelligent design" be part of the teaching of evolution in biology classrooms. There has even grown up a curious reworking of the concept of "academic freedom," making the policy an insistence on the presentation of differing views in the classroom rather than a protection for unpopular academic positions. In other words, "balance" becomes something that can be used as a bludgeon to force a certain agenda, especially (and ironically) in the face of timid attempts to tell the full story. That journalists have fallen for this is pointed to as a prime reason that a public journalism movement is not only warranted but even necessary.

The advocates of public journalism, much more in the tradition of Dewey than of Lippmann, consider themselves as part of the public—and even with an obligation to see their professional lives as *part* of public life, not *for* public life, as many of their contemporaries have seen their role. Dewey believed that the public could be brought into discussions that, all too often, have been happening before anything is presented publicly at all. He saw the press as having an additional role in making sure the public had the information it needs for such participation—and in making sure those debates aren't hidden from the public.

The difference between the two attitudes is, of course, a difference between views of the general public. Lippmann, like much of the press of the 1990s, saw the public as static in its abilities, unable to rise to a level of real participation in a public-owned debate. The role of the press, in this view, is to do most of the work *for* the people. The opposite view is one of working *with* the people, as part of the people of any particular community. It means taking on something of an educator's role concerning rising issues, taking the time to find the information necessary for decision making—but without first framing the debate into an either–or, winner–loser form, for in "matters of the democratic process, such as working out a difficult piece of legislation or consent in a neighborhood group, the winners-and-losers approach is a disservice because it ignores the genius and heart of the process. Sorting winners and losers assumes citizens are one-dimensional in their self-interest and encourages them to be se. Even more distressingly, it is a disservice to the core democratic values of consent and compromise. It sends the message that the process of deliberation will inevitably make some people winners and some losers when, in fact, the nature of consent is that trade-offs are made at many levels and wins and losses are rarely clear-cut."[13]

Public journalism, then, is a deliberate attempt to retool a profession that has lost its way—and that, unfortunately, may be exactly the reason it has never had much traction.

Merritt defines the public sphere, from the view of journalism and for the purposes of democracy, in the following way:

1. Shared, relevant information;
2. A method or place for deliberation about the application of that information to public affairs;
3. Shared values on which to base decisions about that information.[14]

Though public journalism has faltered in the increasingly fractured and contentious political atmosphere ushered in by the 2000 election and only temporarily softened in the direct aftermath of the September 11, 2001 attacks, a related movement taking much of public journalism's philosophy (but not coming from within the journalistic community or expecting to bring change there) may be starting to have an impact in its place. Called "citizen journalism," it is connected directly with the blogs, and not surprisingly, many of its practitioners are people who had dabbled with professional journalism but had been unable to operate within its constraints. Its basic premise, beyond the ideas of public journalism, is that the professional journalists aren't the only ones who can play the role outlined by Merritt and Rosen.

As information becomes more readily available through Internet sources, and often even without being first gathered by professional journalists, the question becomes what to do with that information, how to evaluate it in terms of the necessary debates within the public sphere. Earlier, it wasn't possible for the average citizen to be involved in this process. Technology was unavailable, and distance was great. Those barriers have been erased and with them (in some eyes) has gone any necessity for traditional professional and commercial journalism.

Unlike many journalists, who believe that the decline in their profession isn't their fault at all, but comes from an increasingly and willfully ignorant population, the citizen journalists believe there is a desire in the public for information that allows careful consideration of the issues—exactly as the public journalism advocates argued a decade before the rise of citizen journalism. The citizen journalists, for the most part, do not see themselves allied with the public journalists. The citizen journalists believe that, through utilization of Internet possibilities both for research and for publication, they can sidestep the journalism profession altogether, at the same time getting around the commercial considerations that drive so much of contemporary news media and that encroach on the public sphere.

One of the many citizen journalist groups (there are also quite a few individuals involved in citizen journalism on their own), ePluribus Media, grew out of disgust at the news media's inability to police themselves in the Jeff Gannon affair. Many in the White House press corps had even recognized that Gannon was a ringer, but they had done nothing about it. It took a call to the blog community, at the leftist The Daily Kos by a blogger who used the name SusanG, to set in motion the unmasking of Gannon, whose real name was James Guckert and who had no background in journalism at all (it turned out that Gannon's last job had been as a male escort, with explicit photographs advertised online). The group that coalesced around SusanG, eventually becoming ePluribus Media, saw itself as a replacement for the professional media, but as strictly an amateur group, with a particular focus on research and fact-checking, two areas its members saw as premier weaknesses in the professional news media.

Much of the debate over public journalism was lost in the scramble to get online, when most everyone in the news media suddenly realized that they had to start utilizing the possibilities of the World Wide Web in both reporting and distribution of the news. The new medium, however, requires something more than just skill with the new technology, and here again, the traditional journalists failed themselves by simply transferring their older preconceptions and ethics to a new environment where completely different possibilities require a new and unique mindset.

Though the process has been a difficult one and is still not over, the Internet certainly is providing a means for the public to regain control of the debate within the public sphere through groups like ePluribus Media and others that are finding ways of side-stepping the traditional news media. To work effectively in this new environment, journalists need to accept that they no longer control the conversation by controlling, as they once did, the distribution of the debate. They need to take their cues from the people, not expecting it to work the other way around as it did in the past—for, as James Fallows writes, when "ordinary citizens have a chance to pose questions to political leaders, they rarely ask about the game of politics. They mainly want to know how the reality of politics will affect them."[15] Yet journalists continue to excuse themselves, justifying their excesses by claiming they are simply the surrogates of an inquiring public, though they know full well that no one cares about what they are asking besides themselves and other political junkies. If the profession is going to regain its respect from the public, then, the reporters need to become the public's adjutants, making sure they are putting into public hands the information needed for resolution of the questions the public is addressing. Citizen journalism is attempting to do exactly that, but would certainly welcome the professionals, too.

Chapter 12

THE GROWTH OF THE DISCUSSION BOARD AND THE BIRTH OF THE BLOGS

In the decade before the advent of the World Wide Web, it was certainly possible, with the use of a modem and home computer or terminal, to dial in to a mainframe computer and perform a number of functions, including participation in what were known as "bulletin board systems" (BBSs). These were essentially message sites where responses could also be left, creating discussion threads, and where software could be posted and downloaded. Used for games, news, and discussion, and often serving just local areas, they were also the parents of the blogs.

The model for these BBSs was local, not global. At the time, connection was by phone line alone, and prohibitive long-distance charges made participation in a distant BBS rare—until CompuServe started instituting a system of local access numbers (a system that would be imitated later by Internet Service Providers, or ISPs). Many of the BBSs were run by individuals or organizations without the financial backing for establishment of a national network, so they focused on their own "neighborhoods."

The model of a geographically local online community remained popular even into the 1990s. Writing in 1993 about what may have been the most influential of the BBSs, the WELL, Cliff Figallo, a former WELL director, said,

> In the future, the Internet will certainly feature many small, homegrown, regional commercial systems like The WELL. Such systems will pay for

their own operations and for their Internet connections through user fees, handling all of the billing and administrative tasks relating to their users, developing their own local community standards of behavior and interaction. Their users will often leave the "home" system, going out through Internet gateways to other regional systems or searching for information in the myriad databases of the Net. Internet voyagers will drop in to visit the unique communities they find outside their home systems, sampling the local cultural flavors and meeting and conversing with the individuals who inhabit those systems.[1]

That this "dream" still existed in 1993, when the Internet was exploding through the World Wide Web, and its chaos of connections, its near anarchy, shows the power and attraction of community, even online. What would happen, though, as we now know, is that "community" on the Web would grow with little regard to region. The BBSs certainly did evolve into Internet neighborhoods, the blogs, but the nodes were in cyberspace, not on Earth.

The WELL attracted primarily socially progressive participants who, at first, were often involved with computers or with experimental communities in their own professional and personal lives. Started in 1985 as the "Whole Earth 'Lectronic Link" (WELL), by Stewart Brand, one of the creators of the *Whole Earth Catalog*, and Larry Brilliant, a crusading physician who later headed up Google's philanthropies, the WELL grew into a small but devoted and influential community of users, primarily situated on the West Coast. According to Figallo,

> The WELL Whole Earth parentage brought with it a historical reputation of collaboration between publisher and reader. Whole Earth catalogs and magazines were widely-known for soliciting and including articles and reviews written by their readers. Whole Earth customers knew that the publications had no ulterior motives, were not owned and controlled by multi-national corporations and did not spend their revenues on making anyone rich. Readers supported the publications and the publications featured and came clean with the readers. We strove to continue that kind of relationship with our customers on the WELL although the immediacy of feedback often made openness a tricky proposition.[2]

The idealism expressed here presaged what would happen across the Internet, though it would not be based on such a progressive model as that provided by the Whole Earth publications. Still, the WELL was the closest the BBSs came to an early model of what would happen a decade later.

The WELL, influenced not only by Whole Earth concepts but also by the large, generally unorganized, and idealistic community that had grown up around the rock band The Grateful Dead, was based explicitly on the idea that discussion—or really, anything—starts with the people. Its slogan, "You own your own words," was one of those siren calls that eventually brought the Internet into great demand. For the WELL itself, however, that wasn't quite true: users had to pay to "own" their words, and monitors made sure the words stayed within guidelines.

To be fair, the same was true of all BBSs—and the monitoring is true of the blogs. The difference is that the WELL wasn't part of the extensive panoply of the World Wide Web, so there often wasn't someplace else to turn for the disgruntled user who had found his or her words constrained. The problem of the limits of expression, though, hasn't gone away, certainly not on the political blogs. Like the WELL, most of the blogs are self-policing, with what are called "trolls" run out of the community. There's a certain necessity to this, for all comments on a particular blog (just as the comments on a BBS like the WELL) come to be associated with that blog—and there are views that each community wants to make sure are never associated with it. Figallo talks about how the WELL addressed this problem:

A general aversion to the making and enforcement of rigid rules has continued at the WELL although incendiary incidents and distressing situations have occasionally brought calls for "more Law and Order" or absolute limits to speech. WELL management rejected these calls, resisting being put in the role of policeman and judge except where absolutely necessary, and espousing the view that the medium of online interpersonal communication was (and still is) too immature, too formative to be confined by the encumbrances of strict rules and restrictive software. The imposition by management of arbitrary limitations on language and speech, aimed at protecting the feelings or sensibilities of small groups of people could not possibly protect all people's feelings and sensibilities. Besides, by stifling free and open dialog, we might have lost our chance to discover what kinds of interaction really worked in this medium. Interaction in public access systems seemed to be much more productive, innovative, educational and entertaining where there were fewer prohibitions imposed by system management. If limitations were to be imposed and enforced, they could be handled best from within the user population on a local, not system wide basis. The creation of private interactive areas where such local rules held sway allowed public forums to retain their openness while providing more regulated "retreats" for those who felt they needed them.[3]

Though not an ideal solution, as the problems of both trolls and their handling by user communities has shown, this is the model that most community blogs follow today.

The WELL's discussions may have been the activity that led to the form of much of what happens on the Internet today, but like most of the other BBSs, the WELL was not itself able to keep up with the changing Internet culture or to grow apace with the startling expansion of World Wide Web usage in the 1990s—as Figallo's statement regarding the future shows. Ironically (given its philosophical base), as a closed community of registered, paying users, it could never have become a real part of the freewheeling, much more anarchic Web culture that started to develop in the early 1990s. As a result, by the time it was taken over by *Salon* in 1999, it had become no more than a minor presence on the Internet. Still, its early influence should not be discounted. Another of Figallo's statements from 1993 shows the strength of that influence—and proves that his predictive powers were not always off the mark: "It is my assertion that the actual exercise of free speech and assembly in online interaction is among the most significant and important uses of electronic networking; and that the value of this practice to the nation and to the world may prove critical at this stage in human history. I regard the WELL as a sample of the kind of small, diverse, grassroots service provider that can and should exist in profusion, mutually accessible through the open channels on the Internet."[4] Only it wasn't the *providers* that proved to be "small, diverse, [and] grassroots," but the *user-creators* of the blogs who took what was provided and used it to create something new of their own.

The creators of the WELL certainly understood some of the desires and needs that underlie the public sphere, and they wanted to facilitate them. But their business model and the proprietary nature of the WELL (though the WELL did allow access to USENET newsgroups and provided email services) created a barrier that, though not high (the WELL was never very expensive), kept it from becoming a genuine forum for public sphere discussion. The Internet—which could be accessed in more and more ways as time passed (with the BBSs starting to serve also as ISPs, among other things), with much access being free, such as through schools and libraries—provided a much more open platform for a resurgent public sphere than the WELL or any of the other BBSs could. Not surprisingly, they all faded as the World Wide Web took off—unless they were able to develop new identities as ISPs.

What was unique about the WELL among BBSs was that the WELL was focused on the deliberate development of community more than any of the major BBSs and even more than most of the smaller, regional ones. Rather than being a place where community *could* develop, in the WELL, community development was actively promoted through the various "conferences," as the individual boards of the WELL were known. These encouraged participation in what was hoped (quite explicitly) would become something of a new public sphere. But the WELL, of necessity, was too restrictive both through entry and through its relations to other online entities to have accomplished what the World Wide Web would just a few years later.

The WELL ended up as something of an elite community, though that was never its intention. Regulated and proprietary, it never could reach the level of public "ownership" that, ironically, the Grateful Dead managed, even though it was just that community surrounding the band that the WELL had looked to for inspiration.

Early on in their performance career, the members of the Grateful Dead decided to facilitate, rather than restrict, fans who wanted to record their concerts. In what came to be known as the "Grateful Dead Effect," this ended up helping the band rather than hurting it, as most in the music industry believed (and still believe) would be the case. Like most of those who make their money off media, many musicians feel possessive of their work, wanting to profit from it directly. After all, they are the ones who put in the work. That, however, can limit exposure to their music, restricting return down the road. By allowing people to record their shows and even going so far as to facilitate exchange of tapes (as long as it wasn't for profit), the Grateful Dead expanded their fan base significantly—because those tapes got played, and played. As a result, they became perhaps the most popular live act of their time.

It was a similar openness that allowed for the amazing success of the World Wide Web, starting in the early 1990s. No longer would users be restricted by subscription (though subscription quickly started to show up) or the proprietary nature of a particular site's software. Though there were still access fees, libraries and universities—and even businesses—began to offer access to Internet connection for no cost. Anyone who wanted to could find a way to get online and explore. Because the tools for creation of World Wide Web sites were also open and easily accessible, users could begin to create their own presence on the Web, unrestricted by the economies, philosophies, or other needs of anyone else. The individual could make the rules for his or her own site, no longer having to bow to a community ethic—or could find a site whose rules were compatible with his or her own.

Though many blogs today also have controls not dissimilar to those regulating discussions on the WELL, the sites are not operated on a pay basis (even a nonparticipatory reader, what has come to be called a "lurker" on the blogs, had to pay for the privilege on BBSs) and exist in a milieu where anyone, if they don't like what one site is doing, can go and set up their own blog—for free. They need never feel completely locked out. When alternatives to the WELL started to appear, ones that didn't have to be joined to be read and that were part of a more free-flowing and broader, more open exchange, the WELL, for all its pioneering, quickly fell behind, becoming something of a dinosaur, a subject of nostalgic remembrance for many who had been its members. In terms of the phenomenal growth of the Internet in the next decade, the WELL hardly counted at all. By 1987, it had two thousand users—and only five thousand by 1990, when Internet users (even before the World Wide Web) already numbered in the millions.

Two events in 1991 sealed the fate of the WELL and the other BBSs: First, commercial restrictions on the Internet ceased, opening the door for its usage in profit-making ventures. Second, the World Wide Web was introduced. The already extensive Internet was just too big and too easily accessed not to draw off almost all commercial interest from the BBSs, even the biggest ones, such as CompuServe. And the World Wide Web was too flexible and too inexpensive not to sweep away all competition that might try to stand as alternatives.

Again, like most of the Bulletin Board Systems, the WELL didn't see the Internet coming. That's not surprising. After all, the parent of the Internet, ARPANET—funded by the Defense Department through Stanford Research Institute, which acted as host along with a number of other academic institutions—hadn't been meant as something for the public or home user. In 1969, when it was established, such an idea hadn't yet entered the discourse. Instead, its perceived function was facilitation of institutional research through networking. The Defense Department provided the funding because much of the research that it thought would benefit was work contracted by the department. By the next year, a functioning network was in place for accessing computers from remote locations, and e-mail messaging within the network had been instituted. Soon, more than twenty institutions had been connected.

Though it grew rapidly after that, connecting more and more universities, research institutes, and other entities in the United States and abroad (more than two hundred by the early 1980s—perhaps 100,000 by the end of the decade), ARPANET, though seen as a source of technology for other applications (both Apple and Microsoft would draw on it in the 1980s), wasn't itself viewed as a carrier for commercial applications. For one thing, access was restricted at first to connection through university and government mainframes, limiting commercial value, for it was through charging for access to their own computers that the early BBSs made their money. In addition, most of the BBS services began developing a proprietary attitude toward their software and applications, seeing these as new profit centers, a notion at odds with the noncommercial ARPANET, which had started to be called "the Internet" in the early 1980s.

Each BBS guarded its access and its software jealously. These, after all, were the heart of any profitability that they could see at that time. As the years passed, they all developed better user interfaces, but each was individual. "Open source" was not a concept they bought into—or could afford to buy into while remaining viable. Their jealous guarding of technology, however, was completely at odds with the developing attitude within the universities, where sharing was the byword and the impetus for technological development that would completely bypass the BBSs, though each of them eventually did inaugurate their own graphical user interface (GUI) capabilities and versions of the "what you see is what you get" (WYSIWYG) word-processor screen/printer-output concept.

While the Internet in the 1970s was still far from growing into its behemoth status, Apple Computer was introducing the computer for the home (as opposed to simply a terminal connected by modem to a mainframe, where all the computing was done), and IBM and Microsoft were soon following with the PC and the DOS operating system. These would soon make it possible for the Internet to expand from its institutional base into the home, replacing the BBSs that had been first to take advantage of home connectivity.

The fate of the WELL and the BBSs wasn't unusual. Hundreds of companies and organizations that had worked in the technological vanguard saw their efforts eclipsed by the possibilities inherent in the World Wide Web in the 1990s. Another of the BBSs was CompuServe, which had roots going all the way back to the late 1960s and which might have been best positioned to take advantage of the World Wide Web when it appeared. However, though it had been an innovator in electronic mail and real-time chat in the late 1970s, CompuServe, too, was caught flat-footed by the success of the Web.

Early on, the greatest weakness of CompuServe was that it was expensive to access, though it did develop an extensive network of local dial-up numbers, allowing it to grow into the nation's largest online service as costs to customers went down and home computers became more common. However, it worked on a time-pay basis that kept people from using it as extensively as they might have liked.

CompuServe sponsored WELL-like forums of a wide variety that were particularly popular and that, again, presaged the blogs. Through these, users could communicate and share files (eventually even pictures, when CompuServe developed the .gif picture format). As the WELL would, Compu-Serve also provided a personal messaging (e-mail) service and access to the new USENET newsgroups. With a huge base of users and constantly upgraded technology, it looked for a while like CompuServe would be a primary node for dial-up computer usage into the Internet age. It was undone as an online presence, however, by two factors. First, the newer America OnLine (AOL) introduced a monthly flat-rate plan that proved much cheaper for most users, and, second, though both CompuServe and AOL did eventually begin to offer themselves as portals to the World Wide Web, users began to find that they could connect to the Web directly using Internet service providers (ISPs) and browsers such as Netscape and then Internet Explorer, thus circumventing the much more controlled environments of the two older providers (CompuServe actually blocked certain Web sites, particularly ones with high sexual content). AOL, in addition to offering services at a much lower price, was first to recognize that it was no longer a destination, but merely a gateway. Thus, it soon eclipsed CompuServe, which found it no longer had a role it could promote in the Internet universe. The end of CompuServe as an ISP and host to its bulletin-board-like forums came in 1997, when CompuServe was absorbed into AOL.

Prodigy was another of the BBSs of the late 1980s that looked as though it would be taking BBS technology into the average American home. Its business model was based on the notion of the profitability in providing information and reservation services, shopping, banking, and games along with e-mail. The idea was that income would come through the services provided, not simply through the price of access, which was kept low. This, though, kept the accent on the advertisers and not on the users, making many users feel trapped within a commercial environment. Prodigy did, however, offer the possibility (for a fee) of creating online communities.

The only major BBS that successfully made a transition into the Internet age was America OnLine (AOL), perhaps because it was a latecomer and wasn't quite so saddled with what had quickly become outdated ideas of online profitability. For one thing, AOL worked on a flat-fee system for connection, making it more competitive with the Internet service providers (ISP) that began to appear by the mid-1990s. By recognizing the importance of its role as an ISP, AOL was soon able to provide a portal to the Internet *and* keep users interested in its proprietary chat rooms and other such offerings—at least, until its transformation into primarily an ISP was complete.

The World Wide Web, the innovation leading to an open Internet quickly superseding the BBSs, was built around a number of key innovations and one significant idea. One of the innovations was the development of the "client server" approach allowing different computers to easily share information without human cooperation on each end. There was, then, the "Web browser" allowing the information on those different servers to be accessed. Another innovation was "hypertext," providing something of a shortcut between serves and sites, allowing a jump between parts of documents or between documents, even if housed on different servers. These and other innovations allowed easy communications between connected servers, providing a platform that could sustain the variety of Internet activities and communications that started to appear in the 1990s.

The World Wide Web came about through the work of Tim Berners-Lee, who, working with Robert Cailliau, developed integrated client servers, Web pages, and Web browsers at the beginning of the 1990s. The flexibility of their approach was unlike anything that had been presented before. Most significantly, however, they made the World Wide Web free to use. It was this fact that sounded the death knell for proprietary systems like the BBSs—and that also provided the fertile ground that allowed the blogs to spring up just a few years later.

Once the World Wide Web had been introduced, it didn't take long for the BBSs to realize that they were going to have to meld into the Internet. The first thing they did was add an Internet portal to their services (the WELL did so in 1992, for example). The quick and extensive success of the Internet made any possibility of an alternative system unthinkable: by 1992, the number of Internet hosts was more than ten times what it had been just two years earlier. Anyone could see that there was no longer going to be an alternative base for online activities and that the BBSs would have to move onto the Web themselves or disappear.

Though the blogs really are based on what the BBSs were doing all through the 1980s, it wasn't until 1994 that the first of what came to be known as blogs appeared.

Taking advantage of new possibilities for creating individual Web pages on the World Wide Web, people began to use these Web pages to present their own thoughts on a variety of issues, some set up simply as personal journals and others relating to specific topics. These pages soon came to be called "Web logs." Two years after the first ones appeared, Jorn Barger combined the two words into "Weblog," which, in turn, thanks to Peter Merholz, became "we blog" and then just simply "blog."

The blogs were something of an antidote to the booming commercial usages of the Internet, a result of the huge numbers the Internet was attracting—as many as forty million users around the world by the late 1990s, and perhaps four million Web sites. As the dot-com boom of that time attests, the Internet had become big business. The blogs, on the other hand, were small business—if they were business at all, instead of simply the reflections and rantings of individual bloggers. The lack of a commercial aspect was refreshing to many users, who were tired of being bombarded by e-commerce each time they logged on to the Web.

The first blogs were no more than personal diaries open to anyone to read on the Web. But they also could provide connectivity for the like-minded: one of the things that made blogging attractive was that it could incorporate those hyperlinks, making it easy for readers to jump to other blogs or articles, if so desired. Another was the ability of the blogs to allow a multitude of users or commentators. Politically oriented blogs first gained real popularity after the 2000 election simply for this reason: sympathetic readers could quickly become contributors in their own right. Jerome Armstrong's "MyDD" and Taegan Goddard's "Political Wire" were among the first to utilize this possibility.

The Trent Lott affair first brought the possibilities inherent in the political blogs to national attention late in 2000. Even though the major news media had all but ignored Lott's words, bloggers refused to let drop the comment Lott made at a party for Strom Thurmond—that the United States would have fared better had Thurmond (running under a segregationist Dixiecrat banner) been elected president in 1948. Eventually, the blog drumbeat grew so loud that Lott was forced to resign as Senate Majority Leader, regaining a position of power within the Senate only after the 2006 election.

From that time on, it was clear that something was happing through the blogs that would have an impact on American politics. It just wasn't quite clear what that impact would be.

Chapter 13

9/11 AND THE RISE OF THE BLOGOSPHERE

Soon after World War I, when the world seemed a lot smaller than it does today, Walter Lippmann wrote that all "the reporters in the world working all the hours of the day could not witness all the happenings in the world. There are not a great many reporters. And none of them has the power to be in more than one place at a time. Reporters are not clairvoyant, they do not gaze into a crystal ball and see the world at will, they are not assisted by thought-transference."[1] That is true if "reporters" are separate from "people" and if people don't have the desire or the tools to present the events of their localities themselves. Today they do. Because of the Internet and the blogs, it doesn't even matter that reporters don't have crystal balls or ESP; the combined postings of people (including the press) from every corner of the world are beginning to make it possible to find out what is happening anywhere, anytime. The limitations on the press, to say nothing of its separateness as an entity distinct from the people, are being eroded.

This may be fortunate, and for a number of reasons. Not only could the news media not possibly cover the entire world of 1920, as Lippmann points out, but, by 1990, it was no longer even trying to. After the fall of the Berlin Wall, which made the world seem to get larger, the American news media threw its hands up in despair. Not only was it being hit just then by drastic cutbacks in its overseas operations, but events demanding attention seemed to expand exponentially. At the same time, it appeared that the domestic audience for news had stopped caring about anything happening beyond the borders of the United States. So instead of fighting for continued and increased international coverage or working to develop new ways of gathering foreign news, much of the news media just gave up.

By this time, the American public had been lulled into a certain passivity regarding the news, anyway. Unable to influence the manner of coverage or to participate in the debates being presented in the media, many Americans had decided it just wasn't worth worrying about. And the news media, certainly, didn't care to explore why. But they never would have believed that it was any fault of their own, so this was probably just as well. After all, the news media had a long tradition of refusing to examine itself or see itself as less than perfect. As A. J. Liebling, writing decades earlier, had said, newspapers "write about other newspapers with circumspection."[2] With what bloggers today like to call a little bit of "snarkiness," he says that after reflecting on itself carefully, the press writes about itself with awe. Certainly, many reporters flatter themselves as the carriers of skills and responsibilities that cannot be matched by nonprofessionals. Sarcasm aside, Liebling's analogy likening the reporter's self-image to that of a prize-fighter in a bar, loath to let loose his skills, is apt: like the prizefighter, many members of the press do feel that they have special powers that have to be used with circumspection and that they are somehow different from the "mob" because of their talents. It sometimes seems that journalists never tire of pointing out examples of excesses in the attempts at journalism by those outside the profession.

But people get tired of being looked down upon and taken for granted, and they really get annoyed when they are talked down to by people who believe they know better, especially by people who, fairly clearly, are deliberately withholding information that would bring the people to parity in the conversation. And what happens then? Tom Fenton, a former CBS correspondent, posits that American faith in the triumph of truth comes from the belief that the people can tell the difference between truth and falsehood, but wonders what happens "if, in an apparently competitive media system, the public still only gets inadequate or broadly slanted news."[3] The most positive answer, within the new milieu brought on by the technological developments associated with the Internet, is that the result will be the rise of the blogosphere—of an alternative source of news. If the news is not *given* to them, and a way comes for them to *take* the news, the public will do so. And the news media, unless it really does start on a course of self-examination and change can do nothing but stand helplessly by.

Given the personal nature of blogging, I am now going to change pace in this chapter and make it personal as well, recounting the tale of one blogger with the intent that through his experiences—through my experiences—nonbloggers may get a stronger feel for just what has been happening these past five years and for why so many have been attracted to the blogs. Perhaps, too, I can explain why the personalization of the news through the blogs has proven so seductive to so many.

As David Kline argues, any "serious discussion of the impact of political blogging, of course, must begin with an examination of how it has reshaped the way in which Americans get their political news and discuss the political controversies of the day. Because on that score, at least, political blogs really have become, in the words of *Time* magazine, 'a genuine alternative to mainstream news outlets, a shadow media empire that is rivaling networks and newspapers in power and influence.'"[4] The reasons for this have much to do with each individual personality, with the possibility of individual control of news sources, and with the possibility of the return of the individual to participation in the debates within the public sphere—which the blogs soon expanded. As one of those individual Americans who eventually turned to the blogs, my own experience can shed some light on just what has been happening.

Unlike most movements, the blogs have remained determinedly individualistic. There are no anointed leaders in the blog movement, though real and nascent political operatives certainly have been working through the blogs. The blog movement reflects the Internet itself. The structure is not hierarchical but connective, power coming from the aggregate and not through planning or the decisions of an elite. Success in the blog world doesn't come through working one's way up through the ranks or through the money one can bring to bear. A lot of it depends on luck, on being in the right place at the right time, on talent, on persistence, and on hard work. A successful blogger is constantly writing and making contacts through the blogs, expanding readership through entering into conversations started by others (and not, as many assume, by bringing a "name" from outside to the blogs) and by inviting others into their own. Few of us, myself included, are willing to put in the effort it takes to achieve real status in the blogosphere—but it is important that the possibility is never cut off.

It was soon after I returned from two long stints of living in Africa that I began to get seriously interested in what was happening on the Internet. The year was 1991, and the World Wide Web hadn't yet swept away the independent dial-up BBSs. Through a 1200 baud modem (almost immediately upgraded), I found The WELL, CompuServe, and (a little later) America Online and involved myself in the bulletin-board discussions and then in AOL's chat rooms. Though I was fascinated by what I imagined all of this could become, these weren't particularly satisfying to me, for I wanted more substance than online discussion was providing at the time. Though I could keep a log of them, the conversations were ephemeral and, in many respects, characterless and directionless. The posts tended to be brief and with minimal follow-up, perhaps a result of the minute-by-minute charges that participation incurred.

One of the things I thirsted for was international news. Europe had changed dramatically while I was in Africa, listening in through the BBC as country after country in the East threw off its rulers and turned toward the West. Now, back home, I was finding little enough news from Europe and even less from Africa. Frustrated, I signed up for a variety of USENET newsgroups. The Internet, I hoped, could fill me in on what was going on in the rest of the world.

It did not—not sufficiently, at least. In 1993, I was as shocked as anyone else in New York City when a truck bomb went off in the World Trade Center. Who were these people? Why had I never heard of them? Then, in 1998, explosions rocked U.S. embassies in Dar es Salaam, Tanzania, and in Nairobi, Kenya—something was up, but what? Having been in and out of the Nairobi embassy a number of times, I really did have an interest—but there was little to find out and little follow-up in the media beyond desultory reporting on the misguided retaliatory bombing of a chemical plant in Sudan.

By then, I had completely stopped watching network evening news programs. It was no deliberate decision; they just did not interest me any longer. Why? Because, as Fenton describes the situation, on "some nights prior to 9/11, the network news shows featured no foreign news at all":

> This was a major shift from the heyday of network news in the 1970s, when the networks dominated the airwaves—and almost half the content of most network evening news broadcasts was devoted to foreign news. The same phenomenon occurred in the newspaper business: foreign news fell from 10 percent of the average daily's news content in 1971 to roughly 2 percent [by 9/11]. The major news magazines cut back their foreign news from 22 percent in 1985 to 13 percent in 1995. And yet the popularity of news broadcasts fell consistently throughout those years. The more they dumbed down in the race for ratings, the more viewers they lost.[5]

They certainly had lost me, though I was so uninterested that I did not even bother to think about why. Like so many Americans, I just stopped watching.

Though I knew much more about the wider world than most Americans (I had even traveled to Eastern Europe and Russia in 1992, to see for myself what was going on), I had no real idea what was happening—and the news media weren't helping me learn. I read *The New York Times* daily, but even that often proved fruitless. Subscriptions to *Harper's*, *The Atlantic Monthly*, and *The New York Review of Books* helped, but I felt increasingly out of touch with what was going on in the greater world—more so than I had even as a Peace Corps Volunteer in northern Togo.

For me, personally, the professional news media had failed, though I really had no idea how or why. Certainly, I was not yet at the point of recognizing what was going on—unlike Fenton, who, with many of the old-time correspondents, clearly saw that the press had stopped doing its job: "At the very least, it is our job to keep our public informed of events that will affect them. We should serve as a kind of alert mechanism, an early warning system. Yet we abdicated that position in the months and years leading up to 9/11— and, in real and important ways, we have still not yet returned to the post."[6] He is right—and there were thousands upon thousands like me who thirsted for the news we weren't getting, but who weren't expert enough students of the news media to see what was happening or to do anything about it, just as there were many in the news media who also felt helpless. Like me, many who wanted news were already turning to the Internet as an alternative— though it had not yet reached its stride and was not yet able to offer the panoply of sources for news, from the professional to the personal, from every corner of the globe. It had not yet given *us* a way to replace the failed news media.

It was in 2001 that I first established a blog. It wasn't much: a crude and early blogger.com site—and I posted rarely. I did not fully recognize just what the blogs could do and did not have the time to spend to learn how to manipulate them expertly. Though they were easy to establish and to use, successful blogging was a demanding task even then. One of the things it took, as I have said, was regularity and effort in development of an interested audience. I had the time for neither.

Even so, I knew that the blogs were going to be important, somehow—it was just that my own life (I was running one store, closing another, and beginning to teach for the first time in almost a decade) did not really have room for them. Their flexibility and the already apparent diversity they could encompass made it clear to me that these could develop into an entirely new type of communication. Their public nature, the ability to accept comments, and the fact that multiple bloggers could work from one site added up to something that could only expand the way we presented ourselves as individuals and kept track of our interactions with others.

Because many of the blogs, especially in their first few years, were extremely personal, a stereotype of the blogger was quickly established, helped along by the traditional news media, who, even before the blogs had really entered the political realm, seemed to have sensed that a threat lurked within them. Bloggers were portrayed as people so removed from the world that they could hardly manage to get out of bed—hence the image of the blogger in pajamas. They were imagined to be narcissistic social losers who had to hide behind their Web sites in order to deal with the world. Those who developed or accepted this image, however, had little idea of the reality of what was starting to happen on the web. The bloggers were quite different from the stereotype, of course—they were energetic, inquisitive, and not easily intimidated.

It wasn't until the morning of September 11, 2001, that I finally realized just how important the blogs were going to become, though, ironically, that day also stopped my blogging for three years. I had experienced the cacophony of much less significant "breaking" news events on the web, going back to the death of Princess Diana, four years and a little more than a week earlier, and had not been impressed. At the time of the princess's death, I'd been in an AOL chat room discussing some other topic completely—yet every minute or so, someone would enter the room, type a line about the car crash, and then leave—presumably to do the same elsewhere. All other discussion got completely sidetracked. A level of hysteria that I would not have thought possible on the Web was generated.

I wasn't about to get involved in that sort of thing, not on 9/11, not in face of that event. But I did want to communicate what I was experiencing, walking through Brooklyn close enough to ground zero to watch sheets of half-burned paper flutter to the ground around me, to feel and taste the ash in the air, and—soon—to watch the ashen and ash-covered who had walked across the Brooklyn Bridge and were now trudging down Court Street past my store, heading for their homes in Carroll Gardens, Red Hook, and even further away, many walking to Bay Ridge, Gravesend, and Coney Island.

Unable to listen to the radio with its stunned, nattering announcers—and not having television available at the store—I resorted to my computer for news. There, for the first time, I recognized the incredible power of the Web as a source of information—and misinformation—in breaking-news situations. I also thought immediately of my blog, for I needed to say something, but like those around me, I didn't really want to start talking. Like everyone else, I was in shock; all we could do was look at each other, eyes replacing speech. So, instead, I composed something, there at my store, as people walked by in the lingering dust. I sent it to everyone on my email address list and posted it on my blog.

For the first time, I felt one of the real powers of the blogs, the power to bring people together in a time of tragedy. Over the following days, I posted a couple of further thoughts on 9/11, but even though I now saw how important the blogs were likely to become, my heart wasn't in it, and I felt pulled to deal primarily with the people directly around me. My last post until 2005 came less than two weeks after 9/11.

Coming out of my own shock, I found that the news media were once again focusing on the wider world. Perhaps I thought that the blogs wouldn't be needed, that the news media would once again be doing their job. Though I never got back into the evening news habit, I did find that I could turn on the radio or the television or pick up a magazine and find something about events outside the borders of the United States. However, that wasn't destined to last. American journalism, after seeming to wake from its long nap, soon turned over and went back to sleep, dashing all hopes that a newly invigorated news media would help the American population and government deal with the aftermath of 9/11. By the end of 2001, the news media had fallen back into its old patterns of concentration on the easy stories of missing women and other meaningless (in the larger, cultural terms) fluff.

As those same months passed, I began to get more involved in my new second career as a teacher—extending my classroom work to scholarship. The writing I was doing was directed toward books and journals (some of them online) and not toward what I (in my ignorance) saw as the much more personal world of the blogs. Because coverage continued on U.S. actions abroad in Afghanistan and then Iraq, I was satisfied that there was, at least, a little more coverage than there had been, even though it was again shrinking. So I didn't actively look for alternatives.

Strangely—for I am rather much of a political junkie—I had not participated in the political blogs that had begun to come online in the months before 9/11 and did not do so as they exploded in popularity over the next couple of years. It amused me when the commercial news media made a big deal of bloggers getting press passes to the 2004 presidential conventions—I wondered what the big deal was and why anyone should think bloggers shouldn't be there—but I had no urge to even look at my own blog again, let alone post to it.

I didn't know what I was missing. Having used the blogs as an emotional aide during a crisis, I somehow didn't want to turn to them for anything else, though I certainly knew how powerful that could be. Perhaps I didn't want to lose the emotions of that time in what was sure to be a much more raucous blog experience.

Not surprisingly, what I found when I did start to read the political blogs in 2004 startled me. Here, finally, was opinion that did not masquerade as objective observation. Here, there was no attempt to provide balance between competing views. Though slightly shocking, is was certainly refreshing—even from points of view I disagreed with completely.

More important, no agenda was hidden on the blogs. Everything was right out in the open. Though the arguments were nasty and fierce, at least they weren't cloaked under a mantle of collegiality and false respect. It was then, reading through the arguments on the blogs, that I began to understand the ways in which the professional and commercial news media had failed me. Like much of the public, I had already become jaded to claims of "balance" and "objectivity." No one believed that anymore. On the right, it was all the "liberal media." To the left, it was "the corporate media." Neither side felt any trust at all for the news media, and both were as right as they were wrong in their beliefs. Both saw the news media, also, as essentially commercial, as turning news into entertainment for profit—a much more accurate judgment than simply seeing the news media in thrall to some liberal or corporate establishment that was forcing certain views on a reluctant public. Like millions of others, on discovering the blogs, I felt I had been released from a straightjacket, that I could now move for myself rather than waiting for the media to place me on one side or another. It was exhilarating.

In the preceding two years, the commercial news media had reached a new low, unable to question the administration of a president who, in the aftermath of 9/11, had popularity ratings in the stratosphere, a news media suddenly unwilling to be anything more than a means of transmittal of government-produced statements. There seemed to be only one source of information, really, though it wore a number of faces. I wasn't alone in my increasing frustration. Dissatisfaction with the news media had risen to the point of overt anger with what were seen as the poseurs of feigned neutrality and seriousness who were claiming to bring important information into American homes.

Many of us reacted to this by seeking the other extreme: if we couldn't have neutrality, if we could trust none of those who had once claimed our trust, then as a new venue was established, one that bypassed questions of trust, we would most certainly embrace it and the overt bias it expressed. Furthermore, we were starting to understand that it wasn't a problem with the information we were getting, but rather, what was bothering us was that it was *selected* information. Quite clearly, we weren't getting the whole picture—but we couldn't get anyone in the news media to admit that, let alone address the issue. We were "thirsty for *real* information—news unfiltered by editors who 'know what's best for us,' facts boldly stated and supported, and unvarnished opinion openly expressed for all to see and judge. And blogs gave it . . . in spades."[7]

When I did begin to look in on the blogs, it was not as a diarist or poster of comments, but as a "lurker," someone just reading, not contributing, someone hanging about the edges of the blog world. I had to; I wasn't finding either the news or the comment I wanted elsewhere, but I didn't feel I had anything to contribute. I quickly discovered that there was something refreshing in what I was reading, even though much of it was politically disagreeable to me. For one thing, in terms of the refreshing aspects, many of the posts (though not all, by any means) seemed to reflect real feelings and passions, something the commercial news media certainly lacked. Another plus was that the blogs did not have the sense of being "packaged," as much of the commercial media did, more and more, though the posts were clearly slanted to the views of the diarists. I wasn't alone. One of the reasons that many people began to feel comfortable turning to the blogs for their news is that much of network reporting had devolved into this "packaging," not real reporting. More and more, that packaging seemed stale and all too obvious. And it was boring. There had been no passion in the production, and it showed. On the blogs, on the other hand, there sometimes seemed to be nothing but passion. It was a perfect antidote to a deadening professional media, especially once the information being packaged, including the original video and sound recordings, started becoming available in their raw form on the Web.

More and more, people were also turning to alternatives to the major media news sources. The news media, still filled with keen observers, saw what was happening but did not understand why. Even Fenton, though he is an astute observer of what is happening inside the news media, didn't grasp what was going on beyond. He asks why "else would a nakedly polemical vehicle such as Michael Moore's *Fahrenheit 9/11* do so well, if not because Americans increasingly feel they must look beyond the established sources for their information?"[8] He didn't see that it wasn't information solely that we were seeking, but honesty—even in bias. Obviously, Fenton, like most in the professional journalism world, was a bit flummoxed by the success of *Fahrenheit 9/11*, which flaunted its usage of most of what the profession felt was not "good" practice—just as the blogs did. But the success of the movie was much more than a feeling that new sources of information were needed—again, it was the very "nakedly polemical" aspect of the film that attracted people. They did not, as Fenton's words imply, go to the film *in spite* of Moore's in-your-face propagandizing, but because of it. Everyone knew exactly where Moore stood and what he was trying to do. That, in itself, was refreshing. And it was refreshing, too, on the blogs.

It was in 2004, the year that I started reading the political blogs, that they really started to have an impact on the political and media worlds. The numbers were startling and tell the story. Certainly, I was not alone in turning to the blogs. As Kline records, "during the crucial August period leading up to the 2004 presidential election, the ten most popular political blogs collectively had 28 million visits from readers, which rivaled traffic to the three 24/7 online cable news networks. One of those, the liberal blog Daily Kos, drew 7 million reader visits alone that month, which beat Fox News's 5.7 million online visits."[9]

What was attractive about the blogs was the freedom they represented. There were so many of them, from an infinite variety of viewpoints, that one could always find another if the first did seem agreeable. Though many didn't see it that way (seeing what was happening as a retreat from debate), what was going on was a necessary step toward the reestablishment of a public sphere—and toward a discovery that seems to have been as shocking to American politicians (many of whom believed that Iraqis, for example, wanted to be the same as Americans) as to journalists. The discovery, in Fenton's words, was that the "freer flow of information, apparently, does not lead all societies toward the same values. Given the freedom to do so, we don't even *perceive* the same things. The truth gets fractured, everybody takes sides, no one knows what's going on, *so people watch the news that confirms their views.*"[10] But once they have absorbed that information, people also do start to look around for other viewpoints, if for no other reason than to prove them wrong. People, after all, *like* debate and *want* to be involved personally in the public sphere. Because each blog is limited, and most recycle much of the same set of ideas over and over again, no one blog, ultimately, proves sufficient for most bloggers—not even their own.

Just as no blog in itself will be sufficient for revitalization of the public sphere, not even the blogs as a whole will be able to bring back debate among an engaged public. Even with them, someone doing what journalism is supposed to do will be necessary—for, without that, many people may get stuck watching only "news that confirms their views." For the past two centuries, as discussed in this book and as James Fallows points out, journalism has been "the main tool we have for keeping the world's events in perspective. It is the main source of agreed-upon facts we can use in public decisions."[11] And that tool has been important in focusing the debate. Fallows goes on to say that the "excesses of journalism have been tolerated because no other institution can provide the benefits journalism can."[12] Although that may have been the case once, it may not be today and certainly will not be much longer. People have already started to blog about events they witness, and this will continue and expand. One day, no major event will occur anywhere in the world without people recording it on cell phones and broadcasting it on a blog. In face of this, unless journalists do begin to reform themselves, thereby providing something that these amateurs can't do in the aggregate, the profession of journalism will atrophy.

My own engagement with the blogs as an active writer for a sustained period of time began in early 2005, when I was finally convinced that they could be a venue for sustained discussion of a positive nature—even if each individual blog was a belligerent advocate of just one viewpoint. I had begun to see longer posts based on research by the blogger and thoughtful essays that did much more than cry and scream about this issue or that, and I now wanted to join in the growing discussion.

Along with many thousands of others, that's just what I did.

Chapter 14

RESEARCH, RATHERGATE, AND THE POWER OF THE BLOGS

As of 2006, the blogs still had not matured as a research venue, nor had the Internet as a research tool. This cold fact becomes apparent each time another blog-related scandal erupts, for much of what passes for research on the blogs, no matter the topic, is generally quite shallow, often amounting to no more than a simple Google search or two. Until a means arises of clearly and easily differentiating between diligent and careful research and what might be characterized as bad undergraduate cobbling together of "information" via cut-and-paste, Internet research is going to remain suspect. And for good reason. As Mary Mapes, the CBS producer who lost her job over "Rathergate," writes, "there is a downside to a digital world. We may all be better at exposing secrets and running down information, but we are still beholden to the human weaknesses that lead us to use our new abilities in dark and irresponsible ways."[1] The Internet makes it too easy to abuse the very things it provides, especially when those things are easily counterfeited—with the help of that very Internet.

Not even universities have come up with a good system for evaluating research done through the Internet, for it raises as many problems as possibilities. The sheer volume of information (already of unimaginable extent) crossed with the corner-cutting arising from the ease of information manipulation makes for an unpredictable, chaotic situation.

Two types of bloggers understand best how to manipulate this ocean, one being composed of people genuinely interested in discovery and the other of those simply interested in appearance and surface justification of prior belief.

Both understand the tools of Internet research and their limitations, something most of the public at large does not grasp. But the two, given the way the Internet presents itself, are extremely difficult to tell apart. If college professors are pulling out their hair trying to differentiate between real and pretend research on the Web, is it any wonder that the general public cannot do it at all?

There have been a number of high-profile scandals (and many more that have never made the big splash) associated with the Internet and research. None, however, have gotten more notice than "Rathergate," the brouhaha over supposedly faked letters concerning George Bush's service in the Texas Air National Guard. It was, as commentator on the blogs David Kline writes, "the most famous coup of all for political bloggers."[2]

In a *60 Minutes II* story on George Bush's service in the National Guard, Dan Rather used documents that were immediately called into question, most forcefully by bloggers on the conservative blog site Powerline.com. Though it never was established that the documents were, in fact, forgeries, damage to the credibility of both Rather and CBS was done—leading to Rather's decision to retire.

The incident was complicated by the fact that the most prominent of the bloggers who so quickly "determined" that the documents were forgeries were also Republican Party operatives. One, using the name "Mike," turned out to be Mike Krempasky, political director of conservative direct-mail guru Richard Viguerie's right-wing American Target Advertising. Another was "Buckhead," who posted on FreeRepublic.com; his real name is Harry MacDougald, and he is a lawyer who was involved with the petition to the Arkansas Supreme Court to disbar Bill Clinton. Clearly, there was more going on here than a simple questioning of documents.

This becomes an extremely complex story, almost as complex as the Web's newfound research possibilities themselves. The raw power of the blog assertions about the documents can be seen in the assumption made by Kline[3] (which former CBS newsman Tom Fenton shares)[4] that the documents were in fact forged. Their opinion is one more result of a careful manipulation of Internet "research" leading to assertions that have not, in this case, been proven.

In part because of my own background as a printer and a writer (of sorts) in the 1960s, I have some knowledge of the typefaces available on the type-writers of the time—and was surprised when people started claiming so quickly that the documents under question in Rathergate couldn't have been produced on typewriters of the era. I did all my typing at the time on a huge Olympia office electric that frustrated me, especially when I was typing mimeograph masters for duplication, because as a printer, I quite preferred working with the proportional spacing built into pieces of type and with things such as ligatures. I remember seeing, and wanting, IBM typewriters that not only provided proportional spacing and ligatures, but that, on one machine, could produce documents using multiple typefaces. This was while I was still in college in the early 1970s. Certainly, the military had similar machines available to it at that time, when the Bush documents were supposedly produced.

So I don't assume what so many others assume from the noise on Internet Web sites, that the documents are forgeries instead of copies of faxed and photocopied copies—reproduced too often for provenance to be clearly established. In her book on the subject, Mary Mapes, who like Dan Rather lost her job over the issue, writes that these "Web sites had extensive write-ups on the documents: on type-face, font style, and proportional spacing, questions that seemed to come out of nowhere. It was phenomenal. It had taken our analysts hours of careful work to make comparisons. It seemed that these analysts or commentators—or whatever they were—were coming up with long treatises in minutes. They were all linking to one another, creating an echo chamber of outraged agreement."[5] Two things are significant here. First, there was the speed of the response, which began even as the program was still airing. How could any analysis take place so quickly, and how were conclusions so rapidly drawn? Even with my background, I would have been hesitant to draw conclusions so quickly. I suspect that, having previously gotten wind of the content of the program, the Republican operatives decided to attack rather than defend. Knowing that the documents weren't originals (making it harder to establish their validity), they decided that the best thing to do was raise questions about them. It didn't really matter if the documents were fakes or not, as long as substantial doubt could be inserted into the debate. Then focus would turn away from questions about Bush's service and toward the documents: "There was no analysis of what the documents actually said, no work done to look at the content, no comparison with the official record, no phone calls made to check the facts of the story, nothing beyond a cursory and politically motivated examination of the typeface. That was all they had to attack, but that was enough."[6] Krempasky, MacDougald, and the others who questioned the documents might have been prepared, even before the airing of the show, to attack their credibility—just so that no serious consideration of the contents of the documents would continue.

The trick may have been just that, to use the appearance of research and analysis to raise enough questions to drown out the original argument. If that was the case, it succeeded, in this instance probably beyond the operatives' wildest dreams (Dan Rather had long been seen as a *bête noir* by the right). Substance becomes almost irrelevant when appearance can have such a greater impact. This, then, is one of the greatest dangers presented by the Internet and the blogs: appearance of substance has no tangible difference from substance itself. The resulting potential for fraud appears every day, in everything from "spoof" (seeming from one place, but from another) emails to marriage offers from, say, "desperate" Russian women.

The second significant factor that Mapes brings up is the "echo chamber" effect. This has become a tool for bloggers of all political stripes, and it has been found extremely hard to overcome. This is a tool that even William Randolph Hearst used to great effect through his large number of newspapers and magazines and that (even earlier) networks of Jacksonian papers found effective for making their positions seem a lot more popular and believable than they might otherwise have been.

Spooked by the clamor on the blogs, and now more completely governed by commercial considerations than it had been earlier in its history, CBS set up an investigative panel sure to find targets for blame who could be quickly removed from the organization. On the issuance of the panel's report, Mapes presented her own statement, which said, in part,

> Much has been made about the fact that these documents are photocopies and therefore cannot be trusted, but decades of investigative reporting have relied on just such copies of memos, documents and notes. In vetting these documents, we did not have ink to analyze, original signatures to compare, or paper to date. We did have context and corroboration and believed, as many journalists have before and after our story, that authenticity is not limited to original documents. . . .
>
> It is noteworthy the panel did not conclude that these documents are false. Indeed, in the end, all that the panel did conclude was that there were many red flags that counseled against going to air quickly. . . .
>
> January 10, 2005[7]

Obviously, no clear picture of right or wrong had been established, but the damage had been either done or averted (depending on one's political point of view), the story was dropped, and Mapes and others lost their jobs.

One of the ironies of the Rathergate story is that among the news outlets "reporting" the story itself, one was soon exposed as a fake. Here again, appearance trumped reality. "Talon News" had set up a Web site and had started producing copy, much of it under the byline "Jeff Gannon," but it had no real journalistic bona fides beyond the "look" of a news service.

"Gannon" even started showing up at White House press briefings, taking advantage of a day-pass system set up to allow visiting journalists access to the press room and briefings called (Talon was not able make the case for itself as a legitimate news organization, as necessary for "Gannon" to receive a permanent pass).

After a particularly peculiar question to the president at a press conference, "Gannon" was exposed as a former male escort named James Guckert with no journalistic credentials who had created most of his stories by cutting and pasting from press releases and news accounts—generally giving no attribution and sometimes even implying that he, himself, had conducted the interviews from which he drew quotes. Quite soon thereafter, the Talon Web site was shut down.

The Gannon affair actually provides a clearer picture than Rathergate does of the Internet divide between research and presentation—and of the dangers of the ease with which something can be made to appear to have a legitimate provenance on the Web, a danger that is both a threat and a boon to the blogs. Of course, it has always been possible to set oneself up as a journalist by creating a publication, but never before has it been so cheap to do so or so easy to do it without exhibiting telltale signs of amateurism.

On reading stories on Rathergate such as Gannon's (mostly cribbed, with parts taken directly from a Howard Kurtz story in *The Washington Post*) and the even more strident right-wing blogs, it's no wonder that Mapes, steeped in an older journalistic tradition, reacted with surprise and distrust—and disdain:

> I was watching the birth of a political jihad, a movement conceived in radical conservative back rooms, given life in cyberspace, and growing by the minute. . . . This bias on the part of some viewers had been around for decades. These were people who hadn't forgiven Edward R. Murrow for taking on Joseph McCarthy, people who still referred to CBS as the "Communist Broadcasting System." . . . To these people, there was no such thing as unbiased mainstream reporting, certainly not when it came to criticism of the president, no matter how tepid. To them, there was FOX News commentary and everything else—and everything else was liberal and unfair."[8]

"They do it, so it's only fair that we do it back," was the attitude Mapes saw growing on the right.

Like many who have been the victims of Internet attacks (from both left and right), Mapes did not know how to react effectively, writing, "I was *incredulous* that the mainstream press—a group I'd been a part of for nearly twenty-five years and thought I knew—was falling for the blogs' critiques. I was shocked at the ferocity of the attack. I was terrified at CBS's lack of preparedness in defending us. I was furious at the unrelenting attacks on Dan [Rather]. And I was helpless to do anything about any of it."[9]

One of the things that Mapes did not understand at the time was just how much the climate had changed in the CBS corporate offices. This proved as significant to Rathergate as anything presented on the blogs. The tradition that she saw herself as a part of was no longer important at all to those making the corporate decisions. In fact, as she says, "Les Moonves was telling friends sometimes half-jokingly that he wanted to 'bomb the whole building,' according to *The New York Times Magazine*. It turned out that Moonves wasn't happy simply remaking prime-time television; he wanted to re-create CBS News, making it more entertaining, more upbeat, more fun."[10]

One of the most interesting aspects of Mapes's account of the incident is her depiction of news media that did not seem to know how to comport themselves in the face of these new attacks that utilized evolving technological possibilities to magnify their impact. In fact, her depiction of bloggers is understandably bitter, but also shows some of the fears that other members of the news media hold concerning bloggers. Like Mapes, they see the bloggers as enemies who have, because of the nature of both society and the Internet, certain advantages. For one thing, they can concentrate on a target like CBS, attacking it pretty much constantly. Even a great network cannot fight back the same way. In addition, they aren't constrained by any newsroom culture of accuracy, so they can twist information any way they please. Because of their cloaks of anonymity, they can conduct personal attacks with little chance of being uncovered or of seeing the attack returned. They can use satire and other forms of humor in ways that would be considered unseemly coming from the established news media. And finally, they have no accountability. Mapes describes them as "off the leash and running wild. The mainstream media didn't know what to make of this man-made firestorm, and as they tried to figure it out, it blinded them, too. Where there was so much smoke, wouldn't there be some fire?"[11]

Coming from a milieu of restraint created by centralized corporate control of almost all news media, Mapes and the other news professionals were completely unable to react effectively to this return to a Jacksonian-era type of debate. Cocooned by corporate coffers and the extreme expense of mounting a challenge, their mettle had remained untested. But when an uncontrolled and inexpensive avenue of media access and presentation finally appeared and became the vehicle for attack, the news professionals found they hadn't the skills for fighting back.

The feeling of having been blindsided, of having been attacked by people who just don't fight by the rules, often leads to anger at the vehicle of the attack, as well. Certainly, that was the truth in Mapes's case: "At one time, there may have been a notion that many blog sites were made up of respectful, self-correcting communities of concerned citizens who are strictly interested in the truth and will quickly set the record straight on any issue. That is pure unadulterated horseshit. . . . More likely, bloggers on many partisan political sites cling to their own kind, nurturing their prejudices, shouting down dissent, and promoting hate-speak against any presumed opposition. . . . Far from a place where everyone has a voice, the blogosphere is often about who shouts loudest."[12] Just like those who look back on the writings of Samuel Adams and Alexander Hamilton and are appalled by the vituperation so often in evidence, Mapes does not understand that she is only observing a part of the picture—or that, after all, it wasn't the whole of the blogosphere that attacked her, only a few participants in it. The blogosphere isn't a single entity or even a group that can be controlled by the loudest voice. The greatest impact of the blogs, in the Rathergate instance, was on those *outside* of the blogs, who were not able to see what was going on and react to it intelligently—on those who had not yet learned to participate in the greater public-sphere debates that were evolving on the blogs as a whole.

For a news media unused to having to react to a medium becoming as powerful as their own but completely outside the controls they had grown up with, professionally speaking, the blogs have been a vexation, at best. But they are one the journalists will eventually have to learn to live with.

Just as journalists are having to adjust their attitudes in face of the blogs, so are the rest of us. Some of the signs we used in the past to make our necessary and everyday snap judgments no longer work, at least not on the Internet. This has been noted by those who want to cut out the steps of research, be they students after an easier way to a good grade on a paper or others who want to appear to have done the work but, for whatever reason, don't really want to do it. In the past (and even today), it was expensive, for example, to produce a book or a journal, especially one that would inspire confidence. Today, on the Internet, it costs little to create a Web page that looks "weighty," that seems to have a clear and scholarly standing. As a result, examples of poor use of the Internet for research projects abound, especially projects initiated from a particular political or public-policy perspective. Such studies, along with the more legitimate ones, are part of the world of the blogs, for they provide much of the legitimization of blog diaries and comments, both for good and for bad.

In May of 2006, an organization with the sober-sounding name of American Council of Trustees and Alumni (ACTA) published a report based on online research entitled "How Many Ward Churchills?"[13]—taking its title from a disgraced left-wing professor who was much in the news at the time for disparaging Twin Tower 9/11 victims and for allegations of research dishonesty.[14] The foreword of the report, over the name of Ann D. Neal, President, asks, "Is there really only one Ward Churchill? Or are there many? Do professors in their classrooms ensure a robust exchange of ideas designed to help students to think for themselves? . . . To answer these questions, the American Council of Trustees and Alumni went to publicly available resources. . . . And what we found is profoundly troubling. Ward Churchill is not only not alone—he is quite common."[15] The research for the study was conducted entirely through online resources. At no point did anyone visit the universities, observe classes, or ask for comment from professors or administrators. Even on the face of it, this study is thus another example of mistaking the online world for the real world and of trying to draw conclusions about the real world through false extrapolations. The study is no anomaly, though, but is quite representative of one type of online research, a selection of examples with no attempt to establish a significant correlation between those examples and the whole that is the subject of the study.

The title of the first chapter of the ACTA study is "Ward Churchill Is Everywhere." Yet even that conclusion is unwarranted, for this is a "study" of a limited number of institutions, all of the top rank, and only through an extremely limited information set. The conclusion, again, is only a conclusion for the Internet world. There, by the several million hits a search on "Ward Churchill" finds, it might seem to be the case that Ward Churchill is, in fact, everywhere. In the real world of American colleges and universities, however, Ward Churchill—and even anyone like him—is a rarity.

Another aspect of this "study" that is representative of much that passes for online research is that it is little more than a collection of data," of pieces of information copied from a Web site and pasted into the so-called report. Though a great deal more information on the topic is readily available beyond the Web, none was used. This is a sort of quick and sloppy research aimed to prove a belief. It has little in common with real research on the Web or off—but, unfortunately, it has become the standard behind much of the online political discourse.

There is no real methodology in any of this, just nebulous examination along with information often presented completely out of context (one of the greatest dangers of cut-and-paste writing) and of dubious provenance. For example, the ACTA report claims that, in "course after course, department after department, and institution after institution, indoctrination is replacing education. Encouraging students to think independently has been too often supplanted by the impulse to tell them what to think about some of the most pressing issues of our day."[16] Yet how many courses did they look at? Four at Penn State University, out of the thousands offered there. Furthermore, the professorial acts in the classroom, the putative subject of the study, are never even examined. Essentially, given that it is nothing more than a list, all the study does is show that there is an extremely wide range of course possibilities in American colleges.

The idea of research design is completely missing in this study, as in much Internet research. As a result, there is no dynamic to the final product, no "proving" of anything. This lack comes from the ease of Internet searching, through Google or even through proprietary databases such as LexisNexis. So-called Internet researchers are able to start right in collecting information; there is nothing to stop them from beginning without even formulating a question—let alone establishing that it can be answered through database searches. With no one vetting the projects, there's no need to learn what is needed to design a legitimate research project. In fact, research on the Web is now often turned over to interns and entry-level employees in institutions all over the country. Ultimately, and precisely because of the power of Internet search engines, the concept of "research" has been dumbed down, with expectation of little more than lists and snippets as results.

Because the resources on the Web are so extensive, many assume they are sufficient. Right-wing activist David Horowitz wrote a book, also about university professors, after visiting only one classroom, getting most of the information about his subjects from the Internet. It's as though the cyber-world is becoming, in the minds of some, a wholly sufficient substitute for the real world and actual hands-on research—and as though research design is simply an aspect of search-engine choice and selection of keywords.

This attitude, that the world of the Internet is sufficient and wholly contained, affects the blogs as well, and not just in terms of research. Focus can narrow almost exclusively to what goes on online, leaving out what goes on offline. The situation gets to be a bit similar to the problem with a lot of the news media: if it is not in the media, it is not news. Discussion, in both instances, can get caught up in only what goes on within those universes, with people forgetting that these communities are but poor reflections of the world outside.

There is a great deal of careful research being conducted through Internet resources, even among the blogging world. Whether there are means of easily distinguishing it from ersatz research designed to further tangential goals remains to be seen.

Chapter 15

POLITICAL RECLAMATION AND CITIZEN JOURNALISM

It's impossible to encapsulate the blogs, to say they "are" this or "will be" that. Not even the subset of political blogs can be nicely defined. Differences in political orientation aside, the political blogs range from sheer ranting and expression of anger to honest attempts to promote and present the results of investigation and research and on to cynical attempts to manipulate the public through feigning both anger and research.

The blogs, of course, did not develop by plan, but by opportunity. The possibilities inherent in the new technologies of the Internet and the home computer provided a gateway for people who sought a means of expression and discussion of a type that had been suppressed by the needs of commercial entities and blocked by the entitlements of a growing profession. The fact that governments have been slow to regulate the Internet has also allowed the blogs greater latitude in expression than can be found in other media. Profanity, for example, is commonplace, as is explicit sexual content (though not generally on the political blogs).

Outside of simple formatting, no one has ever developed a template for the blogs. Each individual blogger or group blog site has to develop its own rules. Some have no focus at all, reflecting whatever the blogger happens to feel like writing at the time of composition. Others are quite narrowly directed. From the political left, Professor Juan Cole of the University of Michigan, for example, hosts a blog titled Informed Comment: Thoughts on the Middle East, History, and Religion.[1] The conservative American Council of Trustees and Alumni has its own blog as well, dedicated to "timely commentary on key and current issues in higher education."[2] There are thousands more, of all persuasions, on all topics. The best-known blogs tend to be group blogs, however, where trying to keep to any topic can be rather difficult for the blogs' owners. The liberal blog, The Daily Kos, for example, has a list of twenty-six rules for its diaries, including the following:

12. Diarists are strongly encouraged to back up all assertions with facts (and preferably links to supporting materials) whenever possible. Use reputable sources whenever possible. If you can't find a reputable source that supports your position, then perhaps reconsider writing your diary.

13. As a corollary, diarists should always make it clear when they are expressing an opinion—please do not assert opinions as facts, as this tends to be needlessly inflammatory.

14. Diaries which engage in wild speculation without any proof are strongly discouraged. Repeatedly posting diaries consisting largely or entirely of wild speculation is an abuse of site policy. Bear in mind that extraordinary claims require extraordinary evidence.

15. Diaries which contain hateful or defamatory writing are prohibited.

16. Diaries which are deliberately designed to inflame are prohibited.

17. Deliberately inflammatory titles, or titles which contain attacks, are prohibited. Also, while this site doesn't prohibit profanity, please think very carefully before using any curse words in a diary title. . . .

20. What makes for a good diary: Anything which showcases original research or original analysis. Political calls to action with substantive information on how to get involved. News (plus analysis) on interesting/relevant topics that are not widely discussed.[3]

Of course, a site with 100,000 registered users is extremely difficult to control. Little effort is made to police these rules, most of it being left to the users themselves.

The rules themselves were developed through experience across the first four years of The Daily Kos's existence. They aren't meant to throttle expression, but to avoid "flame wars," online arguments having little to do with the topic at hand and all to do with the contentious personalities of the bloggers. They still happen, rules notwithstanding, and are accepted as a necessary part of what The Daily Kos is.

Even with its rules, The Daily Kos has a reputation as the most vituperative of the major liberal blogs (RedState, by 2006, being its most significant conservative counterpart). A quick look at its posts and comments, however, reveals everything from attack all the way to careful and thoughtful commentary—and even first-rate investigative reporting. Because the main purpose of The Daily Kos is to promote grassroots activism among the Democratic Party and to support progressive Democrat candidates, a high percentage of its discussions focus on specific political races.

One of the things that does unite the blogs is a fierce defense against rules from outside. Although there may be rules from within a particular blog—and even its own "culture" of postings and comments—none wants to be beholden to any sort of outside regulation. This, it seems to me, is part of a negative reaction to media (and not just news media) bound by commercial and governmental restrictions—and results from the desire that had been simmering since the age of Jackson for unfettered public discussion, for a real and free public sphere.

The public sphere in America was hard won and won proudly. In its greatest triumph, it was enshrined in the First Amendment to the Constitution of the United States. By the year 2000, however, it had been debased from noble achievement, becoming primarily a tool of commercial and political interests and not something belonging to the people. As Jürgen Habermas points out, in earlier times "publicity had to be gained in opposition to the secret politics of the monarchs; it sought to subject person or issue to rational-critical public debate and to render political decisions subject to review before the court of public opinion."⁴ Now, however, publicity attempts to hide itself, pretending to come from the people, for example, through what have come to be called "Astroturf" groups, that is, organizations that purport to be "grassroots" but that are actually funded and operated by hidden organizations. Whatever illumination (if any) that is brought to a particular subject is no longer from careful discussion within the public sphere, but from discreet manipulation from behind the scenes. Publicity once meant the promotion of ideas and was the key to successful discussion in the public sphere. Only with the appearance of the blogs has this changed and have "average" citizens once more become a forceful part of public debate—able to raise publicity for their views through the blogs.

How have the blogs succeeded so well and so quickly? The answer, again given by Habermas over forty years ago, is actually quite simple. By the twentieth century, we had altered the nature of public debate, domesticating it: "discussion seems to be carefully cultivated and there seems to be no barrier to its proliferation. But surreptitiously it has changed in a specific way: it assumes the form of a consumer item."⁵ People want to talk, and they want their expression to be unfettered. But the commercial media have slowly and quietly tried to take that ability away, leaving most of the population as nothing more than passive consumers, observers of the conversations of others. This has led to frustration and feelings of powerlessness that had no outlet—until the appearance of the blogs. Habermas goes on: "The world fashioned by the mass media is a public sphere in appearance only. By the same token the integrity of the private sphere which they promise to their consumers is also an illusion."[6] Americans, aware that something was wrong with the public sphere presented to them by the media, simply began to turn away from public involvement as a whole.

There's more: people also want to be heard, not just to have their say. At one point, there seemed to be genuine interest, on the part of politicians and the people in the media, in what "the people" were saying. That, too, changed, as public opinion became something to be manipulated, not simply something to be heard. Habermas harps on this distinction, seeing an older vision of public opinion as something to be respected as a powerful normative influence being replaced by an "object to be molded in connection with a staged display of, and manipulative propagation of, publicity in the service of persons and institutions, consumer goods, and programs."[7] When people are told what's fashionable, what's needed, what their rights are, and for whom they can vote, they stop feeling they have an impact on the world they live in and start to withdraw. Seeing this, the commercial outlets, in a panic, begin to shout louder, using any tools they can to keep public attention.

It was never possible that real public discussion could continue to be toned down to acceptable commercial standards, with an entire side of it lopped off. The Alexander Hamilton of *The Federalist Papers* never could have existed without the Alexander Hamilton of the rough-and-tumble debates in the press. Hamilton needed the latter to leaven the former. The latter, however, has never fit the needs of the commercial world.

In 2004, it seemed that the right-wing political blogs were in the ascendant, shouting, crowing, arguing, and showing just what Hamilton might be writing, were he alive. By 2006, that had changed, and it was the liberal, more Jeffersonian, blogs on top. Both types offend certain sensibilities, just as Sam Adams and Tom Paine did in their day, but both are necessary adjuncts to any real resurgence of the public sphere through the blogs, just as both types were necessary to a revolution that started as minority opinion—a revolution that certainly never could have happened through the emasculated commercial news media that then developed over the next century or so—though that may be the point. A truly free media will always pose a threat to the powers-that-be.

The relationship between the screeching blogs and sober journalism is not that of child and adult, but of different kinds of debate, each one necessary if there is going to be a true public sphere. The screeching, as much as it seems to divide, also serves as a uniter, bringing people of like minds together into a discussion that can then move into the broader debate, and even to greater, more reasoned statements.

In *Democracy in America*, Alexis de Tocqueville discusses how the United States of the early nineteenth century avoided despotism by giving "political life to each portion of the territory in order to multiply infinitely the occasions for citizens to act together and to make them feel every day that they depend on one another."[8] Discussion in the public sphere is a necessary corollary, making it possible for people to, in fact, see that they are acting together. Without the combination of these (though de Tocqueville just concentrates on the political), the likelihood of despotism increases. "Despotism," in de Tocqueville's eyes, is that "which in its nature is fearful, sees the most certain guarantee of its own duration in the isolation of men, and it ordinarily puts all its care into isolating them."[9] He goes on to connect despotism to selfishness and divisiveness, arguing that a despot needn't be loved, as long as the subjects do not love each other—and to argue that the despot doesn't really care what people do, as long as they don't want to be involved in the affairs of the state. A good citizen, in a despot's eyes, is one who tends to his or her own immediate business only. The citizens the commercial mass media posits (and needs) are to be the same as the despot wants from the individual—placid, accepting, and nonargumentative.

Argument (as more than a spectator sport), on the other hand, wakes in people desires that lead to their direct participation in both the public sphere and political life. Without their argumentative side, the blogs would eventually sink into the mire that the commercial news media has found itself stuck in. Without their anger and passion, the blogs would be no more than another new avenue for the same old, same old of the commercial press.

No matter how much the traditional news media has tried to imagine a wall between themselves and politics, the fact remains: the two are inextricably mixed, and they have been (in America, at least) since the founding of the United States. Not even the development of an aggressively commercial press could sever the ties, though it did suppress them for a time. The blogs, unabashedly political, no matter how rambunctious and unseemly they may get at times, are an important aspect of any resurgence of political involvement we may see in America in the future—just as the commercial news media have been a tool for dampening it.

The news media have been loath to recognize the fact of their own symbiotic relation to politics, imagining that they could cover politics without being involved in politics, that they did not, in fact, feed off of politics. Choices made in the coverage, however, always reflect a political orientation of some sort or another; it's impossible to report on politics in a truly objective fashion. Politics is not like a plane crash, where the observer can stand aside and record the event. Politics (and war, which can be seen as politics at its most brutal) isn't a single event, but a panoply of connected actions, each relating to all the others, but in different ways and with various impact. Just by deciding which of these events is important and which to leave aside, the journalist is involved in a political decision. In addition, the press becomes a player whether it wills it or not, with press coverage itself changing the actions "on the ground." By their presence, in other words, the members of the press change the nature of the decisions the politicians make.

One possibility that the news media has not considered for quite some time—because of their aversion to admitting direct political connection—is that good journalism can arise from the political arena. Reporters have long been suspicious of the politicians who occasionally join their trade, however, and have discouraged anyone with an obvious political axe to grind from much of anything but opinion-page commentary. The next generation of reporters, however, will have grown up with the blogs, likely as contributors. This alone will have tremendous impact on the press and the ways it sees itself.

Once the professional boundaries of journalism were broken by the Internet in general and the blogs in specific, the constraints of the profession no longer kept people, politically active people, from also entering the journalism profession not just as bloggers, but as independent "citizen journalists," either on their own or in groups formed through common interests discovered on the Web.

Like public journalism, citizen journalism is an attempt to move news media functions into the public sphere, to connect journalism directly to the debates among the people—but as helpers toward resolution, not as leaders or even as cheerleaders.

One of the citizen journalism groups that grew out of the blogs is ePluribus Media, "a cooperative of citizen volunteers dedicated to researching issues of common concern and encouraging the highest standards of ethics and journalism."[10] In its first year in existence, the group, which runs a journal site as well as a blog site, presented in-depth articles (or series of articles) on Hurricane Katrina, posttraumatic stress disorder, the Ohio vote scandal, and more. One of its rules, one distinct from much contemporary political journalism, is that every statement in every article (even interviews) needs to be fact-checked. A politician who makes a claim that cannot be verified will be contacted before the interview is posted and asked either to provide verification or to retract the claim.

ePluribus Media is composed of nonhierarchical teams responsible for writing, copyediting, researching, fund raising, and managing public relations—each person volunteering and no one running the whole show. Once it had gained enough strength (both financially and in terms of people), ePluribus Media started both the journal and its own blog, where there are statements describing its reason for being, including the following: "The news media is one of the most important institutions of any democracy. Yet, Americans feel inadequately served by our news media."[11] This lack (plus the fact that millions now turn to the Internet for news and along with the natural human desire to impose order) lies directly behind the organization's existence, even more than outrage over James Guckert and his unusual access to the White House.

The citizen journalism movement didn't start, as public journalism did, with a deliberate plan for reconstituting a profession from the top. In fact, there was really no plan at all, but simply a communal feeling that the commercial and professional news media had failed in the American public sphere, that the so-called ethics of journalism were neither sufficient nor effective, and that there are, among the American population, amateurs as talented at writing and as skilled in research as anyone in what the citizen journalists see as the "bankrupt" traditional news media.

In many respects, citizen journalism is simply public journalism removed from the journalism profession. Feeling that the news media no longer functions as an honest purveyor of information for the public sphere, citizen journalists are attempting to take over its role in collecting and presenting information needed for public debate. Because it is the responsibility of individuals, the idea is that the results will be more varied, independent, and (taken as the aggregate) accurate than what the commercial news media is providing. It also is a direct reflection of the needs and concerns of the people involved—of the people as a whole, if the movement becomes broad enough.

Ironically, many of the ideas behind citizen journalism are related to those promoted by people within the journalism profession, especially by the Project for Excellence in Journalism (PEJ) and the Committee of Concerned Journalists (CCJ), both funded by The Pew Charitable Trusts and affiliated with the Columbia School of Journalism. The PEJ has issued "A Statement of Shared Purpose" containing nine points:

1. Journalism's first obligation is to the truth.
2. Its first loyalty is to citizens.
3. Its essence is a discipline of verification.
4. Its practitioners must maintain an independence from those they cover.
5. It must serve as an independent monitor of power.
6. It must provide a forum for public criticism and compromise.
7. It must strive to make the significant interesting and relevant.
8. It must keep the news comprehensive and proportional.
9. Its practitioners must be allowed to exercise their personal conscience.[12]

This list differs significantly from what most professional journalists see as the guidelines for their profession, for it seeks to bridge the gap between the professionals and their audience and to refuse the distinction between "personal conscience" and the possibility for objectivity. What citizen journalists try to do is erase the gap by taking the professionalism out of journalism and returning it to the people—but with intact (though new) ethical standards.

Rather than standing aside from the community it serves, citizen journalism intends to be involved directly, each journalist delving into topics of particular individual interest—and not at the behest of anyone else.

PEJ, in recognizing the importance of the interactions between the press and the people, also presents six "expectations" that the populace should have of the press:

1. Truthfulness
2. Proof that the journalists' first loyalty is to citizens
3. That journalists maintain independence from those they cover
4. That journalists will monitor power and give voice to the voiceless
5. A forum for public criticism and problem solving
6. News that is proportional and relevant [13]

Citizen journalists, as both people and the press, embody this, for it is their interest—from both of their perspectives.

It could happen, but it's not likely that the blogs will ever replace the commercial and professional news media any more than stringers with DVD recorders will replace full-time reporters and chance observers with recording cell phones will become the sole source of spot news. But the news media in America is in peril. Technology has shown that it can be replaced. The news profession will have to do something to prove its worth, or citizen journalists and others will, one day, take over its place.

CONCLUSION

In the early years of the republic, and since the rise of the blogs, it is the contribution of amateurs that has kept American journalism significant to debate within the public sphere. Over the intervening century and a half, the pressures of commercialism and professionalism constrained the public sphere, limiting the ability of the people—the amateurs—to participate directly in the discussions. As much as any other single factor, it is the loss of the ability of the amateur to have a direct impact on the national debates that has increasingly turned people away from both the news media and national politics. With the rise of the blogs, a new venue for direct, amateur participation in both the news media and national politics, we may soon see a reversal of that longtime trend. Rather than being asked to decide simply between two alternatives (or to respond to questions crafted by others), people can now express their opinions exactly as they will—and can draw attention to their ideas.

The impact of the blogs, however, may be even greater than a simple broadening of the debate within the public sphere. With the rise of professional journalism has come the journalist whose expertise is simply in the profession. That is, many journalists today know best the ins and outs of their profession—rarely are they profoundly skilled in the area they are covering. They have been taught the covering, not the topic. Once, people adept in other areas often made the transition into journalism, bringing subject-matter knowledge with them into the field. Today, journalism has its own schools and sense of what makes a professional—and it rarely accepts someone coming in from the outside. The blogs counter the resultant elitism by providing a means for stepping around the barriers of professionalism, allowing media amateurs to participate once more in high-profile discussions.

This is a major change. For the past few decades, even those who have stood as "public intellectuals" in the debates of the day have tended to come only from that single area of expertise, journalism. Not only does that narrow the debate (a result of the singularity itself), but it also reduces expectations of depth and makes the public suspicious of motivation. When the pundits have no reputation outside of the media to protect, they are more likely to fall to the temptation of using the media (the only thing they are expert in, after all) to their own advantage instead of expressing knowledge (that they would have gained elsewhere, had they expertise beyond the media) through the media. Their focus narrows only to themselves.

This is not a book about the future of the blogs, but about the past that allowed them to appear, so I will not try to predict much about what might or might not happen in the next few years. There are major unresolved issues, such as the sustainability of net neutrality, that will have great impact on how the blogs develop, especially in relation to the commercial sphere of the Web itself. And the technology of the Web has not settled into a pattern that can be extrapolated into the future.

At this point, all I am willing to say is that the blogs have shown us just how deep the divide has become between the commercial and professional news media and the people of the United States. If the news media rise to the challenge this realization represents, we could end up with a more fully integrated media mix, running smoothly from the professionals to the amateurs and back, with interaction and connection aplenty. If the news media don't rise to the challenge, they may well find themselves stuck in an eddy to the side of the current, simply spinning around and around again. If that happens, the loss will be not only theirs, but all of ours. For all the problems in the news media today, we do need them as part of the American public sphere.

NOTES

PREFACE

1. Wilson, 13.

INTRODUCTION

1. Warner, 7.
2. Warner, 9.
3. Rosen, 21.
4. De Tocqueville, 176–177.
5. Baldasty, 144.
6. Lippmann, *Public Opinion*, 203–204.
7. Downie and Kaiser, 4.
8. Rosen, 20.
9. J. M. Smith, 498.
10. J. M. Smith, 498.
11. Tebbel, 7.
12. Lippmann, *The Public Philosophy*, 128–129.
13. Downie and Kaiser, 8.
14. Fenton, 3–4.
15. Russell, 292.
16. Anderson, Kurt, "Premodern America," *New York Magazine*, March 14, 2005: http://nymag.com/nymetro/news/columns/imperialcity/11465/
17. Liebling, 7.
18. Liebling, 10.
19. Liebling, 11.
20. Liebling, 191.
21. Fenton, 217.
22. Liebling, 225.

CHAPTER 1: THE CONCEPTION OF A POPULAR AMERICAN PRESS

1. Habermas, 58.
2. Habermas, 48.
3. Isaacson, 60.
4. Habermas, 32–33.
5. Habermas, 42.
6. Starr, 41.
7. Faÿ, 19.
8. Faÿ, 20.
9. Faÿ, 20.
10. *The Oxford English Dictionary*, 2nd ed., "Correspondent," Def. 4b.
11. Burns, 12.
12. Habermas, 60.
13. Burns, 58.
14. "Reporter" in *The Oxford English Dictionary*, 2nd ed., Oxford: The Clarendon Press, 1989.
15. The History Carper, The Writings of Benjamin Franklin: Philadelphia, 1726–1757, http://www.historycarper.com/resources/twobf2/pg1731.htm.
16. The History Carper, http://www.historycarper.com/resources/twobf2/pg1731.htm.
17. Burns, 94.
18. Isaacson, 66.
19. In *New York Times Co. v. Sullivan*, an Alabama official sued the *Times* for libel due to an advertisement paid for, in part, by the entertainer Harry Belafonte. The Supreme Court ruling in favor of the *Times* did not rest on the fact that the *Times* itself had not authored the ad or subscribed to it, but that the plaintiff had failed to show actual malice and that the statements were false—and this was in 1964. The ruling can be found at http://www.bc.edu/bc_org/avp/cas/comm/free_speech/nytvsullivan.html.
20. "Journalism" in *The Oxford English Dictionary*, 2nd ed., Oxford: The Clarendon Press, 1989.
21. Burns, 153.
22. Burns, 137.
23. Warner, 32.
24. Isaacson, 65.

CHAPTER 2: THE RISE OF ADVOCACY JOURNALISM

1. Habermas, 51.
2. Habermas, 4.
3. Kaye, 84.
4. Paine, Thomas, "Introduction to the Third Edition," *Common Sense*: http:// www.ushistory.org/paine/commonsense/sense1.htm
5. Wilentz, 23.

6. Kaye, 17–18.
7. Starr, 67.
8. Kaye, 43.
9. Wilentz, 14.
10. Paine, Thomas, *Common Sense*: http://www.web-books.com/Classics/Nonfiction/Philosophy/Paine_Common/Paine_CommonC4P5.htm
11. Warner, 106–107.
12. Kaye, 51.
13. Kaye, 53.
14. Paine, Thomas, *The Crisis: December 26, 1776*: http://www.ushistory.org/paine/crisis/c-01.htm
15. Paine, Thomas, *The Crisis: Philadelphia, April 18, 1783*: http://www.ushistory.org/paine/crisis/c-13.htm

CHAPTER 3: DEBATE IN THE EARLY AMERICAN PRESS

1. Chernow, 444.
2. Chernow, 59–60.
3. Chernow, 275.
4. Chernow, 70.
5. Chernow, 244.
6. Chernow, 250.
7. Lippmann, *Public Opinion*, 145.
8. Wills, ix.
9. Hamilton, Madison, and Jay, *The Federalist Papers*, #1, 6.
10. Chernow, 274.
11. Starr, 74.

CHAPTER 4: THE VICTORY FOR RIGHTS OF THE PRESS

1. Daily Kos, "This Month's Visits by Day": http://www.sitemeter.com/?a=stats&s=sm8dailykos&r=35 (viewed 11/29/06).
2. Burns, 318.
3. Starr, 83.
4. Habermas, 64.
5. Habermas, 54.
6. Wilentz, 70.
7. Randall, 531.
8. Archiving Early America: http://www.earlyamerica.com/earlyamerica/milestones/sedition/s-text.html
9. Hortensius, 6.
10. Hortensius, 50.
11. Starr, 80.

12. Stewart, 1.
13. Habermas, 58.

CHAPTER 5: THE HEYDAY OF THE PARTISAN PRESS

1. Baldasty, 143.
2. Tocqueville, 177.
3. Wilentz, 247
4. Smith, Elbert, 31.
5. Wilentz, 303.
6. Wilentz, 316.
7. Baldasty, 14.
8. Baldasty 25.
9. Baldasty 29.
10. Baldasty 20.
11. Smith, Elbert, 35.
12. Smith, Elbert, 46.
13. Smith, Elbert, 55.
14. Smith, Elbert, 71–72.
15. Smith, Elbert, 84.
16. Habermas, 183.

CHAPTER 6: THE RISE OF PROFESSIONAL JOURNALISM

1. Habermas, 169.
2. Gordon, 10.
3. Tebbel, 11.
4. Tebbel, 14.
5. Tebbel, 15.
6. Tebbel, 22.
7. Tebbel, 21.
8. Habermas, 184.
9. *New York Tribune*, June 3, 1872, page 1.
10. Baldasty, 138.

CHAPTER 7: THE CREATION OF PRESS EMPIRES

1. Nasaw, 256–257.
2. Habermas, 185.
3. Nasaw, 81.
4. Baldasty, 140.
5. Nasaw, 76.

6. Nasaw, 102–103.
7. Habermas, 165.
8. Liebling, 71.
9. *The New York Times*, August 18, 1896, page 4.
10. Lippmann, *Public Opinion*, 205.
11. Tebbel, 57–58.
12. Tebbel, 70.
13. Tebbel, 61.
14. Tebbel, 141.
15. Nasaw, 190.
16. Tebbel, 69.
17. Lippmann, *Public Opinion*, 104.
18. Tebbel, 113.
19. Lippmann, *Public Opinion*, 155.

CHAPTER 8: DOMINATION OF THE PRESS BY ELECTRONIC MEDIA

1. "Music Wherever You Go," *Radio News*, August, 1920, page 75: http://earlyradiohistory.us/1920WWV.htm
2. "Radio as a Revolutionist," *The Nation*, March 29, 1922, page 362: http://earlyradiohistory.us/1922revo.htm
3. Smith, Sally Bedell, 140.
4. Fenton, 54–55.
5. Smith, Sally Bedell, 164.
6. Merritt, 31.
7. Smith, Sally Bedell, 171.
8. Smith, Sally Bedell, 194.
9. Smith, Sally Bedell, 159.
10. Smith, Sally Bedell, 177.
11. Lippmann, *The Public Philosophy*, 226.
12. Lippmann, *The Public Philosophy*, 48–49.
13. Smith, Sally Bedell, 379.
14. Habermas, 168.

CHAPTER 9: ALTERNATIVE JOURNALISM

1. Cottrell, 17.
2. Cottrell, 43.
3. Cottrell, 87.
4. Cottrell, 79.
5. Merritt, 26.
6. Cottrell, 175.
7. Cottrell, 201.

8. Cottrell, 241.
9. Cottrell, 259.

CHAPTER 10: THE FAILURE OF THE AMERICAN NEWS MEDIA

1. Habermas, 164.
2. Lippmann, *Public Opinion*, 146–147.
3. Fallows, 91.
4. Fallows, 62.
5. Merritt, 14.
6. Auletta, 563.
7. Downie and Kaiser, 219.
8. Rosen, 36.
9. Lippmann, *Public Opinion*, XXIII.
10. Fenton, 70.
11. Habermas, 169.
12. Fenton, 62.
13. Prichard, 7.
14. Habermas, 186.
15. Habermas, 178.
16. Merritt, 4.
17. Fenton, 136.
18. Fallows, 55.
19. Prichard, 8.
20. Fallows, 13.
21. Fallows, 14.
22. Fenton, 45.
23. Mapes, 273.
24. Liebling, 190.
25. Fenton, 66.
26. Habermas, 174–175.
27. Fallows, 127.
28. Habermas, 193.
29. Fallows, 115.
30. Fallows, 117.
31. Fallows, 96.

CHAPTER 11: THE MOVEMENT TOWARD PUBLIC JOURNALISM

1. Meyer, 72.
2. Rosen, 5.
3. Rosen, 262–263.
4. Rosen, 25.

5. Rosen, 182.
6. Meyer, 73.
7. Merritt, 24.
8. Meyer, 232.
9. Merritt, 18.
10. Merritt, 6.
11. Meyer, 233.
12. Dewey, 137.
13. Merritt, 23.
14. Merritt, 7.
15. Fallows, 24.

CHAPTER 12: THE GROWTH OF THE DISCUSSION BOARD AND THE BIRTH OF THE BLOGS

1. Figallo, Cliff. Small Town on the Internet Highway: http://www.eff.org/Net_culture/Virtual_community/well_figallo.article
2. Figallo.
3. Figallo.
4. Figallo.

CHAPTER 13: 9/11 AND THE RISE OF THE BLOGOSPHERE

1. Lippmann, *Public Opinion*, 214.
2. Liebling, 35.
3. Fenton, 110.
4. Kline and Burstein, 5.
5. Fenton, 45.
6. Fenton, 7.
7. Kline and Burstein, 10.
8. Fenton, 18.
9. Kline and Burstein, 5.
10. Fenton, 112.
11. Fallows, 128.
12. Fallows, 128.

CHAPTER 14: RESEARCH, RATHERGATE, AND THE POWER OF THE BLOGS

1. Mapes, 130.
2. Kline and Burstein, 12.
3. Kline and Burstein, 12.

4. Fenton, 96.

5. Mapes, 6–7.

6. Mapes, 7.

7. Statement of Mary Mapes: http://www.poynter.org/resource/public/20050110_182326_18354.pdf

8. Mapes, 9.

9. Mapes, 13.

10. Mapes, 19.

11. Mapes, 193.

12. Mapes, 205–206.

13. American Council of Trustees and Alumni. "How Many Ward Churchills?": http://www.goacta.org/whats_new/How%20Many%20Ward%20Churchills.pdf (viewed 11/29/06).

14. See "Recommendation of Interim Chancellor Phil DiStefano with Regard to Investigation of Research Misconduct." University of Colorado at Boulder Web site: http://www.colorado.edu/news/reports/churchill/distefano062606.html (viewed 11/29/06).

15. American Council of Trustees and Alumni, ii.

16. American Council of Trustees and Alumni, 2.

CHAPTER 15: POLITICAL RECLAMATION AND CITIZEN JOURNALISM

1. Informed Comment: http://www.juancole.com

2. ACTA Online: http://www.goactablog.org

3. The Daily Kos: http://www.dkosopedia.com/wiki/DailyKos_FAQ#Writing_diaries

4. Habermas, 201.

5. Habermas, 164.

6. Habermas, 171.

7. Habermas, 236.

8. Tocqueville, 487.

9. Tocqueville, 485.

10. ePluribus Media: http://scoop.epluribusmedia.org/special/faq#what EPLURIBUS MEDIA (viewed 7/15/06).

11. ePluribus Media: http://scoop.epluribusmedia.org/special/faq#when EPLURIBUS MEDIA (viewed 7/15/06).

12. The Committee of Concerned Journalists and The Project for Excellence in Journalism: http://www.concernedjournalists.org/node/380 (viewed 7/16/06).

13. The Committee of Concerned Journalists and The Project for Excellence in Journalism: http://www.concernedjournalists.org/node/65 (viewed 7/15/06).

SELECTED BIBLIOGRAPHY

Auletta, Ken. *Three Blind Mice: How the TV Networks Lost Their Way*. New York: Vintage, 1992.

Baldasty, Gerald. *The Commercialization of News in the Nineteenth Century*. Madison: University of Wisconsin Press, 1992.

Burns, Eric. *Infamous Scribblers: The Founding Fathers and the Rowdy Beginnings of American Journalism*. New York: PublicAffairs, 2006.

Chernow, Ron. *Alexander Hamilton*. New York: Penguin, 2004.

Cottrell, Robert. *Izzy: A Biography of I. F. Stone*. New Brunswick, NJ: Rutgers University Press, 1992.

Dewey, John. *The Public and Its Problems*. Athens, OH: Swallow Press/Ohio University Press, 1927.

Downie, Leonard and Robert Kaiser. *The News about the News: American Journalism in Peril*. New York: Vintage, 2003.

Fallows, James. *Breaking the News: How the Media Undermine American Democracy*. New York: Pantheon, 1996.

Faÿ, Bernard. *Franklin, the Apostle of Modern Times*. Boston: Little, Brown, 1929.

Fenton, Tom. *Bad News: The Decline of Reporting, the Business of News, and the Danger to Us All*. New York: Regan Books, 2005.

Gordon, John Steele. "The Man Who Invented Mass Media (James Gordon Bennett)." *St. Louis Journalism Review*, 26, issue 184, March 1, 1996: 10–14.

Habermas, Jürgen. *The Structural Transformation of the Public Sphere: An Inquiry into a Category of Bourgeois Society*. Thomas Burger, trans. Reprint ed. Cambridge: MIT Press, 1991. 1989 (1962).

Hamilton, Alexander, James Madison, and John Jay. *The Federalist Papers*. New York: Bantam, 1982 (1787–1788).

Hortensius (George Hay). *An Essay on the Liberty of the Press*. Philadelphia: Aurora, 1799.

Isaacson, Walter. *Benjamin Franklin: An American Life*. New York: Simon & Schuster, 2003.

Kaye, Harvey. *Thomas Paine and the Promise of America*. New York: Hill and Wang, 2005.

Kline, David and Dan Burstein. *Blog!: How the Newest Media Revolution Is Changing Politics, Business, and Culture*. New York: CDS Books, 2005.

Liebling, A. J. *The Press*. Rev. ed. New York: Ballantine, 1964.

Lienesch, Michael. "Thomas Jefferson and the American Democratic Experience: The Origins of the Partisan Press, Popular Political Parties, and Public Opinion." In Onuf, ed., *Jeffersonian Legacies*.

Lippmann, Walter, *Public Opinion*. New York: Free Press, 1997 (1922).

Lippmann, Walter, *The Public Philosophy*. Boston: Little, Brown, 1955.

Mapes, Mary. *Truth and Duty: The Press, the President, and the Privilege of Power*. New York: St. Martin's, 2005.

Merritt, Davis. *Public Journalism and Public Life*. 2nd ed. Mahwah, NJ: Lawrence Erlbaum, 1998.

Meyer, Philip. *The Vanishing Newspaper: Saving Journalism in the Information Age*. Columbia, MO: The University of Missouri Press, 2004.

Nasaw, David. *The Chief: The Life of William Randolph Hearst*. New York: Mariner Books, 2001.

Nye, Russell Blaine. *Society and Culture in America, 1830–1860*. New York: Harper, 1974.

Onuf, Peter, ed. *Jeffersonian Legacies*. Charlottesville: University of Virginia Press, 1993.

Powe, Lucas. *The Fourth Estate and the Constitution: Freedom of the Press in America*. Berkeley: University of California Press, 1991.

Prichard, Peter. *The Making of McPaper: The Inside Story of USA Today*. Kansas City: Andrews, McMeel & Parker, 1987.

Randall, Willard Sterne, *Jefferson: A Life*. New York: Henry Holt, 1993.

Rosen, Jay. *What Are Journalists For?* New Haven: Yale University Press, 1999.

Russell, Bertrand. *Power: A New Social Analysis*. New York: Norton, 1969 (1938).

Simpson, J. A. and Edmund Weiner, eds. *The Oxford English Dictionary, 2nd Edition*. Oxford: The Clarendon Press, 1989.

Smith, Elbert. *Francis Preston Blair*. New York: Free Press, 1980.

Smith, James Morton. "The Sedition Law, Free Speech, and the American Political Process." *The William and Mary Quarterly*, Third Series, IX (October 1952): 497–511.

Smith, Sally Bedell. *In All His Glory: The Life & Times of William S. Paley and the Birth of Modern Broadcasting*. New York: Random House, 1990.

Starr, Paul. *The Creation of the Media: Political Origins of Modern Communications*. New York: Basic Books, 2004.

Stewart, Donald. *The Opposition Press of the Federalist Period*. Albany: State University of New York Press, 1969.

Tebbel, John and Mary Ellen Zuckerman. *The Magazine in America 1741–1990*. New York: Oxford University Press, 1991.

Tocqueville, Alexis de. *Democracy in America*. Trans. Harvey Mansfield and Delba Winthrop. Chicago: University of Chicago Press, 2000.

Warner, Michael. *The Letters of the Republic: Publication and the Public Sphere in Eighteenth-Century America*. Cambridge: Harvard University Press, 1990.

Wilentz, Sean. *The Rise of American Democracy: Jefferson to Lincoln*. New York: Norton, 2005.

Wills, Gary. "Introduction." In Hamilton et al., *The Federalist Papers*, 1982.

Wilson, Edward O. *Consilience: The Unity of Knowledge*. New York: Alfred A. Knopf, 1998.

Zúniga, Markos Moulitsas and Jerome Armstrong. *Crashing the Gate: Netroots, Grassroots, and the Rise of People-Powered Politics*. White River Junction, VT: Chelsea Green, 2007.

INDEX

ABOUT THE AUTHOR

AARON BARLOW is Assistant Professor of English at New York City College of Technology of the City University of New York. He has been involved with blogs since he subscribed to the WELL in the early 1990s, and now continues writing and participating in Web discussions as part of the coordinating group for ePluribus Media, an Internet-based "citizen journalist" group that has grown out of the blogs. Praeger published his earlier book, *The DVD Revolution: Movies, Culture, and Technology*, in 2005.